Addiction Reimagined

Challenging Views of an Enduring Social Problem

Leonard A. Steverson
Flagler College

Cognitive Science and Psychology

VERNON PRESS

www.vernonpress.com

In the Americas:
Vernon Press
1000 N West Street,
Suite 1200, Wilmington,
Delaware 19801
United States

In the rest of the world:
Vernon Press
C/Sancti Espiritu 17,
Malaga, 29006
Spain

Cognitive Science and Psychology

Library of Congress Control Number: 2020932728

ISBN: 978-1-64889-035-2

Also available: 978-1-62273-827-4 [Hardback]; 978-1-62273-953-0 [PDF, E-Book]

Cover design by Vernon Press. Cover image designed by Freepik.

Table of contents

Acknowledgements

I would like to acknowledge all the people (far too many to mention here) who provided the experiences that prompted me to write this book; these experiences allowed me to develop my ideas about the concept of addiction. My field experience provided the exposure to the topic and my academic experience allowed me to reimagine it. Some will agree with the contents and others will not, but that is all part of the process of exploring. And reimagining.

I would also like to express my gratitude to the people who allowed me to get this work in print, such as the wonderful people at Flagler College's Proctor Library who assisted me in the acquisition of my resource material and my colleagues who provided inspiration. And I would also like to thank the crew at Vernon Press for their patient guidance and for making this work available to others.

And, as always, I wish to acknowledge my wife Betty and the wonderful family we have created. This book is dedicated to them.

Preface

Addiction Reimagined: Challenging Views of an Enduring Social Problem provides a comprehensive analysis of the concept of addiction as a social problem, rather than as a medical or psychological issue. The work examines historical aspects of addiction; explores some emerging issues such as the inclusion of behaviors as addictions; discusses diagnosis, treatment, and prevention measures; describes the effect of addiction on the family; explores its relation to the criminal justice system; explains sociological perspectives regarding addiction, and provides strategies for advocacy. The book provides a strong sociohistorical background to better address the current understandings of the ambiguous concept of addiction. Rather than providing only a micro, individual-level perspective of addiction, meso- and macro-level perspectives, such as those involving the role of risks at different levels in society, are included in this examination. The book challenges many current understandings of addiction and calls for a reimagining of the field of addiction.

The impetus for this original monograph is my concern about the addictions field. Prior to my academic life, I was a probation officer, correctional counselor, addictions counselor, and director of a mental health and addiction program for children and adolescents; therefore, my engagement in the addictions field was multifaceted. A recent encounter with the field (after many years) exposed the realization that my work in graduate school provided me with a much broader view of this ambiguous concept that I wish I had as a clinician. Therefore, it is hoped that others will review the book's contents and develop their sociological imaginations on this issue, whether they are counselors, therapists-in-training, addiction program administrators, academics, interested persons, advocates, and, of course, people who suffer with addiction and all others affected by it.

Chapter 1

Introduction

"...the medical profession has officially accepted alcoholism as an illness, and through this fact alone, alcoholism becomes an illness..."

(E.M. Jellinek, 2010 p. 12)

Addiction as a Social Problem

All lives are affected in one way or another by addiction. It is responsible for numerous problems that occur in relationships with families, in broader communities, and work settings, in addition to the tumultuous conditions directly experienced by addicted persons. Overdose and death are undoubtedly special concerns associated with addiction. Some social institutions seek to address the problems informally, as when families or faith organizations encourage people to remain addiction free. Other institutions are more formal and restrict and punish the use of addictive substances as agencies in the criminal justice system or seek to treat behaviors involving addiction through medical and behavioral activity in the mental health system.

So, while addiction is an individual problem, it is a social one as well. The purpose of this book is not to investigate the biological and physiological aspects of addiction; examined instead will be the social conditions that often lead to and are affected by addictive sources that lead to addiction. Using history as a backdrop and sociological insights as a guide, it is believed a better understanding of addiction can evolve and be broadcast to a wide audience of people concerned with the problems caused by addiction. Certainly, social categories involving race, sex, ethnicity, class, religious background, and others are addressed in sociology; however, this work has a more general focus and references these categories primarily in a historical framework.

A sociological perspective moves the focus from the individual to the social. Particularly noted will how socio-historical factors have influenced human's experiences with addiction sources, often as a means of coping in a scary and changing world. Currently new and evolving risks in the contemporary era create the "anxieties of our age" for which people look to new substitutes for the traditional social bonds provided by family, communities, faith organizations, and others that can create forms of social integration that can serve as a protective factor against the use of drugs or other maladaptive behaviors (Alexander, 2000). The chapter on sociological theory, which specifically de-

scribes this perspective, will come later in this text in order to reflect sociologically on basic concepts of addiction mentioned earlier.

This examination also uses an approach known as public sociology, a subfield
of sociology that seeks to move information from academia into the places that
can make direct use of the knowledge. Therefore, the sociological understandings of addiction contained in this book will hopefully move the discussion to
various publics that deal with the problem of addiction on a day-to-day basis
such as, the treatment programs, addictions professionals, the media, communities, advocates, and most importantly, the people who suffer with addictions
and their families. The book, therefore, is for all people concerned with addiction. As readers might encounter sociological terms and concepts with which
they are unfamiliar, efforts are made to explain these terms.

Addiction: Understandings and Examinations

Definitions about what society considers to be addiction have taken many
forms such as, moral failings, bad habits, compulsions, or the results of disease. And ideas about the causes of addiction have also varied, for example, in
the form of demons, sinful excesses, peer pressure, or genes. Ideas about how
addiction can manifest itself are expanding, from substance addictions such
as alcohol and other drugs, to behaviors such as gambling, sexual behavior,
eating, Internet gaming, and many others. Society also grapples with how
addiction can be thwarted (if indeed it can); this is a major political and ethi-
cal concern as strategies of legalization of certain drugs in the continuing
national war on drugs are debated.

To thoroughly examine this idea of addiction, it is beneficial to adopt micro-,
meso-, or macro-levels as our points of analysis. If a micro-level analysis is
used, attention will be paid to bio-psychological factors such as the how addiction affects the individual through the internal mechanisms of drug-taking
or behavioral activity, and the development of craving, tolerance, and withdrawal. The meso-level approach would seek to observe the effects of addiction on an individual's family and community and the effectiveness of certain
community-based treatment and prevention programs. The macro perspective would analyze the effects of addiction at a global level, such as understanding the role of international drug markets, drug trafficking, and the
efforts by organizations such as the World Health Organization to counter the
effect of addictions.

There are many different disciplines that seek to understand the process of
addiction and its consequences at different levels of analysis. Biology, for
example, focuses on the biological and constitutional aspects of addiction;
psychology pays more attention to the cognitive and learning processes that

occur in the addiction process. Political Science and criminology emphasize the connection between the legal and political systems that are often closely connected to criminal behavior that involves addiction as well as the responses to this behavior. This book takes a sociological perspective that seeks to examine the social ramifications and processes that are a result of addiction in its different forms. This means there will be an emphasis on the social and environmental factors that play a role in the addiction process while acknowledging the contributions of the other disciplines mentioned. And due to sociology's propensity to challenge prevailing ideas about social phenomena, the very concept of addiction is confronted. The book takes a socio-historical approach as well to better examine the traditional notions of addiction and provide a more reasoned approach to its study.

Definitions

This section will begin with definitions of terms commonly associated with addiction, starting with the lead concept itself. These terms and their definitions represent formally accepted, standard concepts in the addictions field. Afterward, there will be a reflection on these common understandings, hopefully revealing some additional information and challenge certain assumptions; this is a means to further explore and understand different meanings of common social phenomena. Addiction represents one such phenomenon.

If a casual reviewer seeks information about addiction-related information, a quick Internet search will elicit information from numerous websites that represent providers of addiction services. While some of this information can be relevant and correct, much of it is delivered by private treatment providers geared toward inducing the viewers—presumed to be people who need these services—to choose their addiction program in lieu of a wide variety of others. This information can evade scientific evidence or other possibilities for symptom alleviation. It is somewhat disturbing that addiction prevention and treatment have become such a commercial enterprise that even finding objective data on this common social problem is difficult, especially for someone needing a quick response to an alarming situation, for themselves or someone else. Definitions provided on these sites are often overly generalized with the hope of drawing attention to their own programs. Comprehensive definitions are essential in understanding the broader aspects of personal consequences and social manifestations of addiction. These terms represent common understandings to the field of addictions, but which are not mutually exclusive, exhaustive, or unambiguous. They are listed here to give readers a general overview of the terminology and to provide some insight into the field.

Addiction

The National Institute on Drug Abuse (NIDA), a governmental program whose focus is on health research and its dissemination, defines addiction as a "chronic, relapsing brain disease that is characterized by compulsive drug seeking and use, despite harmful consequences. It is considered a brain disease because drugs change the brain; they change its structure and how it works" (NIDA, 2018b, p. 1). This definition of addiction as a "brain disease" puts addiction firmly under the medical model.

According to the American Society of Addiction Medicine (ASAM), addiction medicines' prominent professional organization, addiction is defined as "a primary, chronic disease of brain reward, motivation, memory, and related circuitry. Dysfunction in these circuits leads to characteristic biological, psychological, social, and spiritual manifestations, reflected in an individual pathologically pursuing reward and/or relief by substance use and other behaviors". In this organization's view, some key components in addiction are:

- craving the substance or behavior

- the inability to control or abstain from the drug or behavior, causing the craving

- dysfunctional behavior associated with the condition

Addiction, under the auspices of the medical model, is considered a chronic and progressive disease and one in which relapse and remission are characteristics requiring medical treatment (ASAM, n.d.).

The Center on Addiction (COA), a think tank formerly known as the National Center on Addiction and Substance Abuse, sees addiction as a complex and chronic disease that affects both brain and body. The consequences of this disease include "serious damage to families, relationships, schools, workplaces, and neighborhoods. The most common symptoms of addiction are severe loss of control, continued use despite serious consequences, preoccupation with using, failed attempts to quit, tolerance and withdrawal" (COA, 2018, p. 1). Viewed as a medical issue by this association, healthcare professionals are tasked with prevention, treatment, and management of addiction, often in concert with social supports.

In its manual the International Classification of Diseases, 10th edition (ICD-10), the World Health Organization (WHO), the health arm of the United Nations, prefers to use the term *dependence syndrome*, defined as "a cluster of physiological, behavioral, and cognitive phenomena in which the use of a substance or a class of substances takes on a much higher priority for a given individual than other behaviors that once had greater value" (WHO, n.d.). WHO abandoned the term addiction (along with the often-interrelated term habituation) in 1964 for the substitute term *dependence*. Relinquishing the term by such a high-level organization reflects the importance of terminology, and while not indicating a rejection of the medical model, it does put the concept in a different light.

Substance use disorder

Substance use disorder is the terminology used in the Diagnostic and Statistical Manual of Mental Disorders, Fifth Edition (DSM-5), the current official diagnostic guide used in making mental health diagnoses. It refers to the "cluster of cognitive, behavioral, and physiological symptoms that the individual continuing using despite significant substance-related problems" (APA, 2013, p. 483). The DSM-5 provides diagnostic criteria about different substances as well as the consequences of use and abuse. A significant portion of the DSM-5 is dedicated to the diagnosis of substance use disorders.

Substance abuse

Sometimes referred to as drug abuse, this term is defined by the National Center for Biotechnical Information (NCBI) as "a maladaptive pattern of substance use manifested by recurrent and significant adverse consequences related to the repeated use of substances" (NCBI, 2005, n.d., p. 17). The definition provided here reflects the diagnostic designation in the DSM-IV-TR (the predecessor to the current DSM-5) and has now been substituted for substance use disorder. However, this term is still used extensively in common parlance, inside and outside the addiction field.

Behavioral addiction

An extension of substance addiction, behavioral addiction (also called *process addiction*), assumes that certain behaviors such as gambling, sex, eating, shopping, gaming, and internet use affect the pleasure centers of the brain (through "natural rewards") in ways that are likened to the ingestion of chemical substances and that produce some similar patterns regarding social consequences, though they come from external processes. Currently, the only non-substance related disorder in the DSM-5 is gambling disorder (APA, 2013).

Disease concept of addiction

The conception of addiction as a disease has a long history and is accepted by many medical associations as well as non-medical organizations. Addiction, according to this model, is like other diseases in that it:

- is caused by biological, environmental, and behavioral features

- affects brain and bodily functions

- and requires medical treatment to stop its progression (CAD, 2017).

The concept is not without many detractors, however, and this will be discussed in more detail throughout this book.

Detoxification

The term detoxification is often shortened to "detox" and, according to the Substance Abuse and Mental Health Services Administration (SAMHSA), it as a "set of interventions aimed at managing acute intoxication and withdrawal" which "...denotes a cleaning of toxins..." from the bodies of those addicted to alcohol and other drugs (SAMHSA, 2015, p. 4). It involves specific actions, supervised by medical professions, to assist them in the deleterious effects of withdrawal from a substance, which can be life-threatening.

Sobriety

Sobriety refers to a state of refraining from the use and effects of addiction sources and indicates the adoption of a lifestyle free from addiction; it is also known as abstinence (from addiction sources). The term also refers to the clarity of thought that accompanies abstinence.

Relapse

Relapse refers to a return to the use of an addictive substance or behavior after a period of abstinence. A *lapse* can refer to a pre-relapse stage that signals a possible return to the addictive substance or behavior, or it can denote a brief return to the use or behavior. The associated term *triggers* refers to stimuli that can promote relapse.

Dual diagnosis

This term refers to a situation in which addiction is a comorbid condition that occurs in conjunction with mental illness symptomology such as depressive, manic, post-traumatic, or other conditions. These co-occurring disorders often result in *diagnostic overshadowing* (Reiss, Leviton, & Szyskzo, 1982), in which certain conditions or disorders receive less attention by diagnostic professionals than other conditions (these can be addictive disorders, other mental health conditions, or neurodevelopmental conditions).

Denial

A common term in the addiction lexicon, denial refers to the rejection of the evidence that someone is addicted to substances or behaviors, even when that evidence is blatantly obvious to others. Denial has connections to psychoanalysis and allows the addicted person to continue the use of drugs or the maladaptive behaviors that result from addiction.

Tolerance

Tolerance refers to a situation in which an addicted person requires more use of an addiction source than was needed previously to achieve the same psychological reward. The body adapts and changes because of the addiction, promoting greater need for the substance or enhanced behavioral activity.

Withdrawal

Another common term in the addictions field and one that is often used in connection with tolerance is withdrawal, which refers to highly uncomfortable physiological and psychological symptoms when someone ceases drug use, and that can result in maladaptive behaviors in one's personal and social life. The symptoms can be manifest in forms from mild to deadly and often differ regarding the type of addiction and substance.

Recovery

The term recovery refers to the discontinued use of the addictive drug or behavior and a return to a non-using lifestyle; it usually implies a process that continues through an addicted person's lifespan. The related term *remission* refers to the cessation of severe and chronic addiction. The term *in recovery* denotes that an addicted person is refraining from use and has adopted an abstinence-based régime. Both terms reflect the medical model of addiction.

Twelve-step philosophy

The most dominant philosophy in the addictions field is the twelve-step model, which also includes a stringent treatment process that includes steps to attain abstinence from addiction sources. The philosophy guides Alcoholics Anonymous (AA) and the many spin-off "anonymous" groups and involves a peer self-help structure that was formed when addicted persons had few places to turn for sobriety (Myers & Salt, 2007). This philosophy is still a significant force in the addictions field and is examined in detail throughout this book.

Harm Reduction

Harm reduction refers to a philosophy that emphasizes a reduction in the use of an addictive source in order to focus on other problems experienced by addicted persons. As such, it does not require abstinence and allows people to make choices rather than strictly follow abstinence-based approaches (Little et al., 2013). This approach obviously differs significantly from the twelve-step model.

Medical-assisted treatment

The term medical-assisted treatment (often reduced to MAT) refers to the use of Food and Drug Administration (FDA) approved medications in conjunction with psychotherapy to alleviate addiction problems. The most common drugs are Methadone, Naltrexone, and Buprenorphine used for the treatment of addiction to opioids (SAMHSA, 2019).

Evidence-based treatment

Evidence-based treatment approaches are those that use up-to-date empirical data derived from scientific research. This information, obtained from research published in academic and professional journals and governmental agency publications, is disseminated to practitioners and clients and is available for all types of mental distress, including addiction.

Differing Views of Addiction

An analysis of any subject requires a meaningful understanding of the terms involved—the names that society has given— for which we, as a whole or part, accept with their connotations. When explored, a definition's implications (and its variants) tell much about the concept. Hidden preferences and expectations in that definition—basically hidden meanings—can reveal much about our understandings and perceptions of addiction. Certain considerations are promoted by individuals and groups to achieve certain ends. A thorough investigation demands that observers tease out these hidden messages; therefore, this work will scrutinize common understandings about addiction, using analogies commonly used to describe addiction.

Readers will note some overlap between some of these perspectives, and this is natural since elements in society are related and due to the social construction of classifications in that people decide how to categorize items based on culturally specific knowledge. For example, it is difficult to totally separate addiction from cultural, risk, and risk categories as these are closely linked in society. However, the distinctions are made to better analyze how addiction as a concept can be understood.

Addiction as Disease

In reviewing the above terms in this analysis, something becomes apparent—the analogy with medicine and the medical profession. Terms such as disorder, disease, detoxification, relapse, recovery, and others certainly reveal a connection to medicine and the medical field. The question is if addiction is a natural fit for the medical model or if it was a rationally planned endeavor so that some might benefit from its placement in the model. This book will explore both possibilities.

Proponents of the disease analogy explain that addiction, like other diseases, has physiological components. It specifically involves the brain and, after the biochemical changes develop for substance use, results in altered behavior that often leads to relapse. When the condition becomes chronic, detoxification (a medical procedure) must take place to get the bodily systems safely stabilized. Recovery can occur if certain physical and psychological conditions take place. As with other diseases, the disorder is progressive if treatment interventions are not appropriately provided. Even if addiction is not viewed as a disease, it still makes sense to many in the addictions field to place it under the auspices of the medical model. Referring specifically to the current opioid addiction crisis, Lembke (2018) feels viewing addiction as a disease opens up insurance potentials and funding for research and, since addiction is well-supported by the strong infrastructure of the public health system (especially in the case of addiction to prescription medications), the health care field should take the lead in reigning in the problem.

Addiction as Habit

Viewing addiction in terms of habits presents an opportunity to explore a functionalist approach, which examines the role of social phenomena to the functioning of society. Habits, defined as actions or behaviors that are prompted by a search for pleasure, become internalized through socialization. Habits, however, can also be viewed as a "friend of social order" (Anderson, 1996, p. S4), in that the regulating social forces that actively interact with habits (such as the licensing of drinking establishments, dispensaries, and gambling casinos) were created to thwart the social breakdown that could occur with excessive drinking, smoking, or gambling. If the driving forces behind the development of habits are analogized as appetites (as mentioned in the next section) which can cause danger as well as pleasure, the type of social control needed can be found in the restoration of "respect for traditions and habits" (p. S7). From this perspective, habits (or addictions) provide both pleasure and harm and require adequate social controls that regulate behavior and mitigate injury.

Addiction as Excessive Appetite

Using an apt metaphor, psychologist Jim Orford (1985) described addiction (in this case in the excesses of alcohol and other drug use, gambling, eating, and sex) as "excessive appetites." Noting the importance of the role of culture, psychological functioning, and human development, an emphasis should be placed on "inclination and restraint," in which these factors "under individual differences of multiple origins are subject to developmental changes" (1985, p. 210), meaning that people at different phases of life encounter circumstances that will depend upon their abilities to accept or reject the choices that can lead to addiction. Also, an understanding of the multitude of factors that contribute to an individual person at a determinate stage making life choices creates a realization that addiction is not an easy thing to adequately define or describe, much less stop or even control. In Orford's metaphorical scheme, "excessive" implies thoughts or behavior that violate some normative social standards. "Appetite" suggests a craving for something that is disproportionate to general standards. Neither the terms 'excess' nor 'appetite' suggest the need for medical intervention. Having an excessive appetite doesn't necessarily make one "sick" unless society makes the connection between excessive appetites and illness.

Addiction as Lifestyle

The lifestyle theoretical model has important connections with the risk society thesis (mentioned in more detail below), which states that as society becomes more advanced, there will be more types of danger, often hidden, to address. With the risk conception of modern life, there is an understanding that there are risks more significant than the individual, which necessitates adaptation. Adaptation requires repetition of certain acts (a lifestyle) deemed to keep people safe but, as lifestyle theorist Glenn A. Walters (1999) notes, "problems arise, however, when a person becomes dependent on a particular lifestyle to cope with fear and the problems of everyday living" (p. 17). Lifestyle often implies choice in that a person chooses between alternatives; those choices can be positive, negative, or neutral, and they can involve the use of addiction sources which can, in turn, produce a lifestyle formed around addiction.

Addiction as Deviance

Deviance refers to behavior that deviates from society's norms. Viewing addiction as deviance exposes the fact that the use of illicit addictive substances or compulsive behavior in some way often violates the social order and therefore requires a system that provides sanctions for the behavior; our criminal justice system has been formulated for that purpose. Deviance as a concept, however, is very ambiguous and relative to time and place as evidenced by the fact that drugs determined to be harmless at some points in time were later considered to be dangerous, possessing the potential to create an epidemic, for example, whereas cocaine was considered a wonder drug with great potential in the early 1900s, it would become racialized decades later as the drug morphed into "crack," creating concerns of an epidemic and what has been considered a "moral panic" (addressed in chapter seven).

Addiction as Symptom

The idea of addiction as being a symptom of a larger social problem is a commonly used metaphor. Berger (1991), using a social psychoanalytic approach, viewed addiction as observable from both the individual (or micro) level in the ways people turn to drugs due to other problems they are experiencing, and the social (or macro) level in which drugs are believed to be a symptom of broader cultural issues. Addiction, then, is perceived as a symptom of personal issues to be addressed by clinical intervention or as social issues to be addressed in policy-based interventions. Also, addiction can be understood as a symptom of these problems or as a cause of them; for example, at the meso-level, the question can be asked: does drug addiction promote the collapse of communities or does a disintegration of communities contribute to drug addiction? In this chicken-and-egg formulation of addiction, the focus is on symptomology.

Addiction as Ritual

A ritual is a set of behaviors that reflect symbolism for deeper, often spiritual values. Emile Durkheim, one of sociology's founders, introduced the notion that common, everyday occurrences (the *profane*) mimic those of religious beliefs (the *sacred*) (Durkheim, 1912/1965). Following this idea, sociologist Erving Goffman (1967) explained how everyday interaction patterns between people reflect religious ritual. More recently Collins (2014) described how ritual is used in drug-related activity; specifically, the tobacco use ritual that involves four-hundred-year-old traditions such as *relaxation and withdrawal rituals* that provide a reprieve from stressful life events; *carousing rituals* that create a sort of rebellious excitement and bonding with other users; *elegance rituals* that promote sociality and display social status; and *ceremonial rituals* including those that symbolize a truce between groups (such as use of the peace pipe). Additionally, in the past, addictive substances such as peyote have been used in religious rituals of indigenous people and considered to be sacred.

It is easy to see how this ritualistic perspective can be used with other substances as well. It should also be evident in the rituals that exist in behavioral addictions such as gambling, in which certain actions or objects are thought to bring about good fortune.

Addiction as Social Construction

The idea of addiction as a social construction has produced a large volume of literature critical of traditional understandings of various social phenomena. For example, the idea of addiction as a disease, best dealt with under the auspices of the medical model, is seen by some as a construction that should be examined critically and not merely taken for granted and accepted. *Moral panics* of drug scares that have occurred throughout our history (discussed in more detail throughout this work) have often been considered constructions since fears of situations that were larger than the drugs themselves, such as racial and ethnic fears and tensions, amplified concerns about drug use.

Addiction as Culture

Culture refers to the way of life in a society. Variations in culture and understandings of cultural phenomena change. New and more expansive behaviors are currently considered or are under consideration for inclusion as addiction sources, such as Internet gaming. The fact that Internet gaming involves relatively new technology is a concern because new innovations also bring to society many fears of the unknown. A *culture lag phenomenon* (Ogburn, 1966) exists in which society advances rapidly in certain areas (such as technology), while the values and belief systems often proceed more slowly than the technology can develop. The Internet gamers, often young, present fears of a group of youthful *folk devils* (this term will be discussed in more detail in chapter 7) engaging in a curious and possibly addictive behavior that might contribute to moral disorganization. The fact that some of the video games are thought by some to contribute to further violent behavior adds to the "panic" component.

Addiction has become a part of popular culture as it is the subject of many books, movies, and songs. In fact, current vernacular reflects this focus: people are considered "workaholics" if they spend too much time at their occupations, or "chocoholics" if they have an excessive love of chocolate. Many people claim to "binge-watch" televisions programs (an obvious reference to binge drinking and eating behaviors). People are "addicted," it seems, to almost anything. In exploring the issues of culture and addiction in literary works, Redfeld and Brodie (2002) comment on our "culture's addiction to addiction" (p. 15). Addiction is part of our culture, which in turn influences our understandings of the phenomenon.

Addiction as Risk

Risk can be understood generally as exposure to a dangerous and anxiety-provoking situation, primarily due to the potential harm that can occur due to this exposure. From an addiction perspective, risk can be observed at the individual level (a micro perspective) as people tamper with addictive substances or behaviors that might create the numerous negative consequences associated with addiction including, the pain-inducing effects of withdrawal, loss of support of significant people in one's life, loss of job and income, and a host of other problems. It can be observed at the community level (meso perspective), as communities, lacking the protective forces needed to guard against it, fall prey to various states of disorganization and crime. It can be observed at the societal level (macro perspective) as newer substances developed through advanced technological knowledge create a situation that puts the entire society at risk; greater risk creates anxiety which can, in turn, cause people to behave in self-destructive ways to deal with the anxiety—through the use of addictive substances.

Addiction as Virtue?

William Glasser (1976), psychiatrist and originator of a well-known therapeutic approach known as reality therapy, proposed that many types of mental distress are in effect the results of "negative addiction," the type of addiction resulting from the use of alcohol, heroin, caffeine, nicotine, and the activity of overeating and gambling. However, he posited that this type of addiction could be replaced with "positive addiction" through will power and the development of a better attitude towards one's life circumstances. Glasser described those addicted to a substance or behavioral addictions as weak and frustrated by the inability to achieve love and feelings of self-worth. The substances or behaviors associated with addiction address these feelings in two ways; by numbing the emotional pain, and providing a pleasurable sensation that reinforces the need to continue with the addictive substances or behaviors. Positive actions such as those involving exercise (specifically running) and meditation were the recommended treatment.

The Stigma of Addiction

Addiction produces a form of stigma associated with people who suffer from the condition. Sociologist Erving Goffman (1963) referred to stigma as a "mark," which creates a spoiled identity of the person possessing it. Again, how social phenomena, and of course, people, are defined and labeled often reflects stigmatic attitudes. People who are addicted to substances or behaviors/processes have had a long list of derogatory labels placed upon them. Labels can be harmful to not only those who carry them but to future generations who have the same or similar problems. Terms like addict, alcoholic, drug abuser, sex addict, etc. (and certainly those that are much more pejorative) will not be used in this book, except to some degree in the discussions in relation to history, as they provide some insight into the current situation. Instead, people-first language will be used, choosing terms such as *addicted persons* or *people addicted to a certain substance or behavior*, in lieu of those that promote labeling and stigma.

The Role of Risk and Anxiety

Fears of risky situations have always been a part of human existence, and these fears were manifested as forms of distress. These feelings of distress became pronounced in America after World War II, and a label was provided: anxiety, which later became a disease ("dis-ease") and fell under the authority of the medical model since diseases are treated in the medical field. Under this model, the disease was treated with medication including the appropriated nicknamed "tranquilizers" and later "antidepressants" (Horwitz, 2013). A growth industry of treatment protocols, the professionalization of treatment providers, and an array of programs and facilities (a therapeutic substructure) emerged (Steverson, 2018).

The idea of anxiety can be observed from both the level of the individual and the social. As the fields of psychiatry and psychology address anxiety as the former level, sociology emphasizes the latter and describes how external problems can influence internal states such as anxiety. Social forces also provide different ways of dealing with the distress caused by risks in the world, and one of those ways is through engagement with addictive sources. For clarity, the term *clinical anxiety* will refer to the anxiety experienced by individuals and *cultural anxiety* for a collective, social form of anxiety. By using the sociological imagination (discussed soon), this analysis can be moved from the individual (or clinical) to the social (cultural) and vice versa.

Clinical anxiety is experienced by individuals as somatic experiences in the form of stomach pain, heart palpitations, and breathing problems, as psychological experiences as fright, worry, dread, and apprehension; and as existential fear over concerns of morbidity and life after death (Horwitz, 2013). Cultural anxiety typically represents a collective malaise, a deeply dreadful social condition. Sociologist C. Wright Mills (1959) defined a situation which can be considered cultural anxiety when he wrote: "...the very shaping of history now outpaces the ability of men to orient themselves in accordance with cherished values" (p. 4). Mills was writing in the 1950s, but many social critics note the same condition today. In fact, Mills described the era as the "Age of Fact" for Americans as when "information often dominates their attention and overwhelms their capacities to assimilate it" (p. 5). In a world more technologically saturated than that of Mill's day, one must ask if today this saturation has produced what is now being described as an addiction to technology (attributed to clinical anxiety). It has most certainly contributed to cultural forms of anxiety in some cases and even perhaps has alleviated it in others. But whether or not extensive use of technology is a contributor to addiction is another matter, but one worthy of consideration.

A Note on Terminology

How phenomena are defined and categorized reveals the existence of the social construction of those phenomena. The fact that the terms chosen for definition in this chapter were selected from a vast number of possibilities reflects a degree of social influence and a stratification system that deems some terms more relevant and important to the discussion than others. An analysis of these influences is beneficial.

For example, terminology might be sought that distinguishes addiction from obsessions/compulsions. The DSM-5 defines Obsessive Compulsive Disorder as having two parts: obsessions, which are defined as "recurrent thoughts, urges, or images that are experienced as intrusive and unwanted," and compulsions, the "repetitive behaviors or mental acts that an individual feels driven to perform in response to an obsession or according to rules that must be applied rigidly" (APA, 2013, p. 235). Interestingly, the condition known as hoarding disorder, in which people feel the need to keep items to the point where the accumulation of these materials becomes hazardous, is characterized in the DSM-5 as an obsessive-compulsive disorder; this condition is considered by many to be closely linked to addiction and will be addressed in chapter 4.

What about the non-clinical and commonly used term "habit" mentioned earlier? A definition offered by Merriam-Webster is "a behavior pattern acquired by frequent repetition or physiologic exposure that shows itself in regularity or increased facility of performance" (Merriam-Webster, 2018). The definition certainly sounds like what is commonly understood as an addiction, and at certain points in history, addiction was referred to simply as an activity involving habit (or "habituation"); even today people speak of a drug "habit." This definition does, however, leave out the issue of craving as well as the fact that reward centers in the brain are activated, resulting from the thing causing the frequent repetition. These issues of language will be considered in this work.

A good question involves how far the concept of addiction extends. It has long been established that addiction involves the use of alcohol and other drugs, but the concept is now starting to include behaviors. Perhaps the definition extends to other behaviors such as religious worship, worry, or the acquisition of money (Schaef, 1987). A key point is that many things could be considered addictions, but the official labeling of these new addictions then creates a system of beliefs and practices that evolve from that labeling. The World Health Organization (WHO) has just officially pronounced gaming and sexual excesses as being addictions. What that means will be explored in this text.

Perhaps society itself is the addict possessing at a grand level the same compulsions, cravings, and addictive behaviors as addicted individuals, rapidly regressing to "hit bottom" and in need of an intervention; in other words, the existence of society-as-addict (Schaef, 1987). A society, thus "impaired" by addiction, according to Peele (1985), is a society that defines addiction in terms of magical beliefs rather than science.

It is often thought that addiction should be defined as a simple biochemical response that occurs within individuals and creates negative internal and external consequences. Increasingly, it is observed that addiction is defined in relation to the social responses to addiction and addiction-related activity. If the latter position is adopted, one must note the role of the terminology in the process of defining the concept and developing treatment measures to alleviate it. The sociological imagination (Mills, 1959) compels people to look at larger social factors that create personal responses within individuals. In highly capitalistic American society, it could be that the treatment industry helps create the definitions to provide remediation (for a substantial fee, of course). If addiction is defined (and widely accepted) as a disease with properties defined as medical in nature, then the methods for providing treatment must be found beneath the umbrella of the health care system, a burgeoning field with high financial rewards for those working in the top tier of the system. Substantial financial rewards create an additional craving for more rewards (which one might observe, sounds like addiction). As noted above, the commonly used terminology reflects this medical model understanding of addiction.

Terminology Used in this Book

As will be explored in more detail in the next chapter, people addicted to substances or behaviors have been described in various ways and reflect the ideas society developed about them at different points in time. Many of these terms and descriptions are derogatory and represent them as criminals, immoral people, diseased, and the mentally ill. The use of derogatory terminology will be avoided unless it helps to describe the mindset of the period in which it was used.

It should also be noted that due to the use of historical quotes in the book, the antiquated term "man" or "men" to refer to all humans will be preserved for context without the notation (*sic*); the understanding of the outdated language is addressed here. In the contemporary material, gender-specific pro-nouns and references will be avoided.

Addicted Persons

The term *addicted persons* will instead be used to describe any person who is experiencing an addiction to a substance or a behavior.

Addiction Source

The term *addiction source* will be used to describe both substances and activi-ties that can result in what is currently understood as addiction. A personal reflection on the use of behaviors as addictions will be addressed in the book.

Mental Distress

This term will be used to describe what is commonly known as a mental dis-order, except in parts of the book that are referring to an official diagnostic category. "Distress" is considered less stigmatizing as all people experience feeling distress, but few would approve of the stigmatic term "disorder."

Behavioral Addictions

This term will be used throughout the book to address the current perceptions of behaviors as addiction sources, avoid confusion with compulsive activity, and to draw a distinction between behavioral and substance addictions.

Organization of the Book

This introductory chapter opened with some basic definitions of the terms encountered in the addictions field because this is the logical place to begin an examination, promoting a better understanding of the terminology that is commonly used; since all terms are socially constructed, a foundation was fashioned upon which to question common assumptions about the concepts. This was followed by an explanation of different perspectives of the concept of addiction, from the familiar conceptualization of addiction as a disease to the less familiar representations such as addiction as risk, addiction as a social construction, addiction as lifestyle, and others.

The second chapter of the book provides a short socio-historical examina-tion of alcohol and alcoholism—although alcohol is a drug, humanity's unique history with it is examined separately. Chapter three continues the socio-historical examination of other drugs, shedding some light on the user's relationship with substances of abuse. A historical view adds insights about our earlier perceptions of the concept to allow a reflection on current and possibly future understandings.

The fourth chapter examines the concept of behavioral addiction, which involves those behaviors that have now been classified officially as addiction, such as gambling, or unofficially, including internet gaming, compulsive sexual behaviors, and problematic eating behaviors among others; it also explores how inclusion of these behaviors as addiction has enhanced or complicated understandings of the concept. Chapter five is a discussion on the processes of diagnosis, treatment, and prevention as components of the addictions field, again using a socio-historical perspective that describes the evolution of these processes.

The sixth chapter explores the issue of addiction in the family and takes a systems perspective which sees families as "bundles of relations" (Rapaport, 1968) in which addiction affects all members—this section includes the Adult Children of Alcoholics (ACOA) movement and other familial concepts, and their effects on the field of addiction.

Chapter seven examines the role of addiction as deviant behavior and addressed in the criminal justice system; it also explores how fears involving addictive behavior in the past have helped develop what is known as moral panic theory. The eighth chapter describes sociological perspectives of addiction through an examination of the contributions of sociological theory: it introduces readers to a perspective that will hopefully allow greater reflection on our understanding of addiction.

Chapter nine includes a discussion of advocacy measures by people and groups with addiction to further enhance how the concept has been and continues to be addressed. The final chapter concludes our discussion with an examination of the meanings of addiction and related concepts from a sociological perspective in a changing world full of risks and social anxieties.

Conclusion

Addiction, as our society has identified it, has been determined to be of two types: substance addiction and, more recently, behavioral addiction, the former requiring the ingestion of an external substance (alcohol or other drug) and the latter relating to behaviors or experiences (gambling, sexual behavior, overeating, Internet gaming, to name a few). The concept of addiction is an important one due to the consequences for individuals, their families, communities, and society at large; therefore, it is important to examine addiction at micro-, meso-, and macro-levels of analysis. Although several natural and social science disciplines address the concept, this work takes a sociological approach by examining the social and environmental conditions surrounding addiction and challenging certain commonly accepted notions of the concept.

An understanding of a concept's terminology is vital in understanding the concept itself. Examining and analyzing terms and concepts and their relationship to similar and related terms and concepts provides a more comprehensive inspection. Much of the standard lexicon in the addiction field reflects current understandings, and this lexicon reveals a very close connection to the medical model. An examination of this connection with medicine and the medical field will be offered in the chapters that follow.

The history of society's past experiences with addiction provides important information to assist in fully understanding the subject, so next to be explored is a socio-historical analysis of addiction sources for a foundational examination of the concept as a major social problem.

Chapter 2

A Short History of Alcohol and Alcoholism

"Perhaps we should consider how the knowledge of historical determinants in both the moral and medical model can be of theoretical and practical use not only to research and treatment professionals but to problem drinkers and their families as well."

(Genevieve M. Ames, 1985 p. 37)

A Socio-Historical Examination

Starting with a socio-historical examination of addiction provides a strong foundation of how addiction has been understood in the past, the measures that have been taken to address it, and how these past understandings affect our current ones. The attention paid to the physical effects on the body and the psychological effects on the mind are important in understanding addiction, however, by using a sociological framework within a historical backdrop, it can be observed how not only how individuals are affected by alcohol and other drugs, their production, and their addictive processes, but also how society has been affected by these factors, on a larger scale. And, more about addiction can be learned. This chapter will be dedicated to the social history of alcohol.

A Global History of Alcohol

Alcohol is so pervasive that it exists in the far reaches of the galaxy; in the form of methanol, ethanol, and vinyl alcohol clouds. With the omnipresence of alcohol, it is no wonder it has affected homo sapiens, or to use McGovern's terminology, "homo imbibens" (drinking human). As McGovern (2009) notes, "some four billion years ago, primitive single-celled microbes are hypothesized to have dined on simple sugars in the primordial soup and excreted ethanol and carbon dioxide" (p. 2); therefore some forms of alcohol might have been here from the start.

The history of alcohol, its production, use, and its consequences, is extensive throughout human existence. Though there are several types of alcohol, the type used in beverages that can cause intoxication is ethanol. Ethanol alcohol has long been consumed since antiquity in different forms. Alcohol is produced through fermentation, distillation, and brewing. Alcohol in the form of wine, liquor or "spirits," and beer have been a part of the global landscape in terms of its addiction-related properties. Worldwide, alcohol is associated with a wide range of human experiences, including celebrations, religious rituals, adaptations to stress and grief, and an assortment of social movements that have supported the consumption of alcohol and those that have sought to control it. It has some potential health effects, such as creating a calming effect, promoting communion with others, and acting as a preventative agent against heart disease when used in moderation. Alternatively, when used to access it can cause damage to many organs, including the liver, pancreas, heart. And of course, it can cause major damage to the brain in the form of problems in memory formation, abstract thought, problem-solving ability, attention and concentration, and emotional regulation ((Kuhn, Swartzenwelder, and Wilson, 2008).

Wine

It has been surmised that fermentation is the earliest form of energy production. Wine, the product of the natural fermentation of grapes, has contributed heavily to Western civilization through its role in religion and spirituality, medicine, war, and other phenomena (Esteicher, 2006). The fermentation of grapes was probably discovered by accident (Barr, 1999). Wine production (called viticulture) probably began between 6000 and 4000 B.C. in the area currently known as Armenia, and its use spread around the globe. It was readily adopted by some regions of the world but rejected in others on religious and moral grounds (such as in Islamic countries) or reasons having to do with the adverse effects of wine on certain populations (primarily Asian nations). Christian nations were more readily receptive to wine consumption due to its relationship to ritual activity—with wine representing the blood of Christ (Courtwright, 2001). Noting the habit-forming effects wine, Swedish physician Magnus Huss described the condition as "alcoholism" in the mid-1800s (Lesch et al., 1990).

Wine comes in many different types and has been associated with a long history of social conventions. Champaign, the bubbling French wine, associated with a highbrow, indulgent, and lascivious lifestyle, became a fixture in European cities in the early eighteenth century (Ehmer & Hinderman, 2015). Despite its elite associations, it is also associated with the image of addicted persons becoming intoxicated and living on streets (creating the derogatory term "winos" for this group).

Distilled Spirits

Distilled spirits, or liquor, consist of several different alcoholic beverages, including rum, gin, brandy, and vodka. Distilling alcohol was used by early Greeks and Romans, further developed in the Middle East, finding its way into

Europe in the 12th century, with Holland becoming a main producer and distributor (Courtwright, 2001).

Rum's association with seafaring travel is well-documented. The drink, derived mostly from sugar cane, is closely linked to global commerce. Rum rations were provided to sailors transporting the cargo for its perceived health benefits. Also, alcohol was important in preserving the fruits on board, causing them to stay fresh longer. Drunkenness unsurprisingly became a concern on the ships, and rum was often diluted with water in what became known as "grog," a term derived from the nickname of the admiral who issued the order for the weakened substance. The beverage is also associated with the disturbing history of colonization of the West Indies and Central America, areas that provided sugar cane to produce rum as a reward for slaves on the Caribbean Islands. The spirit was called "kill devil" and later "rum" from "rumbellion," a portmanteau for rum and rebellion (Ehmer & Hindermann, 2015)

Gin, distilled grains flavored with juniper berries, was the subject of a period of British panic known as "gin mania" or the "gin epidemic" in which the areas rapidly industrializing between 1720 and 1750, notably London, felt the effects of unrestrained capital through a host of social problems such as homelessness, crime, poor health, and addiction to spirits. The potent effects of gin added to urbanites' woes, as was depicted in the Hogarth engraving "Gin Lane" in 1751. While gin was used in the colonies, it was never consumed in large amounts as it was considered an "urban drink," and there were few large population centers, though, after prohibition, it would enjoy more popularity in the form of the martini (Lender & Martin, 1987). Governmental attempts to control its use backfired, causing only a very slight decrease in use followed by a sharp upturn; unexpectedly, a decline in consumption followed the repeal of the gin laws. This suggests that legislative attempts to control a substance's use are often ineffective since there is a complex of social values that reflect the desires of the community (Warner, Her, Gmel & Rehm, 2001). This is a phenomenon that has been observed with similar types of legislative action to addictive substances and social responses to that action.

Beer and Ale

Early hunter-gathering societies learned to process grains for both bread and beer. The predecessor to what is now known as beer was gruel or porridge, which was created by soaking the grain in water and allowed the early people to digest them more easily. Grinding and heating produced changes that enabled the establishment of yeast, which released ethanol. In addition to the health benefits of sanitized liquid, the gruel beer also acted as an intoxicant, as the early societies discovered. Different grains were used, but barley became especially popular (Sinclair & Sinclair, 2010).

Beer and brewing also have a long history. Produced from fermenting starches, the brewing process that creates beer, it is believed, began in the Near East, where barley and wheat were in large supply. Africa had large supplies of millet, also used in beer production (Sinclair & Sinclair, 2010).

A National History

All nations have a long history with alcohol, and its ramifications in America is no exception. Before the American Revolution, alcohol use was not considered a problem of social concern (Gusfield, 1986); this is not to say alcohol was not used in the early years of the nation, it was, and in large amounts. The amount of alcohol consumed in the nineteenth century, in fact, astounded luminary visitors such as Charles Dickens, Alexis de Tocqueville, Harriet Martineau, and Frances Trollope, who dutifully documented American love of intoxicating beverages in the period (Mitenbuler, 2015).

Alcohol in the colonies

When the settlers arrived on the shores of what would become the United States of America, they brought with them a taste for "strong drink." The colonists, as with people in the Old World, had to deal with polluted water, and various forms of alcohol were safer and seen as a healthier alternative. Since water often spoiled in wooden kegs during sea transport, alcohol traveled better. Liquor was shipped to the colonies, and the settlers maintained their close and enduring relationship with Old World drinks. With high shipping costs, the colonists turned to brewing, distilling, and fermenting their own beverages from local sources, creating distinctive drinking preferences and customs. Brewing and drinking homemade beer became commonplace in early America. Though it would come later in the Western parts of the country, wine production did not catch on initially; therefore, imported wine was consumed by the wealthier residents (Lender & Martin, 1987).

"Strong water" was initially not as popular as beer in the New World but increased in popularity in a few decades. Gin was cheaply produced and available for the working classes. But while gin was popular in some quarters, it suffered the bad reputation it had received in England during the British gin epidemic. Indigenous resources such as pears, apples, peaches, corn, rye, potatoes, berries, and honey (used in the production of mead) created some uniquely American beverages; applejack, hard cider, brandy, and other drinks became local favorites. "Demon rum" became quite a hit for Eastern colonists averting their tastes from beer to the more potent drink. However, the frontier people who moved westward had less access to the rum that arrived by sea, so they turned to the local grains, especially corn, to create their alcoholic indulgences. Bourbon, an indigenous drink of the frontier of Kentucky produced with corn and other grains and aged in charred oak barrels, had a distinct flavor and dark color and became quite popular (Lender & Martin, 1987). Bourbon's influence would become so great in a developing nation's economy; it is claimed that "like no other American product, it embodies capitalism" (Mitenbuler, 2015, p. 4).

The use of alcoholic beverages in the colonies was considerable, and workers and family members (including children) drank regularly. Celebrations of different varieties often called for alcohol as well. Drinking establishments such as taverns and inns provided social interaction and were placed in different types of buildings, from simple structures to elaborately decorated enterprises. Some of the colonists' drinking patterns mimicked those of their forebears, but others did not. New norms in the field of drinking supplemented older ones, and while colonists were serious drinkers, they were not problem drinkers to the extent that legislation interfered with their drinking patterns. As Lender and Martin (1987) notes, "a general lack of anxiety over alcohol problems was one of the most significant features of drinking in the colonial era" (p. 14). However, social anxiety over "imbibing" did begin to emerge in the decades after colonization.

Although alcohol was considered a normal and practical aspect of life with most colonial Americans, there were controls on its use. Puritans legislated attempts to limit consumption by creating laws introduced to stop sale to Native Americans, African slaves, servants, and apprentices, and established a colony (Georgia) with controls over liquor. Also, protectionist policies were established in some areas to promote beer and liquor production for national and international trade reasons. In addition, licensure for inns and taverns helped encourage innkeeping, to provide revenue for the government, and to control alcoholic distribution (Thornton, 1991). However, Gusfield (1986) noted that taverns were governed by local licensure, but this was not to limit or control but to provide for the protection and satisfaction of traveling customers.

Taverns modeled on retreats in London became very popular in New York, Charles Town, and Annapolis. Their numbers grew quickly, prompting upperclass concerns to be able to control them; they were, in fact, considered by some to uncontrollable. However, these taverns were "certainly seed beds of the Revolution" or "nurseries of freedom" (Rorabaugh, 1979, 35) for the patriots plotting independence from England. Quakers and Methodists were the primary religious institutions that were concerned with the negative effects of taverns and the excesses of imbibing.

Consuming strong drink became increasingly linked to deviance and crime, signaling to the citizens the emergence of social disorder, so dangerous to a newly forming society. Colonies developed local codes and ordinances over the use of alcohol. Incarceration, flogging, shaming, surveillance, and the imposition of fines were levied on those who disturbed the public order due to drunkenness (Lender & Martin, 1987). By the end of the eighteenth century and during the early nineteenth century, concerns over the abuse of alcoholic beverages continued in several states (Gusfield, 1986). Other concerns to the social order involved "othered groups"—Native American inhabitants and African slaves—who were thought to be driven mad by strong drink. A "firewater myth" fostered a belief that Native Americans, due to their biological constitutions, were ill-equipped to drink rationally. The highly controlled "celebration days" for African slaves were created to keep them complacent when laboring, therefore representing how racial and ethnic stereotypes fueled the concerns of alcohol use by those that did not derive from good Old Country Caucasian stock (Lender & Martin, 1987). Alcohol consumption decreased after the American Revolution but picked up after 1800, resulting in what has one scholar called "the great alcoholic binge of the early nineteenth century" (Rorabaugh, 1979) and fell sharply again during early temperance efforts.

Temperance

Preserving the social order in the colonies was of utmost importance to the social activists of the period as inebriety was perceived as one of the evils that could result in the collapse of society. Concerns over the loss of social stability and cohesion over the issue of drunkenness and other ill effects of strong drink led to a series of actions to thwart their use. Activists such as Portland mayor Neal Dow, creator of the Maine Law that sought to remove spirits from his city, and health advocates such as Benjamin Rush, a Philadelphia physician and so-called Father of Psychiatry, sought to educate citizens on the physical and psychological abuses of alcohol and to treat and prevent these abuses (Lender & Martin, 1987). These early attempts at forcing abstinence from alcohol consumption (called temperance) would continue in American history, rising at various times and culminating in Prohibition in the twentieth century.

Temperance's humble beginnings have been considered by some scholars (Tracy & Acker, 2004) to have begun with Rush's work *An Inquiry into the Effects of Ardent Spirits upon the Human Body and Mind* in 1784. In this work, Rush referenced the same problems that occurred during Britain's gin epidemic and implored citizens to abandon all "ardent spirits" except for a few alcoholic drinks he felt were important for their medicinal value (Musto 2002). While Rush's message in *Inquiry* was written from a physician's perspective, he offered several alternatives to strong drinks, such as plain water, cyder, malt liquors, wines, coffee, and combinations of water and molasses or maple. However, people who are already addicted to ardent spirits, he warned, should not wean off them gradually but "abstain from them suddenly and entirely" (Rush, 1785, cited in Musto, 2002, p. 43). In addition, Rush made a plea to the clergy "of all dominations to aid me with all the weight you possess in society, from the dignity and usefulness of your sacred office, to save our fellow men from being destroyed by the great destroyer of their lives and souls" (cited in Musto, 2002, p. 38).

Famed seventeenth-century reverend Increase Mather believed spirits were a gift from God and, if used in moderation, had important medicinal and nutritional benefits. His equally famous son, Cotton Mather, adopted his father's viewpoint but was more concerned about the harms of alcohol to the overall social structure of the New England colonies, especially regarding drunkenness among the upper classes (Rorabaugh, 1979).

Some factions of the clergy also intervened in their efforts to eradicate the use of alcohol, even despite the pessimism that "tippling" (another term for drinking) would continue as a major component of the culture. Reverend Lyman Beecher was one of the most notable voices of the church denouncing alcohol use, in addition to his status as the father to social reformers, including Harriet Beecher Stowe. In his small book *Six Sermons on the Nature, Occasions, Signs, Evils and Remedy of Intemperance* (1826), he argued that only total abstinence from alcohol would suffice in eradicating this evil and that total abstinence was essential and possible (Musto, 2002). He proclaimed, "the effect of ardent spirits on the brain, and the members of the body, is among the least effects of intemperance, and the least detrimental part. It is the moral ruin which it works in the souls, that gives it the denomination of giant-wickedness" (Beecher, 1926, p. 46, cited in Musto, 2002). As Musto (2002) notes, Benjamin Rush saw the natural end of inebriety as death from punishment or suicide, Beecher saw it as damnation to eternal hell.

Beecher's voice was not alone in a growing chorus of opposition. Still, alcohol use and abuse did not assuage its use in the nineteenth century. It has been suggested that the period from the 1790s to the 1830s was the country's zenith regarding the use of strong drink, eclipsing that of the colonial period. The arrival of Irish immigrants in the mid-century created a unique dynamic in American alcohol consumption. The Irish, predominately Catholic in a new nation occupied by Protestants, rejected assimilation measures early on and formed enclaves whose Old-World traditions (including the hardy consumption of alcohol) were maintained. Irish staples such as whiskey, gin, and malted beverages were the main beverages consumed. German immigrants brought beer-making skills to the New Country and established many breweries still in existence, which embodies what is currently known as "American beer." As the Germans' drinking patterns approximated those of the "native borns," they did not receive the stereotypes given to the hard-drinking, uncultured Irish newcomers (Lender & Martin, 1987).

Several groups were established in the ninetieth-century to oppose alcohol consumption. In Baltimore, an anti-liquor movement began in 1840 with a group calling itself the Washingtonian Temperance Society, or the Washingtonian Movement (named after George Washington). This group achieved such initial success that it created many spin-off groups. Their focus was on helping individuals by providing social support for total abstinence; in this, they differed from other temperance groups whose mission it was to reform drinking laws. Despite its popularity, the movement was short-lived, though its ideals continued to other organizations (Lender and Martin, 1987).

With urbanization and industrialization that occurred after the American Civil War, the social problems of crime, poverty, violence, and public health problems were viewed in terms of citizen's relation to alcohol and other drugs; they were very visible in the "skid row" and "bowery" areas of American cities that clearly exposed saloon life and the intoxicated "bums" that inhabited the street corners. The appearance of prostitution in "red-light districts" further drew the attention and ire of people seeking to maintain order (Lender and Martin, 1987). Transient populations in the seaborn towns also intensified the image of the Eastern skid row areas (Gusfield, 1986).

Groups such as the Women's Christian Temperance Union (WCTU) rallied aggressive (but primarily non-violent) attacks on saloons and taverns, which were perceived to the cause of many social problems, including unemployment and conflict in the home (Musto, 2002). The powerful Anti-saloon League (ASL) was formed in 1895 in the nation's capital and centered around the abuse of alcohol. Political pressure continued to grow against alcohol use and the prohibition of alcohol in the United States.

Prohibition

The "noble experiment" (as it has been called) of prohibition was an attempt to legislate alcohol consumption. Named after U.S. Representative Andrew Volstead (even though it was drafted by Congressman Wayne Wheeler), the Volstead Act, or the National Prohibition Act, was the legislation that outlawed the manufacture, sale, and transport of alcoholic beverages in the country. Prohibition began in 1920 and lasted until 1933.

While research studies have produced conflicting results about the effectiveness of prohibition, it does seem that consumption and alcohol-related problems were lowered, at least in some areas of the country. However, consumption did not cease entirely. In rural areas, sellers of illegal alcohol called "bootleggers" produced this illicit produce known as "moonshine," which contained a variety of different ingredients and was often lethal. People in the moonshine trade became adept at constructing cars fast enough to outrun the police. They also became proficient in their driving skills; stock car racing would eventually develop from this activity of running from the police in modified cars.

In more populated areas, underground "speakeasies" where people socialized and partied with alcohol, hidden from the watchful eye of police, replaced the pre-prohibition taverns and saloons. Of course, crime establishments sprang up to deal with the demand for alcohol through black market operations (gang activity in Chicago became legendary). The "gangster era" became a period known for its violence, creating a popular culture craze that could be found in songs, novels, and movies.

The "noble experiment" of prohibition ended in December of 1933. It seems Americans did not want to give up their alcohol and had hoped that the economic devastation wrought by the Great Depression might be alleviated once alcohol was again legal and order restored.

The Disease Concept of Alcoholism

In the seventeenth and eighteenth centuries, alcohol intoxication (normally called drunkenness) was not directly linked to a disease. In fact, as described earlier, drinking was considered normal and imbibing an activity performed out of affection and love of drinking. It was not perceived as an overpowering, all-consuming force. Addiction, as is understood today, did not exist in colonial America. This doesn't mean drinking was not a problem for some citizens, but their actions were generally tolerated. However, concerns were growing within the clergy of the effects chronic drunkenness was having on society. Strong desires for alcohol were thought to produce "habituation" in some people, but this habituation was connected to the act of drinking, not to alcohol itself. Drunkenness began to be perceived as sin, and movements were forming to deal with it. In the late eighteenth century, the idea of powerlessness over excessive drinking began to germinate, even before Benjamin Rush began to describe the concept of addiction and its classification as a disease (Levine, 1978).

As described previously, early temperance movements accepted Rush as their founder and his philosophy as their guiding vision. Only through abstinence, the early temperance movement followers began to argue (changing an earlier principle of moderation) would the evil of alcohol be defeated. Many people made the pledge to remain alcohol-free. "Reformed drunkards" gave testimony in speeches and autobiographies of their reformation through abstinence, and the concept of drunkenness as a disease begins to appear in speeches and literature. The idea of this disease as a heritable condition also became popular. Most temperance organizations, such as the fraternal organizations that formed during the nineteenth century, were supportive of those addicted to alcohol. This would change, however, when a new generation of temperance groups organized around principles of science and pragmatism in the following century. These groups were more coercive in their attempts to bring about a nation of abstainers, focusing more on the evil of alcohol than addiction. Those considered drunkards were perceived as nuisances and less as victims of a disease. Addiction was considered more of a problem with other drugs, notably opium, in the early years of the twentieth century (Levine, 1978).

Prohibition's focus, guided by the abstinence ideal, was centered less on addiction and more on legislating American consumption of alcohol. Americans did not accept the idea, however, and in the aftermath of prohibition's repeal, another transition took place which has had a lasting effect on society's understanding of alcohol, alcoholism, and treatment protocols. Research studies were conducted in the mid-twentieth century to establish a more scientific grounding of addiction. The "alcoholism movement" began in this milieu, and the idea of addiction to alcohol as disease took root (Ames, 1985).

E. M. Jellinek at Yale University adopted a medical approach of medicine that was extended to the World Health Organization (WHO), the American Medical Association (AMA), and to Alcoholics Anonymous (AA). Research in this area, driven by renewed funding, pushed the idea of addiction as a disease subsumed under the "medical model," one that competed with the narrative of the "moral model" which put emphasis on personal agency in the choice to avoid drunkenness (Ames, 1985). Of course, this idea was a reappearance of the early ideas of Benjamin Rush and was not really that novel. Jellinek was the most notable expert on alcoholism in America during the 1940s and 1950s (Musto, 2002). Although it has been claimed by some scholars that Jellinek stated alcoholism was "like" a disease, he clearly stated in *The Disease Concept of Alcoholism* (1960/2010) that he adopted the "majority position" of the period that "analogous forms of the injection of narcotics and alcohol, such as drinking with loss of control and physical dependence are caused by a physiopathological process and constitute diseases" (Jellinek, 1960/2010, p. 40). It is therefore clear that alcoholism, in the more noxious forms in his typology, were considered diseases; this typology (or "nosology") of addiction types is how he is most remembered and consists of these categories:

The disease model has five main assumptions:

- There is a biological cause

- Once addiction is activated, it is no longer dormant and will follow a predictable course

- Total abstinence is the only way to quell the symptoms

- There is no cure

- Any exposure to the drug will reactivate the condition and re-sult in relapse (Berger, 1991).

It is often believed that the idea of addiction as a disease (in this case, alcohol addiction) began with AA; however, the idea of the disease conceptualization of alcoholism was already in existence in the medical community in the nineteenth century (Barr, 1999). It was not an idea; however, that made its way outside the medical field until AA brought it into the public view. The disease concept fits well within the AA philosophy on several counts; for example, the idea of powerlessness that was expressed in the first of the twelve steps absolved the addicted person of moral failings. Similarly, the older idea of alcoholism as an "allergy" under the medical model assumed a predetermination for addiction, reduced self-blame, and was accessible for the redemptive force of submission (Bahr, 1973).

In the 1940s, a change was evident as the disease concept of addiction found its home in the obvious place. As the medical profession took on the newly established disease, practitioners had to adjust to the new skills needed as well as to the consequences of working with people who were previously considered degenerates; this was also a concern for health practitioners (Ames, 1985).

Conclusion

Addictive sources come from many different types, and the one with the greatest ubiquity and most remarkable history probably belongs to alcohol. Alcoholic beverages, in the form of wines, distilled spirits, and beers and ales, have been used as a source of recreation and socialization for eons. They have also been a source of addiction, affecting not only addicted individuals throughout history, but changing the way societies have dealt with the regulation of those considered to have abused the drug.

The United States certainly has an interesting history with alcohol and alcohol addiction. In the colonial era, newcomers to the country drank often and heavily. As time progressed, Puritan clergy grew increasingly concerned with the disorganization perceived to be taking place, activity that threatened the very foundation of social order. Temperance movements were organized to confront the problem, starting with a tempered strategy but evolving into an abstinence-based one. Temperance movements became a powerful force in American perceptions of alcohol and drunkenness. The idea of an overwhelming force and powerlessness to this force compelling people to drink began in the late eighteenth century, only to reappear in the early twentieth century in the form of addiction as a disease and placed under the medical model.

The "noble experiment" of prohibition in the early 1900s proved that Americans were not ready for changes that regulated their drinking patterns. The notion of addiction to alcohol, or alcoholism, has been a major concern, however, throughout most of the country's history. As Levine (1978) argues, colonial ideas of excessive alcohol consumption as simply nuisance behavior and nineteenth and twentieth-century notions of the same behavior as constituting addiction existed side by side for some time. If newer models of addiction appear on the scene (and it is assumed they will), they will likely exist for some time alongside the current medical model.

Chapter 3

A Short History of Other Drugs of Abuse

"Here was a panacea…for all human woes; here was the secret of happiness, about which philosophers had disputed for so many ages…carried in the waistcoat pocket."

(Thomas De Quincey, 1822/2009 p. 68)

A socio-historical approach will be used in our examination of drugs of abuse, this time, those other than alcohol. The history of how drugs have altered individuals (and society), how and when they arrived on the scene, the various "moral panics" that resulted (often based on race and ethnicity), and the measures taken to diagnose, treat, and prevent them paint a more vivid picture of the current scene today.

Hillman (2008) notes the role of drugs in the ancient world. The extreme threats to life that came from disease, including various types of epidemics; war and other forms of violence; malnutrition; and dangerous animals, reptiles, and insects all added to the fact that life was consistently precarious and often short. Experiments with various herbal remedies resulted in relief from painful occurrences and the vicissitudes of life. Various concoctions derived from plants, animals, and minerals were experimented with, and potions, balms, and other drug forms were created; in fact, "drug craft was arguably the classical world's greatest resource" (Hillman, 2008, p. 33). Although still a rudimentary science (or better, "pseudoscience" in many cases), the early Mediterranean healers used all the resources at their disposal for their remedies, as Hillman notes, "instead of Pfizer, they had Mother Nature" (p. 34).

Some of the ancient creations had properties other than curative. The Greek writer Virgil extolled the virtues using poppies (which produce opium) for its euphoric properties rather than its pain-relieving effects. Those in the classical world also sniffed fumes from burning plants such as cannabis. They also liquified certain plants such as different types of woodworm for potent mind-altering drinks. They also enjoyed the "nightshade" plants—jimson weed, belladonna, henbane, and mandrake—despite their knowledge of the potentially fatal side effects. In addition, the ingestion of mushrooms was common for its hallucinogenic effects, despite its potential for death. Even hemlock, so well recognized as a method of execution (well-illustrated in the story of Socrates), was also a sedative when used sparingly. The use of these mood-enhancing agents is well documented in the literature in the form of "narco-mythology" (Hillman, 2008). In literature and philosophy, drugs played a major role in the classical era.

Drugs of Abuse

Nicotine and caffeine

These two categories are linked together in this section as they, like all drugs, have the potential for abuse, despite the fact they are probably not the first drugs that come to mind when considering the link between drugs and social problems. Tobacco was a curiosity to European explorers when the leaves of the plant were rolled and smoked by the Tainos Indians in 1492 (Courtwright, 2001). Still considered exotic during the sixteenth century, tobacco quickly spread throughout the world, being cultivated in various places and enjoying a robust global market; it was used in the form of pipes, cigars, cigarettes, and in the smokeless form known as "snuff." Despite protestations by critics of its unappealing effects of bad breath, stained teeth and clothes, and the unsightly release of mucus and spittle, as Courtwright (2001) noted: "nothing checked tobacco's progress" (p. 16) as its use grew, eventually becoming fashionable around the world. Tobacco produced an industry that grew exponentially despite the growing acknowledgment in its role in causing cancer and other serious health effects.

Caffeine is an extremely popular drug with a very long history of use. This use began in Ethiopia with the chewing of coffee beans and was later drunk in Yemen around the fifteenth century after infusing the beans. It became traded globally, and Europe became its epicenter. Coffee houses spread around the world, representing the popularity of the beverage. Its use became a major part of the American experience as the frontiers were settled, and growth and expansion were emblematic of the new world (Courtwright, 2001). The use and production of tea developed in India and China as the plant was used for medical and spiritual purposes. Its use also spread quickly and became a major player in the global market, especially noted in the eighteenth-century American rebellion against taxes on tea, resulting in the Tea Party uprising and a subsequent preference of coffee over tea (Kuhn, Swartzwelder, & Wilson 2008). The history of chocolate, from the cacao plant in Africa, was another introduction of caffeine to the world; initially prepared as a beverage mixed with spices and served with tobacco, chocolate became the beverage of choice among the exalted classes (Courtwright, 2001).

Though not associated with the major social problems that form the focus of this book, caffeine and nicotine are popular addictive substances that can cause major health problems. Nicotine, especially, is a major concern that claims the lives of many people, resulting in numerous prevention and cessation programs in the form of psychoeducation, psychotherapy, and medications. Especially troubling is the use of tobacco by young people. The use of electronic cigarettes (also called e-cigarettes or e-cigs) are a growing concern as well; these devices heat nicotine or other substances instead of burning, and users inhale the vapors (or "vape"). E-cigs have become increasingly popular among young people despite the fact they are not a healthy alternative to traditional cigarettes as the Federal Drug Administration (2019) has warned that the recent increase in e-cigarette use by both middle and high school students has many consequences including problems in brain development, chronic impulsivity, mood disorders, and, of course, addiction. As the FDA warns, "no tobacco products—including e-cigarettes are safe for youth to use (FDA, 2019)."

Narcotics

Derived from the Greek term for stupor, narcotics originally referred to a wide range of drugs that were used for pain relief. The term was initially used to refer to different drugs (particularly opium, cocaine, and marijuana), but today they primarily refer to opium and its derivatives and semi-synthetic substitutes. Currently, the term narcotics has been primarily replaced by the term opioids, referring to heroin, codeine, morphine, methadone, fentanyl, oxycodone, and hydrocodone, among others (dea.gov, n.d). Before discussing narcotics as a class, considered will be the background of opium and cocaine separately, then narcotics as a general classification of drugs.

Opiates

Opium is probably the world's first discovered drug other than alcohol, and though its origins are dubious, it is likely that its cultivation and use began in eastern Europe and spread outward to the Middle East and North Africa, and to the rest of the developing world (Booth, 1996). This drug provided users with both medicinal relief for various ailments and euphoric escapes from everyday life; it also created serious problems with addiction in many users.

Extracted from the sap that comes from the poppy plant, opium was traditionally eaten or smoked. Later it was mixed in various liquids (including alcohol to create laudanum), and when the hypodermic needle was created, it allowed intravenous injection, causing a more rapid and intense feeling of euphoria. Swallowing opium, which in its pure form was bitter enough to induce vomiting (which is why various spices and other flavors were added), resulted in a moniker for users: "opium eaters." Its use by swallowing continued for hundreds of years in parts of the East and India, but it was consumed in a mixture of wine, sugar, or honey in Europe, and smoked in China and other parts of the East. Elaborate pipes were made for smoking the drug and rituals developed in which the smokers reclined on their sides, drawing in the smoke that created a deep but short period of slumber and euphoria; "opium dens" were founded for users to drop in and smoke opium (Booth, 1996).

In the West, the use of opium was notably related to Asian culture but did not garner much notice until the publication of *Confessions of an Opium Eater* in 1822 (Hickman, 2007). Speaking elegantly and enthusiastically about the effects of opium (especially in contrast to the effects of wine), Britain's Thomas de Quincey explained his experience with the drug after experiencing the pain of a toothache: "...the opium eater...feels the diviner part of his nature is paramount—that is , the moral affections are in a state of cloudless serenity and high over all the great light of the majestic intellect" (de Quincey, 1822/2019, p. 72). His accounts of coming off the drug, however, along with similar reports by era physicians, caught the attention of an interested (and often fearful) public, especially due to its connection with an encroaching fear of foreigners (Hickman, 2007).

Morphine (amply named after Morpheus, the Greek god of dreams) was isolated from opium around 1805, became available for medicinal use in pill form, and later prepared as an injectable. Initially seen as a great cure for many ills, its addictive properties quickly became known and resulted in a name—morphinism. Laudanum, made by mixing opium with other ingredients such as nutmeg and saffron (among an assortment of many possibilities), was formulated into pill or liquid form. Heroin was introduced in 1898 by a chemist at the Bayer Company and used to treat respiratory conditions; as its additional effects (the drug was stronger than morphine) was quickly discovered, its use as a medicine was discontinued.

Though it might be difficult to realize today since the *over*prescribing of opioids has become such a current issue, there was a time in the recent past when opioids, it was believed, were being *under* prescribed. In the 1980s and early 1990s, there existed a state of "opiophobia" in which patients were being prescribed the drugs for postoperative care and cancer. The push for more aggressive treatment as a humane practice began in the medical field, augmented by pharmaceutical companies. Advancements in the field appeared in such forms as extended release oxycodone (better known by its brand name OxyContin); oxycodone prescriptions were often increased due to a seriously flawed belief they were less likely to be abused (Jones et al., 2018).

Beginning in the late 1990s, upon assurances to the medical profession by the psychopharmaceutical industry that opioids as a pain reliever were safe and did not pose serious threats of addiction, these drugs began being increasingly prescribed (NIDA, 2018a). As the consequences of addiction and overdose became broadcast widely through professional publications and the media, physicians, and pharmaceutical companies were reprimanded for the over-prescription and false claims of opioids. Federal regulations were quickly promulgated to reduce the number of opioids being prescribed (Jones et al., 2018).

In recent years, there has been a major focus on opioids. According to the Centers for Disease Control and Prevention (CDC), in 2017, opioids accounted for almost 68% of drug overdose deaths, making it a significant area of social concern in America (CDC, 2019). Currently, the most frequently prescribed opioids include hydrocodone, oxycodone, oxymorphone, morphine, codeine, and fentanyl and the most abused non-prescribed opioid is heroin. (NIDA, 2019).

Cocaine

Originating in South America from at least 1800 BCE, the coca plant was chewed to produce a feeling of euphoria by local laborers. Spanish conquerors rejected the use of the drug, but its properties intrigued the people back home in Europe who were able to isolate cocaine, then add a chemical to produce water solubility. The concoction was used for some medical procedures but also found its way into a host of different "elixirs" that would reportedly cure a variety of ailments.

Cocaine was widely believed to be a beneficial medicine and was available, pure, and cheap in the nineteenth century. Early on, it was used as a tonic for sinus problems and hay fever, and to cure addictions resulting from alcohol, opium, and morphine. It was touted in medical journals and achieved praise from many in the medical community (most famously, perhaps, was Sigmund Freud). In was available in many forms, including tablets, injectables, ointments, and sprays. In addition, it was available non-medically in liquid form and placed in sodas, wines, and various elixirs.

Around the turn of the twentieth century, the drug became associated with the loss of control by users. Whites, especially in the South, feared uprisings by African Americans who used cocaine, which was thought to increase their cunning and efficiency and produce almost supernatural strength (including being resistant to bullets). These fears corresponded with the enactment of suppressive voting laws and legal segregation, and with the horrors of lynching (Musto, 1973).

The classification of narcotics in historical perspective

The classification known as narcotic drugs will be used here because of its historical significance, important to understandings of addiction. As mentioned previously, the term narcotics moved beyond its usual reference to opium and its derivatives morphine and heroin to other addictive substances such as cocaine and even marijuana (Musto, 1973). The term is often used in the convergence of these drugs in twentieth-century drug policy; narcotics control was a big part of law enforcement efforts of the era. The term also conjures up a specific image in American drug history; therefore, although these drugs were previously discussed separately, the following section examines narcotics as a collective group due to their influence on a rapidly modernizing society.

Addiction to drugs, other than alcohol, affected society differently than alcoholism. Narcotics reflected a significant change in culture; the potential for drugs to do great things in the increasingly industrial period of the nineteenth and early twentieth century was tempered by the potential for unimaginable social maladies. Conditions of mental distress of different types were invented to make sense of the new modern period—one example was neurasthenia, a multi-symptom disease thought to be caused by the fast-paced lifestyles that were contributed to and were a consequence of by narcotics use (Hickman, 2007). Another condition known as Mania Americana was similarly a disease of modernity. Both of those new conditions had a potential cure in narcotics, but there was a downside: they helped produce more anxiety in this anxiety-ridden period (Hickman, 2007). Narcotics seemed to be a miracle cure for these constructed ailments.

In the nineteenth century, narcotics addiction had several names, based mainly on the primary drug of abuse. Therefore, the categories of morphinism, opium poisoning, and opium inebriety were replaced later in the century by simply "addiction," and the disease concept in the following years guided a new way of seeing the former "habits" (Hickman, 2007).

After the American Civil War, narcotics use became more visible and viewed as a social problem, not due to the development of battlefield medicine (as once thought), but due to increased medical knowledge and the rising addiction to narcotics. The hypodermic syringe had a part to play as well as it allowed the quick release of the substance into the bloodstream. As the 1800s drew near its end, the primary constituents of narcotics changed from higher-status women, who had received them as prescriptions for their various ailments, to lower-class men, which had the effect of establishing narcotics as street drugs. The idea of addiction as disease began to grow. Although the narcotics' addictive potential had been noted earlier, it remained "in the shadows" until this time, and it came to the attention of the legal system (Hickman, 2007) and the criminal justice establishment increasingly committed to professionalization.

Hickman (2007) relates many of the concerns regarding narcotics addiction to modernity; life in an increasingly industrializing and urbanizing world manifested in physical form in factories, trains, cars, and symbolically, the

syringe. In a transforming world where independence, industriousness, inge-
nuity, and self-mastery helped form a personal (and national) identity, narcotics offered both a remedy and a threat to social progress and growth.
Narcotics abuse, which evolved from medical or personal intervention, was
different from alcoholism which had a very long history; narcotics abuse represented a transformation from the old to the new. Opium, morphine (also
called morphia at the time), and heroin were joined by a new drug called
cocaine in the 1850s, bringing narcotics into the modern world (Hickman,
2007). Medical and popular writers of the 1800s broadcast to the public greater attention to the habits of opiates and cocaine; these habits would get a new
label—"narcotics addiction."

In the late nineteenth and early twentieth centuries many doctors and medical researchers (including many charlatans) answered the call to find answers
to this new problem of narcotics addiction, perhaps none better known than
Dr. Leslie Keeley and his legendary Gold Cure, in which gold (emblematic of
the period) was actually injected into patient's bodies to restore to the body
the will power that was taken by narcotics. The cure had no positive effects on
patients, but it did make Keeley wealthy (Hickman, 2007). Another figure in
the history of narcotics was Charles B. Towns, described as the "undisputed
king, or perhaps emperor…of all the cure proclaimers" (Musto, 1973 p. 79). At
the dawn of the twentieth century, Towns, a salesman with no experience or
interest in addiction, claimed to have developed a miraculous remedy which
after its use would produce a mucous lined stool which, upon passing, would
relinquish the pull of the narcotics habit. The cure, of course, was a sham, but
by the 1920s, when he was discovered to be a con man, he had become a major national and international figure in the field of addiction legislation
(Musto, 1973).

The issue of race and ethnocentrism also played a key role in this growing
concern over narcotics. Both medical and popular writers related narcotics to
the fear of "others" in the mysterious regions of Asia, the Middle East, and
Africa, even more frightening to an American way of life (Hickman, 2007;
Musto, 1973). Asian Americans and those of Middle Eastern descent were
depicted as lazy, opium den frequenting "others," African Americans were
stereotyped as excessively violent and uncontrollable when they came under
the influence of cocaine, always possessing the potential for attacks on white
women (Hickman, 2007, Musto, 1973). These ideas further cemented the notion of the racial inferiority of these "othered" groups.

Gender, too, played a key role as women were not spared the effects of the
stereotypes promoted by the fear of drugs. The perceived weakness of femininity, characterized by a "delicate constitution" that made women prone to
hysteria, hypochondria, anorexia, and various other forms of emotional dis-

tress in late 1800s America, was conceived by male physicians as being both biological and environmental; resulting in a weakness they claimed which was worsened with the introduction of narcotics. Women, who have historically been blamed for social ills, were thought to be vulnerable to narcotic addiction, creating disruptions in the home—their area of domestic responsibility (Hickman, 2007).

The first major piece of legislation intended to stem the tide of the growing drug fear was the Harrison Act of 1914. This act was promoted by both media depictions of the problem and the decision by the rapidly professionalizing American Medical Association (AMA) to become involved; after all, many prescribing physicians contributed to the narcotics addiction problem. The bill required narcotics dealers to become licensed, keep records of all transactions, have all narcotic medicines delivered by physician prescription, and proposed legal sanctions to be leveled against non-registered persons in possession of drugs. The act promoted an increase in the power of the already increasingly powerful medical establishment to police the medical professions, especially the pharmacists who dispensed the drugs (Hickman, 2007, White 2014).

Prior to the establishment of the pharmacy field, medical doctors often dispensed drugs but eventually turned this function over to the druggists (Musto, 1973). In Hickman's (2007) view, due to the Harrison Act, dependence was transferred from narcotics enforcement to the medical profession, which was still dependent on the Federal government. Physicians were required by the government, especially by the powerful Treasury Department, to progressively lower dosages of narcotics until the medications were discontinued altogether. The misrepresentation of success rates of addiction hospitals and asylums made it appear they were a better choice for getting clean.

Doctors were often jailed for not following the act, or they just stopped dispensing the drugs. The extreme nature of the Harrison Act was driven by fear: fear of children getting access to drugs, fear or gangs and crime, and fear of racial and ethnic "outsiders," among others. Clinics that dispensed drugs were closed. The Harrison Act and the other harsh control measures served to criminalize narcotics addiction. Research on drug addiction, along with various treatment strategies, continued over the next few decades (White, 2014).

Users of these drugs in the twentieth century also found themselves with a new label: "addicts," which created the idea of a new menace forming in the minds of citizens. Narcotics would come to be known as "junk," and the people who become addicted to narcotics bore the name "junkies" or "junkers." The narcotics scene was amplified by writers who associated this new problem with other problems of modernity.

The drug scene became fascinating to a public caught up in the conservative post-World War II period. There were books, television shows, movies, and other forms of media that depicted the mystical world of narcotics. Novels from the so-called beat writers of the 1950s described a new, carefree lifestyle that frequently included drug use. William S. Burroughs was one such writer who wrote over two dozen books, most of them dealing with different extents of addiction and narcotics. However, it was his first book published in 1953, initially named *Junk*, later renamed *Junky*, which later provided the subtitle *The Definitive Text of "Junk"* (Harris, 2003). Certainly, at least partially biographical, the work takes the reader to a world of narcotics using, narcotics dealing, and narcotics "scoring," and describes not only addiction ("junk sickness") but the wide variety of drugs available at the time. Much like De Quincey's expose on opium over a century earlier, *Junky* illustrated the shadowy side of life but at another historical point in time.

Certainly, popular works like *Junky* captivated lay readers, but the dryer, more tedious academic works found their way into the lives of professionals interested in this new and frightening cultural change. For example, Finestone (1964) constructed the social type of the "young colored drug users" (p. 282) and introduced the lifestyle of African American males, or "cats" in their attempts to get "kicks" (highs), through a variety of "hustles" (means to get money). This new vocabulary was also reflected in the other forms of media at the time, likely played a role as well. Television shows such as Dragnet and Adam-12 during the 1950s, 1960s and early 1970s showed the police and their struggles with criminal offenders, with many episodes dedicated to crime control over those addicted to narcotics

Marijuana

Marijuana's centuries-old cultivation can be traced to Central Asia. Cannabis was found to be a durable and hardy plant used in rope production, as cooking oil, and as a food product. And, of course, its psychoactive potential was known as well. Its intoxicating properties were likely first employed in India, but it spread throughout Europe, the Middle East, Africa, into the Caribbean, and the Americas (Courtwright, 2001). Physicians in the United States were able to use extracts of the drug as a recognized medicine for various ailments until newer drugs with fewer problems with preparation were found (Himmelstein, 1983).

In Central America and Mexico, cannabis was used for its psychoactive properties, and its use crept across the border into parts of Texas. The drug picked up a new nickname, "killer weed," as it was thought the drug made the Mexican workers aggressive and prone to kill American whites (Himmelstein, 1983). The drug became part of the jazz subculture in the 1930s and would become part of the "beat" generation in the avant-garde centers of cities such as New York and San Francisco in the 1950s. It would also become a symbolic image in the counterculture movement of the 1960s and early 1970s (Himmelstein, 1983; Courtwright, 2001).

Marijuana was given many nicknames such as "reefer," "grass," "Mary Jane," and "weed." It was emblematic as a drug of the 1960s hippie culture that rejected racism, materialism, and the Vietnam war. The young users, often college students, were the children of a more economically comfortable era who traveled more than their forebears, spreading the influence of the drug to new areas (Courtwright, 2001). The use of marijuana by this youth counterculture became associated with the use of other drugs, especially psychedelics (Musto, 1973).

Amphetamines

Amphetamine and its herbal relative ephedrine were introduced in the early twentieth century. Identified in the 1920s by a Chinese American scientist, ephedrine was found to be an effective remedy for asthma symptoms, but the main ingredient, mahuang, a Chinese plant also known as ephedra, was in short supply, so a chemist attempting to create a synthetic form of ephedrine produced amphetamine. Inhalers with the drug became very popular because they possessed both stimulant and euphoric properties (Kuhn, Swartzwelder, & Wilson, 2008).

Amphetamines' popularity grew in the 1930s, and during World War II, soldiers from many countries used the drug to remain awake during military operations (Kuhn, Swartzwelder, & Wilson, 2008). After the war, its use continued among several groups that desired to remain active such as truck drivers, college students, veterans, inmates, celebrities, and experimenting teenagers, resulting in what Courtwright (2001) referred to as an "amphetamine democracy" (p. 79). It was also popular in the 1960s as a symbol of a growing drug revolution; the famous slogan "speed kills" (referring to a common nickname for the drug) reflected concerns over the substance (Kuhn, Swartzwelder, & Wilson, 2008).

As amphetamine use decreased and cocaine use increased, a derivative of amphetamine, a more volatile form called methamphetamine (commonly known as "ice" or "meth"), appeared on the scene (Kuhn, Swartzwelder, & Wilson, 2008). Methamphetamine is very potent and can be swallowed, smoked, or injected (Courtwright, 2001). Amphetamine use can be defined in three postwar waves: the first being the movement of the drug from military to civilian populations, the second being the 1960s use as a countercultural phenomenon, and the more recent recreational use of methamphetamine can be considered the third (Kuhn, Swartzwelder, & Wilson, 2008).

Armstrong (2007) describes a methamphetamine scare of the late 1990s and the first decade of the 2000s. Methamphetamine, an illegally produced form of amphetamine that has the same stimulant qualities of amphetamine, was described in media outlets as a "new drug." Methamphetamine was hardly new on the drug scene, but ongoing exaggeration about its use in rural America created a strong reaction and hence has been described as a moral panic (this will be discussed soon). Known by the nicknames "meth," "ice," "crystal," "crank," and "speed," it seemed mysterious and foreign; however, nothing strikingly differs from it and other forms of amphetamine. The focus on the truncated name "meth" seemed to create an image of something new and frightening.

Barbiturates

Created in 1864 by German chemist Adolf von Baeyer, barbiturates are derived from barbituric acid and at low doses act as sedatives, at medium doses are hypnotic or sleep-promoting, and at high doses are anticonvulsant or anesthetic. In contrast to amphetamines, which were commonly called "uppers" for their stimulant effect, barbiturates and other sedatives were given the street name "downers" for their opposite effect. Highly lauded upon their discovery in the mid-1800s, barbiturates offered the promise of relief from seizures and anxiety in controlled doses. A problem with barbiturates is that at high doses, they depress brain functions, most notoriously those that govern breathing. In 1957, Lithium was produced, which reduced anxious conditions without suppressing respiration or causing drowsiness (Kuhn, Swartzwelder, & Wilson, 2008).

In the 1930s, there were over a dozen different forms of barbiturates that were being heavily prescribed. By World War II, abuse of the drug was widely known. Termed a highly addictive substance, serious legislative debates were carried out over who would control their use—the pharmacies, federal law enforcement, or prescribing physicians; the medical establishment would emerge the victor. The drug was nicknamed "America's opium" and "devil's capsules" as fears erupted that barbiturates would unleash a host of social maladies on society (Rasmussen, 2017).

Inhalants

Inhalant use of different substances has been around since at least the time of the ancient Greeks but because of the advancements in production of new materials not used for medical purposes such as gasoline, glues, solvents, paint, and various commercial sprays, the inhalation of toxic chemicals has been a special concern, especially regarding children and adolescents due to their easy access and the effects on the developing body, particularly the brain (Kuhn, Swartzwelder, & Wilson, 2008).

Regarding chemicals for medical use, the introduction of substances such as nitroglycerin and other anesthetic drugs such as ether were groundbreaking advancements. Other chemicals, such as nitrous oxide ("laughing gas"), were used more often for entertainment than medical purposes. While the inhalant category consists of both of those for medical use (nitrites and anesthetics) and solvents (gasoline, paint, cleaning fluids), the latter category should never be used for human consumption (Kuhn, Swartzwelder, & Wilson, 2008).

Hallucinogens

It is noted that hallucinogens are not reported to produce addiction. However, they are included here because they reflect an important component in the evolution of drug use and because it has been argued that seeking altered levels of consciousness has implications for addiction.

The hallucinogens are a class of psychotropic drugs that are also known as psychedelics or psychic deviators. They come from plants such as psilocybin (mushrooms), mescaline (San Pedro cactus buttons), and harmine (found in different plants) and produce perceptual effects such as visual and auditory hallucinations, heightened perception, exaggerated emotion, changes in cognition, and the alteration of a sense of time and place. These effects were often part of ritualistic behavior in early peoples who used a shaman guide to help them frame the effects in a spiritual manner. Therefore, the presence of cultural attitudes and perspectives have been an important feature in the experiences of the users of hallucinogens (de Rios, 1984).

Mescaline in the form of peyote was used for hundreds of years in Central America before moving north into what is now the American Southwest. If it was used for medical and religious purposes and the top of the plant, the peyote "button" was removed and dried. Indigenous people chewed the drug, drank it in a tea, or ingested it with water during religious services in which it was believed to lead users down a spiritual path. Peyotism (or the Peyote Religion) became a contested subject as America began its battle against drugs in the twentieth century (Maroukis, 2013).

In 1953, British novelist Aldous Huxley took mescaline under the supervision of psychiatrist Humphry Osmond, the person who coined the term "psychedelic drug." Osmond was one of a small number of psychiatrists who were studying the use of psychedelics, especially LSD in the treatment of mental distress in the 1950s, but in 1962, research was stifled in the United States by the Food and Drug Administration. In 1963, LSD moved out of the labs and into the streets, was liquefied, dipped into sugar cubes, and sold in communities, especially to young people who were interested in the drug's potential to alter individual consciousness. LSD became associated with the growing 1960s counterculture, antiwar demonstrations, and college campus unrest, and was outlawed in 1968, thwarting further mental health research (Costandi, 2014).

Perhaps the greatest challenges to our understandings of the effects of hallucinogenic drugs were provided by academic psychologists Timothy Leary and Richard Alpert (who later changed his name to Ram Dass) and a legion of others in the counterculture era who followed their lead in advocating the use of the drugs. Another person connected to the study of hallucinogens is Andrew Weil who, writing during the counterculture drug milieu of the 1960s, published *The Natural Mind: A New Way of Looking at Drugs and the Higher Consciousness* (1972) which provided an alternative explanation for drug use—the existence of an innate human desire to seek out alternatives to regular consciousness. According to Weil, from youth onward there is an attraction to those activities that reveal other forms of consciousness, from enjoying hallucinogenic pre-sleep patterns, spinning, participating in activities such as the "pass out" game (in which children use air compressions by squeezing other kids from behind, sending a rush of air to the brain and causing a short fainting spell), among others. As the child matures, other mind-altering states are sought out using alcohol and other drugs, according to this thesis.

Certainly capturing the spirit of the counterculture era, Weil explained how "straight thinking" in the form of traditional means of promoting drug abstinence and waging war of drugs by cutting off supply has been ineffective and should be replaced by "stoned thinking," which does not suppress drug use but rather stresses education about the effects of drugs and their relation to consciousness. Later, Weil would replace the outdated and conflict-laden term "stoned thinking" with "deep thinking" (Weil, 2004).

Weil's second book (1980) further explored the issue of consciousness with an exploration of psychedelic experiences with substances in different parts of the world. Weil's thesis of addiction, resulting from this quest for consciousness-altering, has been both praised and condemned, and through its revisions, has tamed some of its revolutionary rhetoric (Weil, 2004). The core idea, however, has remained the same and has presented a challenge to our understandings of drug-seeking behavior that has the potential for addiction. Certainly, the current focus on Eastern meditation practices as a way of alleviating certain mental health conditions, including addiction, seems to suggest movement in the direction of Weil's thesis. Expanding this idea can also be applied to behavioral addictions as well.

Club Drugs

Club drugs are not a specific class of drugs but are included here under this informal category due to their involvement with a cultural pastime—specifically the use of certain drugs, complete with cultural byproducts (explained shortly) at all night club events called raves. This grouping consists of different drugs, some of which fall under other drug categories, but get their name from the fact that they are often used by young people while engaging in club activity or in other party environments. Examined briefly will be a few of these—GHB, MDMA (Ecstasy), Rohypnol, and Ketamine.

GBH, gamma-hydroxybutyrate, is a sedative that gained national attention when the 1996 death of an athletic young woman and good student who had taken the drug was broadcast in a popular magazine. GBH is a drug often used in "raves," analysis dance parties, or for enhancement in bodybuilding activity. Possibly the drug most associated with clubs and rave parties is MBMA, with the extremely long official name methylenedioxymethamphetamine, but frequently used nickname "ecstasy" was created in 1912 but not tested on humans until mid-century (Kuhn, Swartzwelder, & Wilson, 2008).

Sometimes known as party drugs, these substances were a drug phenomenon of the 1990s and are still used today. The sedative Rohypnol, a benzodiazepine with the street name "roofies" and known for the amnesia-like symptoms, gained notoriety as the "date rape drug" in the late twentieth century as it was often placed in the drinks of unsuspecting people (normally women) often at parties, to incapacitate them as a prelude to sexual assault. Due to the common use of the drug, it was considered by some scholars to involve "the worst kind of drug abuse because it is inflicted on someone who does not choose it" (Kuhn, Swartzwelder, & Wilson, 2008).

Users of club drugs developed a series of risk management practices to deal with the adverse effects of the drugs—some were adopted from strategies of the harm reduction movement (mentioned in more detail in chapter five) while others were created through the experiences of the users. Included in these strategies were the consistent intake of water to prevent dehydration; the use of dance breaks to keep from overexertion, dehydration, and muscle cramping (some parties had "chill out" rooms for this purpose); controlled and moderate use of the drugs; and the avoidance of alcohol due to potential problems with dehydration and worrisome after effects. Other strategies included the use of other drugs before or after the parties to mitigate the effects of neurotoxicity and depression (called "pre-" and "post-loading"); the use of social media to spread drug effect information; and the strategy of "pill-testing" to ensure the legitimacy of the substance, including the use of ecstasy pill testing kits which confirmed the identity of the drug but unfortunately not its purity level (Kelly, 2007). Drug using ravers often used objects to assist with the teeth grinding that often occurs with use such as lollipops and pacifiers, which became a fashion trend in the era.

Conclusion

Americans also have a long history with drugs of abuse rather than alcohol, a history that, with few exceptions, had its start in other countries. A socio-historical investigation traces the influence of nicotine, caffeine, narcotics, marijuana, amphetamines, barbiturates, inhalants, hallucinogens, and club drugs not only on individuals but also on culture. They have assisted people with medical needs, provided recreation, created comradery, but also have promoted addiction and many different but associated social problems. Some drugs are naturally occurring, and others are produced synthetically, but all have had an impact and often in culturally significant ways.

The appearance of different drugs on the scene represents different cultural shifts in our society. The various drugs have been introduced into bodies by eating, snorting, smoking, injecting, drinking, and sniffing in many different settings, including coffee houses, bars, streets, opium dens, jazz halls, hospitals, religious events, countercultural gatherings, and dance clubs. A variety of factors at different points in time, especially involving race and ethnicity, have allowed Americans to view the issue of addiction and the advent of new and foreign substances as reasons to panic—this will be addressed in more detail in chapter seven on moral panics.

Chapter 4

The Emerging Issue
of Behavioral Addiction

"The addict, heroin or others, is addicted not to a chemical, but to a sensation, a prop, an experience which structures his life."

(Stanton Peele & Archie Brodsky, 2015 p. 43)

A New Idea: Addictive Behaviors

To fully analyze addiction, it is beneficial to see how newer interpretations have developed and extended our understandings of the concept (correctly or mistakenly). External substances of various types, whether consumed in drinkable, smokable, inhalable, or injectable forms, have long been considered the source of addiction, as explored in the previous two chapters. However, newer conceptions have emerged and will be considered here to further our investigation into the meaning of addiction. These newer notions suggest that perhaps not only substances can be addictive but that the actual experience of certain behaviors can be addictive as well. The DSM has expanded to include non-drugs as addiction sources and incorporated the idea of certain behaviors, or "new things to be addicted to" (Tunney & James 2017, 1720).

In 1975, Stanton Peele and Archie Brodsky, perhaps most famously known as the addiction scholars who challenged the highly popular twelve-step programs, wrote a book entitled *Love and Addiction* in which they labeled certain behaviors as addictions. In a 2015 update of the book, the authors bemoaned the resistance of the mental health and addiction fields to accept behaviors other than gambling and potentially online behaviors (which will be explained below) as addictions. They wrote, "psychiatry still has not acknowledged sex, love, shopping, eating, electronic, and other potential addictions…, and so it continues to lag behind" (Peele and Brodsky, 2015, p. 3). These scholars reject the term behavioral addiction as they feel it relegates this condition to a curious subcategory that is not an authentic addiction like substance addictions. The use of other terms is recommended: "consuming experiences" and "non-drug involvements," for example. While the authors consider these behaviors in the same context as substance addictions, theses terms, considered on their own, reveal an important potentiality—as a means of removing them from the category of "addiction"; this point will be reex-

amined later in this work, and the terminology will be used, though not always with the original intention of the writers.

In this chapter, the two conditions that have received attention by the American Psychiatric Association will be examined initially: gambling, which has
received an official designation, and Internet gaming, which is set to receive the
next designation. Then examined will be activities not yet so designated by the
association in its official manual, the Diagnostic and Statistical Manual of Mental Disorders, 5th edition (APA 2013), but that are considered by many in the field
to be addictions. Next will be considered a host of other behaviors that might at
some point receive the official classification, or at least could be potentially
considered addictions, based on the logic behind the classification of behaviors
as addictions. Questions of whether these behaviors should be viewed as addictions or better explained by some other phenomena, have caused a long-
standing debate and will be discussed at the end of this chapter.

Official Non-Substance-Related Disorders

The DSM-5 created a new category, "Non-substance-related Disorders" in the
section of the manual known as Substance-related and Addictive Disorders
(APA, 2013), wording which seems a bit contradictory on its face. As previously noted, the first condition to receive the designation is gambling, therefore
first considered will be this activity before proceeding to others that not yet
been given the official seal of clinical addiction.

Gambling

In the Western world, gambling was considered sinful and banned on religious grounds until the seventeenth century. The activity was particularly
viewed as aberrant during the previous century's Protestant Reformation,
which stressed the importance of hard work in obtaining wealth and prosperity; gambling was, therefore, an affront to this ideology. During the Enlightenment Period of the seventeenth century, the orientation toward rationality
and away from spirituality shifted the idea of gambling-as-sin to gambling-as-
break-from reason-and-sound mental health (Reith, 1999).

The element of chance is a common feature of gambling. Risk, another key
and related feature, is a major factor in someone's decision (at the individual
level) to continue the practice, but large-scale gambling (at the cultural level)
provides more insight into how the personal is affected by the social. Gambling is not only a leisurely pastime for people but also involves decisions
based on legislative concerns and pecuniary interests. Therefore, risks associated with gambling occurs at national and state governmental levels through
the calculus of how much and what type of gambling can be considered ac-

ceptable leisure and at what point the consequences to the citizens become too cumbersome. It occurs at the local governmental level as the quest for profit by financial interests must be tempered by the response of the communities. And, of course, it occurs at the personal level as people must weigh the joys of the activity with the potentially negative consequences to family and other close relationships, employment, finances, and social status. At all three levels, risk is involved, and rational choices must be made regarding the activity—from the large level casinos, called *risk institutions* (Cosgrave, 2006) to local governmental entities, to individuals.

There are many forms of gambling, such as casino gambling, athletics betting, slot machine use, card games, lotteries, board games, online gambling, and many others. Gambling has certainly been a popular pastime of many people throughout societies, providing fun and social engagement. Gambling has also been associated with many problems for people who get caught up in a compulsive need to continue the behavior despite losing money, family, friends, and respect. At various times, this problematic behavior has been termed heavy gambling, compulsive gambling, pathological gambling, and gambling addiction. Declaring the condition as pathological has placed it firmly under the umbrella of the medical model. Labeling it as an addiction solidifies its categorization as a medical disorder since the concept has long been in the DSM series, in various forms, prior to its new status as addiction.

Gambling's history is somewhat unique in its universality. Present in all societies throughout history, understandings of it is rooted in culture; whether it is seen as a positive leisure activity or a social problem with criminal implications depends on the cultural manifestations at the time under study (McMillen, 1996). On the negative end, gambling, along with abortion, prostitution, pornography, homosexuality, and illicit drug use, even constituted one of the six "classic vices" in the United States beginning in the 1960s (Dombrink, 1996). Throughout history, changes have been made regarding the legalization of gambling, such as in the 1980s, when state legislatures sought legalization to improve revenues when other sources were unavailable (Rosecrance, 1985).

If the practice of gambling was considered a vice, heavy gambling was viewed as a sin in the eighteenth and nineteenth centuries. It emerged as a sickness with the popularization of psychoanalysis and the psychoanalytic view of human behavior. The initially perceived etiology of problem gambling was mania, followed by compulsivity. The DSM-III, published in 1980, categorized the condition as an impulse control disorder, along with kleptomania (theft of items based on compulsion rather than need or desire of the object stolen). The DSM-III R published seven years later, moved the disorder closer to substance dependence based on similar criteria (Walker, 1996). However, it wasn't until 2013 that the DSM-5 classified it as an official addiction.

Sociologists have been providing the field's unique perspective to the study of gambling only since the late 1940s (Bernhard & Preston, 2007). An early sociology examination of gambling (Bloch, 1951) perceives it as a function of a rapidly industrializing society that demands conformity but rewards risk-taking and material acquisition. Block, situating the practice firmly in a socio-logical framework stated: "unlike excessive drinking, drug addiction, or sex demoralization, gambling produces no directly deteriorating effects upon the human organism or the social group. Its danger lies in the fact that it inter-feres with the normal assumption of responsibility which organized society compels" (1951, p. 216). This perspective conveyed a belief that the "extreme" gambler requires rigorous psychiatric care. That came to pass because prob-lem gambling is now a clinical diagnosis in the prominent DSM.

In its official designation in the DSM-5, gambling disorder has certain diag-nostic criteria such as consistent gambling behavior that leads to significant functional impairment or anguish over a 12-month period that contains four or more of these attributes:

- The use of more money to obtain the desired gambling exhila-ration

- Restlessness or irritability when the behavior has ceased

- Unsuccessful attempts to control the gambling

- Preoccupation in thought, memory, or preparation for future events

- Gambling when exhibiting distress

- Retaliatory gambling behavior after losing money from the ac-tivity

- The use of deceit to hide the level of gambling involvement

- The loss of or potential loss of a significant personal relation-ship, job, or the neglect of professional, or educational oppor-tunities

- Reliance on others to provide monetary assistance due to fi-nancial need, often as a result of incurring gambling debts (APA, 2013).

In addition, for a diagnosis of gambling disorder, it is not to be better ex-plained as a manic episode resulting from bipolar disorder. There are specifi-ers as well, including differentiation between whether the activity is episodic or persistent, in early or sustained remission, and whether the severity level is mild, moderate, or severe (according to the number of above criteria being met). These factors, notably the concept of remission, firmly place the disorder under the medical model. The DSM-5 also distinguishes gambling disorder from a manic episode, a personality disorder, or other medical conditions. Most interestingly, the manual also notes a distinction must be made between this condition and either "professional" or "social" gambling (APA, 2013).

Elster (2003) notes that differing from other addictions, the status of "professional" (as in "professional gambler") does not exist for substance use or compulsive eating as it does for this behavior. He also provides a stage model for compulsive gambling that can be useful in understanding the condition:

Stage one—moderate, occasional use motived by a desire for entertainment and financial payoff

Stage two—more frequent and higher stakes gambling triggered by near-wins and social acceptance by gambling peers

Stage three—more intense gambling behavior derived from higher arousal levels, the development of irrational beliefs about the chance of financial gain, and manipulation from gambling entities that provide incentives and triggers for betting

Stage four—intensive levels of gambling, creating a situation like tolerance, motivated primarily to win back money that was lost (called "chasing your losses") and to become free of gambling debt

The key focus, according to the model's creator, should be the transition from stage two to stage three as the gambler develops a rationale for continuing the process that sets the compulsive behavior in motion (Elster, 2003).

Treatment for gambling disorder often follows the same regime as other addictions and mental distress conditions—participation in a variety of therapeutic modalities, including self-help (twelve-step) programs, cognitive behavioral therapy, motivational enhancement therapy, various types of brief, and family therapy, and natural recovery for some sufferers. Though there are no currently approved psychopharmacological remedies, there are drugs such as opiate antagonists, mood stabilizers, and antidepressants that are being used. (Karim & Chaudhri, 2012).

Of note in the treatment field is the twelve-step program known as Gambler's Anonymous, or GA, modeled after Alcoholics Anonymous. Started in 1957 by two chronic gamblers, the program took some time to gain much attention, as gambling behavior was not initially thought of as a source of addiction, like alcohol and other drugs. Decades later, when the problem became more evident in middle-class communities, the focus was directed on the problem along with a demand for something to be done to prevent or control it (Gambler's Anonymous n.d.). By being placed under the medical model, compulsive gamblers were able to receive some similar benefits as those addicted to substances, including a reduction in stigma, a reprieve from responsibility for actions, and the acceptance by health insurance companies for coverage (Castellani, 2000). Through its inclusion of the DSM, gambling, as other conditions considered addictions and mental health disorders, had entered the professional field of addiction treatment.

Internet Gaming

The most likely disorder to be designated as such in subsequent editions of the DSM is internet gaming, which is mentioned in the DSM-5 as deserving attention for possible inclusion in the manual. Described in the DSM-5 as a persistent and repeated use of the Internet to play a variety of games, often with other people, that leads to impairment and suffering in the user's life, the criteria are as follows:

- Preoccupation with Internet gaming to include thought, memory, or preparation for future gaming opportunities

- Intense and emotional withdrawal symptoms

- Tolerance involving engagement in online gaming

- Inability to control the behavior

- A decrease in previous recreational interests

- Continued online gaming activity despite deleterious consequences

- Deception to others regarding the extent of time spent in the activity

- Use as an escape from negative feelings

- The loss or potential loss of significant personal relationships, jobs, or the neglect of professional or educational opportunities

The primary specifier is the current severity of the activity, whether it is mild, moderate, or severe. The DSM-5 notes that gambling, as specified elsewhere in the manual, is excluded. Also excluded is Internet use as part of one's work life, other recreational or social media activity, and the viewing of online pornographic sites (APA, 2013).

The DSM-5 also states the disorder has received much attention in medical journals and has been declared an addiction by the Chinese government, which has established a treatment protocol to deal with it (APA, 2013). The condition is certainly of concern regarding younger people who spend a good deal of time online.

Some scholars believe there are many good reasons for "erring on the side of caution" (Rooij et al., 2018) rather than prematurely reacting to create a formal diagnosis of addiction for this activity. For example, the concept of Internet gaming disorder is too ambiguous, too multifaceted, and lacking the robust scientific validation needed for official mental health diagnosis. The authors, therefore, call for careful reflection before an official classification.

A review of effective treatments for the forthcoming official designation found that despite the interest that has been generated for Internet gaming, most psychological and psychopharmacological approaches have yet to conform to the evidence-based standards criteria. It is possible that cognitive-based treatment, family therapy (especially in relation to problem online behavior by adolescents), motivational interviewing, and perhaps some medications might be of some value (Zajac, Ginley, Chang, & Petry, 2017). While medication for Internet gaming addiction or other problematic online behaviors might be recommended, these are used to treat underlying behavior and not the condition.

Potential Addictions Without Official Designations

There are other activities that have been generally considered behavioral addictions that are not officially classified as clinical disorders by the DSM. At some point, these may also be added to the panoply of official behavioral addictions, or they may be deemed to be unfit, for various reasons, to be so labeled. Or perhaps a reconsidering, or reimagining, may occur about what constitutes a behavioral addiction, or any type of addiction for that matter. In any event, at the present time, there are many categories of activity that many consider addictions.

Sexual Behaviors

Sexual activity has resulted in prohibitions since antiquity due to fears of a breakdown in social functioning if sexual behavior is left unchecked. Problematic sexual behavior by individuals, despite its historically high levels of concern, has only recently (since the mid-twentieth century) become determined by some to be an addiction. Krafft-Ebing's famous work *Psychopathia Sexualis* (1886/1997), first published in the late nineteenth century, vividly described sexual deviations and used the term hyperesthesia for abnormally high levels of sexual desire (Riemersma & Sytsma, 2013). In the early part of the twentieth century, founder of psychoanalysis Sigmund Freud developed his seminal ideas that many psychological problems are the result of re-pressed sexual feelings. In the later part of the century, social philosopher and sociologist Michel Foucault also contributed to understandings of human sexuality from a socio-historical perspective, highlighting the attempts by societies to control human sexuality.

In the late 1970s, the idea of a medical response to address "dangerous and uncontrollable sexuality" (Irvine, 1995) began to take shape and in the next decade scholars such as Patrick Carnes developed the concept more fully (Levine, 1995, Birchard, 2011); in fact, he helped move the concept "out of the shadows" (Carnes, 2001) and into the rapidly expanding addiction treatment industry. Clinics for sex and love addiction, bestselling books, treatment manuals, and addiction medicine programs sprang up within this industry despite questions by some sexologists of sexual addiction's scien-tific credibility and concerns over the reignition of sex-related fears as "cul-tural anxieties" (Irvine, 1995).

Fueled by the AIDS crisis, changing sexual mores, and a moral panic involv-ing "false memory syndrome," a backlash sprang up in response to what many perceived as sexual immorality. In the early 1980s, some notable psychiatrists began to suggest to patients that the causes of their psychological problems were due to experiences of child sexual abuse, which they had repressed, although they reported no memory of such abuse. The patients were told they had to reveal the experiences for healing to occur and encouraged to address the abuse, even though such abuse often did not occur. A form of treatment called recovered memory therapy, which contained different treatment mo-dalities, developed from this concern and received positive recognition by some institutions in the field of American psychiatry, including mental health hospitals, teaching programs in universities, and even the National Institute of Mental Health (NIMH), despite very little evidence that patients with cer-tain psychological problems commonly repressed memories of abuse (McHugh, 2008). Legal battles and negative media attention exposed the mat-ter, and the mental health field eventually rejected the improper inducement of memories by therapists.

The backlash over sexual mores, along with the emergence of "sexual purity feminism" that linked many sexual behaviors to female victimization, helped create conditions that bolstered the medicalization of non-traditional sexual behavior, relating it with addiction in the public eye. This new focus created problems for women, as Levine notes, "medicalization inevitably focuses on the individual body and psyche as the site of disease and the locus of inter-vention. This presents a profound reversal for feminism, a movement dedicated to continually politicizing individual experience" (Levine, 1995, 448). Emphasized is the personal, not the political.

The term hypersexuality has often been used to describe sexual addiction or compulsion. The term removes the question of whether the behavior is more accurately characterized as one or the other but suggests a normative sexual pattern for which deviations are clinically problematic, a difficult stance due to the personal nature of sexuality. Another term, "addictive compulsive pattern of sexual behavior" has been considered "to embrace this double aspect of this pattern of behavior" (Birchard, 2011, 164); however, the question about this type of behavioral categorization remains—as well as its designation as clinically problematic behavior that is influenced by culture. Although discussed for inclusion in the DSM-5, its addition was never agreed upon.

The diagnosis of sexual addiction is not referenced in the DSM-5. It is mentioned casually in the DSM-III TR but was dropped from the DSM-IV. In the International Classification of Diseases, 10th ed. (ICD-10), it is described as an excessive sex drive with the forms of satyriasis and nymphomania—the former term refers to having a succession of objectified sexual partners and the latter term, more familiar, is outdated and sexist. The World Health Organization (WHO) has now described a compulsive sexual behavior disorder in the ICD-11 (WHO, 2018).

The DSM-5 has two primary sections dealing with clinically problematic sexual behaviors—one is Sexual Dysfunctions which includes a variety of conditions that inhibit normal sexual functioning—in which people are unable to "respond sexually or experience sexual pleasure" (APA, 2013, p. 423); however, conditions that might signify sexual addiction are not listed there. Another section of DSM-5 is related to sexual problems and is titled Paraphilic Disorders. Paraphilia refers to "any intense and persistent sexual interest other than sexual interest in genital stimulation or preparatory fondling with phenotypically normal, physically mature, consenting partners" (APA, 2013, p. 685). The term "normal" in this definition is not congruent in today's current notions of a "spectrum" of sexual behaviors and a denial of binary understandings of sexuality. However, the conditions referenced in this section include a number of behaviors commonly understood as unacceptable such as voyeurism, exhibitionism, frotteurism (touching or rubbing against non-consenting others), masochism, and sadism, pedophilia, fetishism, transvestism, and a few sub-categories. Paraphilic behaviors are certainly problematic, especially those that victimize others, and many have been deemed criminal; however, behaviors in this section are also not described as addictions.

In contrast to older "classic" descriptions of problematic sexual behavior, Riemersma and Sytsma (2013) propose a new category—a "contemporary" form of sex addiction categorized by "chronicity, content, and culture." It is hypothesized that the enhancement of vivid sexual imagery produced by the Internet technology viewed consistently over time, produces effects that are influenced by a highly sexualized culture, creating a "perfect storm" that leads to sexual addiction. This new technology is problematic to young Internet viewers whose immaturity and vulnerability are molded by the ubiquity of online graphic sexuality. As with other conditions labeled addictions, this perspective emphasizes the neurochemical changes to the brain's arousal system.

While traditional strategies of classical forms of treatment included trauma processing, cognitive-behavioral therapy, twelve-step programs, group treatment, contemporary formulations are so recent, they have not received appropriate attention, but Riemersma and Sytsma (2013) recommend a treatment protocol that reaches younger populations through early intervention and prevention programs, with strategies that replace abuse-as-trauma techniques with pornography-as-trauma approaches, and parental interventions that block online sexual content, as well as providing skills training. Regardless of the responses to this dual classification scheme, it is certainly important to consider the current role of technology in understandings of problematic sexual behavior. Time will reveal the impact of online sexual imagery on populations, especially impressive youth, but the close connection between the personal and social, will undoubtedly be exposed in an increasingly online cultural landscape.

Many practitioners cite their clients who are using compulsive sexual behaviors to relieve negative emotional states rather than as a healthy relational experience. As research points to problematic attachment histories in sexually compulsive individuals, treatment may one day proceed in this area (Benfield, 2018).

Eating Behaviors

There are several types of eating behaviors that have been considered manifestations of addiction, though not officially classified. Like sexual behaviors, eating is a natural human activity (indeed, essential), but when used in access or in non-socially approved ways, it has been given various medical diagnoses. Disordered eating behaviors come in a variety of forms, such as overeating, anorexia nervosa, and bulimia nervosa. Anorexia nervosa, more commonly referred to simply as anorexia, involves to a condition with these main elements: persistent restrictions on energy intake (in the form of food/nutrition), strong fears of weight gain, and an incongruent self-image based on weight or body shape (APA, 2013). More common in females, this disorder's addictive source, according to Brumberg (2000), is starvation.

In her work on the history of anorexia, Brumberg (2000) notes that the condition does have certain properties that resemble substance addiction:

- it has a habitual activity (consistent denial of food)

- alters the affected person's emotional and physical states

- produces feelings of normality over time

- promotes and is maintained by denial defenses

- continues despite severe consequences from the continued restriction of food

The social and personal are connected in her position as "recruitment" to fasting occurs early on in a person's life due to cultural messages in the "sociocultural stage" and continues into a "career" stage where the psychological and physical manifestations of the condition occur; the discipline of history, she notes, is interested in the first stage and the mental health field is interested in the second (Brumberg, 2000). Both fields are of interest to sociology and other social sciences as the interplay of social and individual processes are evident in the analysis of disordered eating.

Bulimia nervosa, a term often shortened to bulimia, is also described as an eating disorder and is a condition defined by:

- recurrent binge eating (consumption of food in larger amounts than necessary for satiation)

- compensation behaviors (such as vomiting, exercise, the use of laxatives, and fasting)

- an incongruent self-image based on body weight and shape (APA, 2013).

Vomiting is the most common compensatory activity, and again, females are more likely than males to be bulimic (APA, 2013). The food preferred by those who binge is high-calorie "junk food," though other types of foods are also favored. Food that can be quickly prepared and consumed, especially in private, is the most valued (Boskind-White & White, 2000). If the addictive agent in anorexia is starvation, the source in bulimia is bingeing. The binge-purge cycle has been seen by some as analogous to the addictive process started by the ingestion of chemical substances.

Taking a psychodynamic approach, feminist psychotherapist Kim Cherlin believes a better understanding of eating disorders, which she describes as "the most spiritual and political and deeply psychological issues that women face today" (Cherlin, 1985, p. xiii), will provide insights into the true gendered meanings on selfhood and femininity. Personal identity is indeed affected by culture. The personal is political.

A stage approach is beneficial in examining treatments for eating disorders. At the prevention level, younger people can be provided with psychoeducation, especially from a social cognitive approach that exposes the cultural influences promoted by media sources, that thinness is a sign of beauty for girls and women. At the intermediate prevention level, therapists and counselors observe developing manifestations such as excessive dieting, bingeing, or compensatory behaviors. At the psychotherapeutic intervention stage, people who have developed eating disorders can be exposed to a host of strategies such as cognitive-behavioral therapy, dialectic behavioral therapy, and family therapy. Motivational interviews, also used with other compulsive disorders and addictions, have also been identified as strategies for eating disorders (Schwitzer, 2012).

Some suggest that correcting overeating behaviors by dieting is not the same as recovery. As Katherine (1996) notes, diets have failed persons addicted to food; those persons did not fail at dieting; therefore, long-term treatment instead of dieting is needed. This idea reflects the effectiveness of treatment and recovery, again defining the problem as a medical one rather than one that can be solved through the power of will.

Disorders on the Edge

Other forms of activity have been generally considered by some in society to be addiction. Internet use (other than gaming), exercise, self-injury, shopping, hoarding, and even love have been described as having addictive properties. Society deems human classification systems as being legitimate if they are given an official classification as such. Understanding why or why these have not been granted such access provides more information and understanding about the validity of the concept itself.

Problem exercise

Excessive exercise has also found its way into the addiction scheme. Like eating, sex, recreational gambling or gaming, normal consumer behavior, and others, exercise is a common activity and normally perceived as promoting positive health benefits. In fact, as noted in the introductory chapter, the use of exercise through running or other physical activity ("positive addiction") has been described as a recommended substitute for other addictions (Glasser, 1976). The frequently described "runner's high" is often found in other types of exercise as well and refers to the exhilaration of an endorphin rush that sometimes occurs concurrently with extensive exercise; this might mimic addiction but is not normally considered problematic unless physical injuries occur during this "high."

Recent conceptions of exercise addiction are also called exercise dependence, obligatory exercising, exercise abuse, and compulsive exercising, and refers to the use of physical activity to cope with external stressors and which possesses the core features of other addictions (Berczik et al., 2012). It has not received an official label of addiction by the DSM-5 or other official designators.

As with the consuming images of size and attractiveness that have been posited with the etiology of certain eating disorders, there is also extensive cultural messaging that promotes exercise as a means of obtaining better health, physical appeal, and self-esteem. However, this activity can also provide problems with other compulsive activities when performed to excess. Commercials and other forms of media present a message that "common people" can (and should) run, bike, or participate in other activities, pushing themselves to break personal records (this is, of course, to sell exercise equipment). The "highs" that are often described that come from the activity, combined with these external messages, create the "thinspiration" (Schreiber and Hausenblas, 2015) that often leads to processes resembling addiction.

Workaholism

Excessive time spent on occupational matters has been given a name—workaholism. The "ism," of course, reflects a connection to the addiction of alcoholism. It was introduced into mainstream American vernacular in the early 1970s in the book *Confessions of a Workaholic* (Oates, 1971), a work whose title has direct associations to de Quincey's *Confessions of an Opium-Eater*. Griffiths (2011) correlates the spending of excessive amounts of time and energy on occupational pursuits with six factors:

- salience (or how a person's life can be consumed by work activity or thoughts about work)

- changes in mood which include feelings of intoxication or escapism when involved in occupational activities

- internal and interpersonal conflicts

- tolerance

- withdrawal

- relapse

Building on the idea of work addiction, a certain personality type has been posited that is associated with those entrepreneurs whose ruthlessness and authoritarianism create a "dark side of entrepreneurism" (Miller, 2014). Spivack and McKelvie (2018) suggest the existence of addiction to entrepreneurship, an addiction characterized by a pathological desire to become involved in and to increase "experiences and investment in venture creation activities" (p. 360).

Related to work addiction or workaholism, there has also been discussion regarding whether excessive studying in educational settings (also called "study-holism" or "problematic overstudying") is an addiction or something better characterized as a form of obsession (specifically obsessive-compulsive personality disorder). Loscalzo & Giannini (2018) agree with the latter conception.

Non-suicidal self-injury

Non-suicidal self-injury, referred to previously as self-mutilation, refers to several different types of activity (often conducted by younger people) that include self-inflicted cutting, burning, picking the skin, hitting and stabbing the body, and pulling hair, that are not motivated by the intent to cause life-threatening injury or of suicide. The activity is listed in the DSM-5 under the category of Conditions for Further Study (APA, 2013) and is engaged in to relieve negative feelings or cognitions, to resolve personal problems, and/or to create an emotional reward. As it is a behavior repeatedly performed to relieve negative feelings or invoke positive ones, it has often been considered to resemble an addictive act. The DSM-5 adds this note in its proposed criteria for this possible disorder: "the desired relief or response is experienced during or shortly after the self-injury, and the individual may display patterns of behavior suggesting a dependence on repeatedly engaging in it" (APA, 2013, p. 803). The issue of dependence asserted in the manual certainly appears to suggest addiction potential. An argument for the inclusion of non-suicidal self-injury is the existence of certain elements:

- compulsivity

- the loss of control (including craving behavior)

- continued use of the activity despite negative consequences

- the presence of tolerance (Buser & Buser, 2013).

The negative consequences of this type of behavior could be considered more directly linked to medical problems than some of the other behavioral addictions (excluding eating disorders) since the act involves the infliction of harm to the body.

Hoarding and compulsive shopping

Hoarding is listed in the DSM-5 not as an addiction but as a compulsion in the Obsessive-Compulsive and Related Disorders section of the manual. The creation of the formal diagnosis of this condition in the DSM-IV signaled a new disorder which "rendered unsound certain relations to certain personal property" (Herring, 2014, 1). Specifically, hoarding refers to hanging on to possessions despite excessive accumulation and related potential health hazards. It differs from collecting (of items like coins, stamps, etc.) due to the lack of organizing activity that is characteristic of those hobbies. Discarding items that have some intrinsic value results in great distress in some people; the resulting clutter resulting from accumulation creates physical congestion and often interferes with movement in the homes of sufferers or visitors. The activity persists despite consequences such as loss of family and friends, loss of residence, exposure to hazardous materials, vermin, and insects, and potential arrest if the accumulated items are found to be a threat by authorities and not discarded.

Hoarding is obviously related to cultural patterns and ideas about materialism and the value placed on certain items deemed worthy of maintaining, despite the myriad associated problems with overaccumulation. It has cemented a place in popular culture through a popular television show called Hoarding and in other media depictions. It is ultimately linked with the concept of "clutter addiction," and the study of it has been dubbed "clutterology." In 1981, a group patterned after AA going by the whimsical name Messies Anonymous (MA), formed and continues to exist. Other groups such as Clutterers Anonymous (CLA) that were started later promote the twelve-step philosophy, reinforcing the idea of hoarding as an addiction (Herring, 2014). Even though not designated by the DSM as an addiction, many popular books imploring people to break the clutter habit have promoted the disease model to an interested public.

The idea of compulsive shopping behavior has also been considered by some to be an addiction and, in the acquisition of items, resembles hoarding—if those items are not used or discarded. Therefore, compulsive shopping differs from hoarding in this key respect. Compulsive shopping has gone by many names—impulse shopping, addictive buying, addictive shopping, compulsive consumption, and even an early name, onomania (buying mania) (Lo & Harvey, 2014). Compulsive shopping has not yet found its way into the DSM, but if a therapist wanted to provide a mental health diagnosis for this behavior, presumably, it would be in the "unspecified" section of obsessive-compulsive and related disorders.

Excessive love

The issue of addiction that includes the experience of love was proposed by Peele and Brodsky in *Love and Addiction*, originally published in 1975. In this work, the authors identified love or as an addiction source. Obviously, the idea of love (or "interpersonal addiction") as an addiction source is difficult for many to accept and contributes to the idea that all "consuming experiences" are addiction sources. Love can certainly fall into this category, but its ambiguity, relativity, and various categorizations make it a difficult fit in an increasingly scientific field. However, if one believes the medicalization of normal experiences (such as love) is occurring, scientific validity is lacking in the field increasingly filled with a host of routine activities and experiences.

Compulsive use of tech: Internet and cell phones

Internet use in general (not for the purposes of gaming behavior) has received its share of attention. Constant attention to social media sites and online videos, literature, music, podcasts, etc. has resulted in a concern of people (normally younger people) becoming too attached to Internet technology. The much talked about faux disorder known as FOMO (Fear of Missing Out) reflects the level of concern about Internet usage as well as the idea that so many behaviors are given a diagnostic label. A current, popular book (Price, 2018) explains how cell phone technology is addictive by design (through dopamine rushes) and implores users to "break up" with these devices.

Excessive tanning

Tanning, the darkening of the body through sun-seeking, the use of tanning beds, or other means such as sprays or oils, has also been suggested as a possible behavioral addiction (Kourosh, Harrington, and Adinoff, 2012). The persons who most compulsively tan are white females, adding to the argument that a gendered society can create or reinforce what seems to be psychological problems. While the underlying causes of problematic tanning are important to examine sociologically, the idea of the behavior being considered a true addiction is certainly controversial.

Criminal behaviors: Kleptomania and Pyromania

If excessive shopping, running, or love can be considered addictions, there are obviously other candidates if current interpretations of the concept are expanded. For example, the DSM-5 lists another two candidates that could fit into this category (if such expansions are continued). In the Disruptive, Impulse-Control, and Conduct Disorders section, kleptomania is defined as the "recurrent failure to resist impulses to steal items even though the items are not needed for personal use or for their monetary value" (APA, 2013, p. 478); if the activity is recurrent and there is a failure to resist impulses, this condition could meet the addiction criteria. Also, pyromania is defined as "multiple episodes of deliberate fire setting" (APA, 2013, p. 476) propelled by a fascination or arousal with fire—the "multiple episodes" requirement suggests a compulsion to continue the activity, despite serious consequences. In both kleptomania and pyromania, there is a tension that arises before the activity, a reduction in that tension afterward, and continued return to the behavior despite the consequences that are criminal in nature—theft, and arson. This is not to suggest these should be considered addictions but to draw attention to the ways in which behaviors are categorized to fit a pattern.

Conditions Related to Behavioral Addictions

In this section, some additional considerations will be provided to phenomena that are correlated in various ways to the concept of addiction. Specifically, the concept of flow and responses related to trauma, albeit in very different ways, are potentially associated with the mechanisms of addiction. An analysis can hopefully offer more insight in this area.

The Issue of Flow

Many people have experienced what is referred to in common parlance as being "in the zone" when there is deep concentration in an enjoyable activity to the point of experiencing an altered state of consciousness. Mihaly Csikszentmihalyi, a scholar who researched this experience by studying the activities of rock climbers, athletes, dancers, chess players, and many other groups, developed the concept of "flow," which describes how people "concentrate their attention on a limited stimulus field, forget personal problems, lose their sense of time and of themselves, feel competent and in control, and have a sense of harmony and union with their surroundings." He further describes a flow activity as an activity that makes these experiences possible (Csikszentmihalyi, 2000, p. 182).

Csikszentmihalyi posited a connection between flow and addiction by noting that certain people become so involved in a task that the psychological experience is comparable to the effects of taking heroin or other drugs. Almost all flow activities have the potential to become habit-forming, making flow a "dangerous resource" (2000, p. 139). In an early article in which he sought to understand the intrinsic psychological rewards of play, Csikszentmihalyi (1975) mentioned that the reinforcement provided by gambling does not normally include potential payoffs from financial gain, but rather *autotelic* benefits, referring to the internal benefits of the activity itself without specified goals for external rewards. Some flow activities, such as gambling, have clearly defined rules which allow the person engaged in the action to concentrate solely on the flow activity, narrowing the stimulus field to allow greater focus and consciousness alteration.

Csikszentmihalyi and a colleague later argued that television viewing, more than gambling or sex, is an addiction-oriented activity in that some people are unable to decrease their level of TV viewing; the addictive features of television, it is posited, come from an instinctive biological attraction to audible or visible novelty. The scholars fall short of recommending that TV "addiction" should be a clinical diagnosis and even believe it has some positive benefits (Kubey & Csikszentmihalyi, 2004).

Since flow involves so many activities that are common in everyday life, concerns about addiction are ever-present. Recently many researchers have studied the possible effect of flow on addiction in various human activities. Studies have focused on gambling, especially online gambling or other online activities, in their relationship to flow experiences; these studies have produced some disparate findings and a need to study the issue more fully (Trivedi & Teichert, 2017).

Whether flow activities have enough in common to warrant a serious analysis with behavioral addiction processes is, at this point, debatable. Perhaps these two things are just human reactions to various forms of stimuli with little more in common that the degree of focus and engagement with the activity. Or maybe an examination of comparison and contrast might open new lines of inquiry about what are termed behavioral addictions. Further analysis could shed some new light in this area.

The Role of Trauma

Listed in the DSM-5 as mental disorders (not addictive disorders), trauma-related responses are given different classifications, the most notable perhaps in this regard is Posttraumatic Stress Disorder or PTSD. PTSD is described as exposure to a trauma-inducing situation that causes disturbances such as:

- flashbacks of a psychologically disturbing event

- fear

- avoidance of associated events or people

- other physical and psychological responses (APA, 2013).

Again, the issue of trauma maladaptation is described in the DSM-5 as a mental disorder, not an addiction. However, there are some potential associations with addiction that should be explored.

Trauma survivors normally experience many cognitive and physical sensations and altered states of consciousness. These include:

- detachment

- depersonalization

- numbness

- dissociation

- helplessness

- heightened perceptions

- distortion of time (Herman, 2015).

Efforts at reducing the torment of remembering the tragic events often result in the use of alcohol and other drugs (Herman, 2015). In this situation, trauma and its responses could potentially be an addiction source.

Janet (1925) described the traumatic experience as one in which a traumatized person is unable to play a "satisfactory part, one to which his adaptation has been imperfect, so that he continues to make efforts as adaptation" (p. 603). The key term here is adaptation—people normally find themselves in traumatic situations and are later forced to adapt to the changes they experienced because of the event. People react to and adapt to trauma differently based on many factors. Maladaptive attempts sometimes are manifested in what Sigmund Freud termed the repetition compulsion or compulsion to repeat. The idea promoted over a century ago, refers to phenomenon in which trauma responses, especially from traumatic actions experienced at early developmental stages, create a process where survivors continue to reenact the trauma-producing behavior, often metaphorically, presumably in order to gain mastery and some control of a disturbing and confusing event which left the person vulnerable and helpless.

In an essay entitled *Remembering, Repeating, and Working Through*, Freud (1914) explained the development of psychoanalysis to that point, from its early use for traumatic processing in the form of hypnosis and later free association, interpretation, and insight. However, the memories and the reenactments are both unconscious to the traumatized person. Freud gives little detail in this short essay about the forms the repetition might take but describes how the psychoanalytic technique can turn the compulsion into a "motive for remembering" (p. 154), through overcoming resistances over time.

A modern definition of the compulsion to repeat is "repeatedly enacting, experiencing, or ending up in situations that are unpleasant, painful, or self-defeating" (Zellner, 2014, p. 2). This definition obviously only partially correlates with the current understandings of addiction. However, the notion of the repetition of behaviors, as well as the experiencing of similar consequences resulting from addiction, can be found in trauma reenactment. Noting that research on repetition compulsion is difficult due to the ambiguity of the concept, there are some potential neurobiological relationships involved in the process (for a general description, see Zellner, 2014); findings in this regard could further lead to a greater connection between the addictions and compulsion to repeat processes. Herman (2015) also notes that reliving trauma for many traumatized people is a disturbing, even horrifying activity; therefore, many people avoid it at all costs. However, those who do "return to the scene of the crime" often end up in a cycle of behavior that, in some ways, mimics addiction.

Conclusion

The idea of behaviors or experiences as addictions is relatively new on the addictions landscape. Also called process addictions, these involve behaviors that some believe are equivalent to substance addictions. At this point, only gambling has been officially recognized in the DSM as having properties that can be considered addictive. It has been placed in a new category called "Non-substance Related Disorders" in the Substance-Related and Addiction Disorder section of the manual. The next entrant into the DSM series will likely be Internet gaming, reflecting current observations of how technology might serve as an addiction source.

Many behaviors and conditions in society considered addictive without official designation involve sex, eating, exercise, voluntary overwork, voluntary overstudying, excessive entrepreneurial strivings, non-suicidal self-injury, hoarding, compulsive shopping, love, cell phone use, tanning, and even some behaviors that have direct links to criminal activity such as kleptomania and pyromania. These are certainly activities that are common in society, and which have some similar manifestations with addiction. The legitimacy of these behaviors as being considered addictions is controversial.

Related to the notion of behavioral addictions are the concepts of flow, a state of consciousness that happens when one is "in the zone," and traumatic response, which sometimes includes the psychodynamic concept of the repetition compulsion, in which a traumatic experience produces a mental, and sometimes physical, revisiting of the event. While these are not considered addictions, they have the potential to offer some insights into the concept and worthy of further exploration.

Chapter 5

Diagnosis, Treatment, and Prevention

"The evolution of psychotherapy is both the development of a field of expert knowledge and a process by which a culture interprets and defines itself."

(Robert L. Woolfolk, 1998 p. 130)

Substance use disorders and the disorders considered to be behavioral addictions by the mental health treatment enterprise are considered mental disorders, and as such, they are subject to diagnostic, treatment, and prevention measures like other health conditions. These three areas will be analyzed as they relate to addiction.

Diagnosis

Diagnosis is the beginning phase of a treatment process. The term diagnosis, or assessment, implies addiction is a medical condition to be treated like other medical problems. Another term often used is nosology, which refers to the classification of diseases. Before investigating current diagnostic conceptualizations and practices, some historical aspects of diagnosis will be reviewed.

A Short History of the Diagnosis of Addiction

Early psychiatrists, or "mad doctors" as they were known, initially had little use for classification systems and relied instead on what knowledge they possessed, which often had little scientific basis. It was difficult to use a classification system for states of mental distress when very little was known about what caused them (Grob, 1991). Early attempts in the 1800s provided two categories of mental "disease"—neurodevelopmental and neurocognitive conditions. This would change, however, and early diagnostic categories appeared for a variety of mental health, as well as physical health conditions.

The U.S. Census, conducted every 10 years beginning in 1790, created a rudimentary system of mental health classification and by the 1880 version, had these categories:

- dementia

- dipsomania

- mania

- melancholia (depression)

- monomania (comparable to today's obsessive-compulsive disorder)

- paresis (bodily weakness due to nerve damage) (LaBruzza, 1997).

Two of these: dipsomania, which is alcohol addiction, and monomania, which is comparable to obsessive-compulsive disorder (some forms of which are currently considered behavioral addictions), would fall into the classification of addictions, or at least relate to the concept.

E.M. Jellinek developed a new system in 1960 that received much attention in the addiction community. Jellinek (1960/2010) started by defining alcoholism as "any use of alcoholic beverages that causes any damage to the individual or society or both" (p. 35). Acknowledging this very vague definition, he believed it created space for a useful classification system of "species" of alcoholism. Using the Greek alphabet in his typology, Jellinek (1960/2010) posited five types (or stages) of alcohol addiction:

- alpha type—addiction resulting from "undisciplined drinking" that represents dependence on alcohol to quell physical or emotional pain; there are no withdrawal symptoms, tolerance, or progression with this type

- beta type—addiction with various physiological problems but without physical or psychological dependence on alcohol

- gamma type—severe addiction with psychological dependence progressing to physical dependence, withdrawal symptomology, and loss of control, which can result in damage to health, finances, and social status (this is the most severe species, and the one Jellinek claimed was the type designated by the AA as alcoholism)

- delta type—heavy alcohol consumption and withdrawal symptomology, though the addicted person maintains the ability to control the amount consumed

- epsilon type— or "periodic alcoholism" or binge drinking (the type "least known" at the time, according to Jellinek, but that results from "episodic drinking" in which a person can desist from drinking for a sustained period)

In addition, in this work, Jellinek mentioned other types of alcohol consumers: explosive drinkers, excessive weekend drinkers, fiesta drinkers. All these types cause much damage to self and others—these he calls "alcoholized" drinkers. Jellinek's model contains much overlap and ambiguity between the types, primarily due to his broad definition of addiction; however, it was an early attempt to make sense of alcohol overuse.

An early study of addiction in Sweden based on family adoptions produced a well-known classification system—a dichotomy of Type I and Type II forms of addiction, which would later be designated as "episodic" and "continuous" types. Type I users consisted of people who began use in later life; binge consume, experience addiction only after decades of use, are dependent, and are anxious and inflexible in deportment. Type II users consist of those who begin their use early in life (before age 20), have few periods of abstinence, and are aggressive and impulsive in their conduct. Type I users were found to be children of alcoholic mothers, and Type II users were found to be children of alcoholic fathers (Henderson, 2000). In addition to the obvious gender biases, this classification scheme does little to provide any useful diagnostic knowledge.

It is possible that other classification systems might be employed, such as this very simple typology by Fatayer (2008), that reflects on Jellinek's early formulation:

- Beta addiction—substance addictions

- Gamma addiction—behavioral/process addictions

- Delta addiction—addictions that are of at least two of the other types (which includes a distinction between primary and secondary types)

While the nosology seems overly simplistic, it does promote the idea of dividing substance and behavioral addiction into two separate categories, with a third inclusive category. This idea might have some merit and could deserve attention in the addictions field.

The DSM Series

Although the DSM has been discussed already in this text, it is important to explore how other behaviors, labeled mental health problems in the official manual, differ in ways than those considered addictions. Other nosologies were created that sought to classify mental health conditions in the nineteenth and early twentieth centuries, but it was the Diagnostic and Statistical Manual of Mental Disorders (DSM) and its editions and revisions that became the official classification system for all conditions associated with mental health. The original DSM, produced by the American Psychiatric Association in 1952, was created to provide a more systematic nosology, prompted in part by the concern over mental health issues of soldiers in the period surrounding World War II (Malik & Beutler, 2002, Clegg, 2012). This original DSM considered substance addiction (classified then as alcohol addiction or simple drunkenness) as an acute and chronic brain disease resulting from the use of alcohol and other drugs and the ingestion of poison. Interestingly, it was also classified as a "personality disorder."

The second edition of the manual, the DSM-II, was produced in 1968 and attempted to align more closely with the international health care nosology produced by the World Health Organization known as the International Classification of Diseases (ICD) (Clegg, 2012). In the 1960s and 1970s, some members of the psychiatric community (as well as scholars in other fields) began to question the growing influence of the DSM, a controversy that continues today and which will be discussed in more detail later.

The third edition of the manual was published in 1980. The DSM-III differed markedly from its forebears as it included more disorders and a multiaxial diagnostic system, provided a more scientific demonstration of contemporary mental health understandings, discarded the theoretical basis of the first two (which primarily had psychoanalytic underpinnings), and sought to conform to requirements from the insurance industry for more reliable diagnoses, treatment plans, and outcomes that were more predictable than in the past. And as the world entered an era focused on technology, precision, uniformity, and predictability, the new manual, with its perceived cookie-cutter format, was a cause for concern for some mental health professionals. There was a feeling by some that human intuition in dealing with complex psychological problems, many of which involved social factors, had ended (LaBruzza, 1997).

The American Psychiatric Association continued its revisions of the manual in 1994 with the DSM-IV, which included cultural factors to consider when performing mental health diagnoses (Clegg, 2012). It contained a system of five axes, the first of which included substance-related disorders, eating disorders, and other addiction-related problems. It included more scientific data and dropped and added disorders of earlier versions from its classifications.

The DSM-5, the current edition, was published in 2013 and the workgroup who decided the mental disorders for inclusion reviewed much scientific data to derive these categories (APA 2013):

- *Neurodevelopmental Disorders*

- *Schizophrenia Spectrum and Other Psychotic Disorder*

- *Bipolar and Related Disorders*

- *Depressive Disorders*

- *Anxiety Disorders*

- *Trauma- and Stressor-Related Disorders*

- *Dissociative Disorders*

- *Somatic Symptom and Related*

- *Elimination Disorders*

- *Sleep-Wake Disorders*

- *Sexual Dysfunctions*

- *Gender Dysphoria*

- *Neurocognitive Disorders*

- *Personality Disorders*

There are also disorders in the DSM-5 that are specifically related, in various ways, to addiction:

Substance-Related and Addictive Disorders. This category covers a large section of the DSM-5. In over 100 pages, there are 10 substance abuse disorders based on these drug classes: alcohol, caffeine, cannabis, hallucinogens, inhalants, opioids, sedatives, hypnotics and anxiolytics, stimulants, tobacco, and other or unknown drugs. As mentioned earlier, gambling is the first behavioral addiction designated in the guide, with others likely to soon follow.

It should be noted the following are **not** considered by the DSM to be addictive disorders but are included here because some of the features of these conditions have some similar characteristics of the behavioral addictions and necessary for a comprehensive analysis of addiction.

Obsessive-Compulsive and Related Disorders. The disorders in this section refer to conditions in which the sufferer has persistent or troubling thought patterns (obsessions) in coordination with behaviors (compulsions) that are insistently performed to relieve the obsessive thoughts. Included in this category are Obsessive-Compulsive Disorder (or OCD), Body Dysmorphic Disorder, Trichotillomania (hair pulling), Excoriation (skin-picking), and the newly added Hoarding Disorder. The obsessions and compulsions addressed in this section often mimic some responses considered behavioral addiction.

Feeding and Eating Disorders. The disorders in this category contain all psychological and related physiological disturbances involved in the process of eating, such as Anorexia Nervosa, Bulimia Nervosa, Binge-Eating Disorder, Rumination Disorder, and Avoidant/Restrictive Intake Disorder. Anorexia, bulimia, and binge eating are often correlated with addictive responses involving food and have the unofficial designation as food addictions.

Disruptive, Impulse-Control, and Conduct Disorders. These disorders are indicative of problems with impulse control and often include acts of aggression and violence that result in the violation of the rights of others. Examples are Oppositional Defiant Disorder, Intermittent Explosive Disorder, Conduct Disorder, Antisocial Personality Disorder, Pyromania (fire-setting), and Kleptomania (compulsive stealing). These disorders often involve the criminal justice system due to their close connection with injury to others (physical or psychological), destruction of property or other forms of behavior deemed criminal. Again, these are not considered clinical addictions but include behaviors often associated with addictive disorders, co-exist with addictions, and usually are addressed in the criminal justice system.

Paraphilic Disorders. The disorders in this section, Voyeuristic Disorder, Exhibitionistic Disorder, Frotteuristic Disorder, Sexual Masochism Disorder, Sexual Sadism Disorder, Pedophilic Disorder, and Fetishistic Disorder, are sexual behaviors often that are considered deviant and that involve harmful or potentially harmful consequences to others. These disorders are the ones that are considered by some to be sexual addictions, thought the DSM does not make this official classification. Like disruptive, impulse control, and conduct disorders, the conditions in this section closely tied with the criminal justice system as others are often harmed in the commission of paraphilic behaviors.

Addictions Treatment

A Short History of the Treatment of Addiction

Early "treatments" for mental health conditions other than addictions throughout history consisted of a host of various oddities. Those thought to be "mad" were often placed in jails and workhouses due to concerns over dangerousness or deviance. The rather benign use of amulets, potions, charms, magnets, soothing baths, and chants and incantations on one end and the more extreme use of dunking, shocking with cold water, terrorizing, bleeding and blistering, inducement to vomit or sweat, beating and psychosurgery on the other were all strategies to cure those deemed "mentally ill" (see Steverson, 2018).

Most people who were addicted to alcohol and other drugs prior to the professionalization of the addictions field did not receive treatment and, instead, like those with other conditions of mental distress, were placed in jails and poor houses. And in Colonial America, similar strategies were used on those with addictions, such as leeching, blistering, forced perspiration and vomiting, and exposure to frightening situations, much like people experiencing other mental distress. Later, with the disease concept of addiction, things would change regarding the treatment of addicted persons, though it has not been without controversy.

Alcoholics Anonymous, and its many spin-off programs, was normally not intended to be led by professional therapists; however, the twelve-step models are now often incorporated in a broad therapeutic program. As can be noticed in its name, it allows (and recommends) that people remain anonymous; therefore, people often use only their first name or first name and first initial of the last name. This movement has a very rich and interesting history.

Two unlikely contributors to AA philosophy were the psychoanalytic psychiatrist Carl Jung and philosopher/psychologist William James. Jung's influence can be found in his relationship with a businessman and former politician Roland H. in 1930, who sought out the doctor's help as he was undergoing major problems with his alcoholism. Jung worked with Roland for a lengthy period, then provided this remedy: undertake a spiritual journey that leads to a revelation that creates a rebirth; the ideas of rebirth and redemption found their way into the AA philosophy. Like Jung, William James had an interest in spiritual phenomena; his work *Varieties of Religious Experience* (1902/1985) is a standard text in the psychology of religion. James, who was trained in medicine, espoused the idea of addiction as a disease, which would become a key component of the twelve-step ideology. James also became involved with a group called the Emmanuel Movement that sought to help people with emotional problems (including alcoholism) through a strict code of religious adherence, confession, and spiritual cleansing. The movement was a major influence on a person named Richard Peabody, who started the most successful alcohol treatment program until the founding of AA. James' ideas on the "hot flashes," the sudden conversion experiences alcoholics experience before sobriety, certainly was appealing to Bill W. (Finlay 2000).

Addiction became medicalized in the mid-twentieth century and continues today. A more scientific approach to diagnosis and treatment developed, which firmly place addiction in the medical model, though this model has been challenged and adapted. An emphasis on addiction and family dynamics occurred toward the century's end with the codependency movement, which will be explored in more detail in the next chapter. Treatment has changed in the twenty-first century with new models and concepts. The twelve-step programs are still a very popular treatment philosophy and treatment modality, but there are a variety of others currently in use, and these will be discussed soon.

Treatment Settings and Providers

There are different settings in which substance abuse treatment occurs. For example, there are formalized institutional in-patient, outpatient, group, and individual formats in which treatment is provided in hospitals, clinics, private offices, community-based therapeutic residential programs, and even online. Some settings are much more informal, such as those that use the twelve-step approach and can be held almost anywhere people wish to gather—specified buildings, private homes, places of worship, businesses, and others.

Therapists who are trained in addictions treatment must be cognizant of the specific problems with different drugs and behaviors and need to have a good understanding of other mental health conditions as well. They are trained in aspects of addiction, such as knowledge of current information on drugs of abuse and their effects, addictive behavior, cravings, triggers, relapse potential and consequences, and family dynamics. Addictions training also involves an understanding of the criminal justice system since many addicted people are involved with that system and are mandated to receive treatment.

Many different types of professional psychotherapists work with addictions, both substance and behavioral, and the list includes psychiatrists, psychologists, social workers, marriage and family therapists, professional counselors, psychiatric nurses, and religious-based counselors. Therapists working with addictions clients should have a license in their field and/or a certification in addiction treatment. Some addictions professionals work in private practice, some in clinics of different types, and some work in institutional programs. Many therapists of addiction work in general mental health programs with an addictions component, though some work in addiction specific programs. The different types of therapists that work with addicted clients have different treatment orientations, use a variety of treatment modalities (such as those listed below), and use individual, group, or family treatment. Their therapeutic practice is governed by different professional organizations. For a more detailed list of general mental health providers, see Steverson (2018).

Benefits of Therapy

The benefits of treatment for substance and behavioral addictions for addicted persons are many and include:

- facilitation of insight into addiction-related thoughts and behaviors

- contemplation of problems caused by addiction

- identification of triggers that promote a return to addiction

- provision of coping skills to resist an addiction-based lifestyle

- engagement with social supports that provide resistance to addiction (Myers & Salt, 2007).

Involuntary Treatment

Not everyone entering treatment does so voluntarily. They often do so due to desperation when the level of emotional and often physical distress becomes too great to tolerate, or the fear of losing important people or things is a real consequence of the continuing behavior. In AA terms, a person at this point has "hit bottom" and has few choices (Myers and Salt, 2007), but fortunately, one of those choices is treatment. Involuntary or mandatory treatment is another reason people enter addiction programs, and this type of treatment is more common for drug addiction than other mental health conditions. Drug treatment coerced through the court system only began in the United States in the early 1960s, and more treatment options were available to drug offenders for a brief time. In the 1970s and 1980s, punitive measures rather than treatment options became the focus in dealing with addicted offenders (Tiger, 2011). Drug courts, which came about in the early 1990s, promoted a treatment focus in lieu of traditional court sentencing by focusing specifically on the needs and risks of defendants with addiction problems.

Since participation is mandatory, there is monitoring by outside agencies such as parole, probation, or child welfare agencies, creating a degree of "therapeutic leverage" to ensure compliance with treatment plans (called "raising the bottom" in AA lexicon). There is also a high level of resistance that comes with mandated treatment that must be overcome for the therapy to be effective. Mandatory treatment is carried out through various "referral pathways," such as:

- the criminal justice system, in which treatment is used as an alternative to sentencing, incarceration, or due to a child protective service mandate

- employer/workplace, through an employee assistance program (EAP) referral

- school, through a school counselor in a student assistance program (SAP)

- family, friends, or child welfare programs (Myers and Salt, 2007).

It is true that sometimes people "mature out" of the use of addictive substances or addictive behaviors. This process of "natural recovery" is often disavowed by treatment providers due to fears that failing to complete a regimented treatment program will result in serious consequences to both individuals and society (Myers & Salt, 2007).

As changes in society occurred, changes in addiction treatment have followed. Very early pre-scientific "treatment" modalities have fortunately ceased to exist and have been replaced by others, depending on how society's ideas about addiction have changed. Some current treatments specific to addiction will now be reviewed.

Contemporary Addiction Treatment Approaches

Substance abuse treatment borrows heavily from other forms of mental health treatment. There are standard treatment modalities (or specific types of treatment) used in mental health practice such as psychodynamic therapy, cognitive behavioral therapy, brief models, group therapy, family therapy, and newer models such as mindfulness approaches. In addition, there are modalities that are more focused specifically on addictions treatment such as twelve-step based movements—these are considered "self-help" but are often used in clinical practice and in many treatment settings—and newer addiction-focused therapies such as harm reduction, motivational interviewing, and contingency management. All of these are examined below.

Psychoanalytic models of therapy

Most people have heard of psychoanalytic theory and its founder Sigmund Freud, who developed a theory of bringing information buried from deep in a person's subconscious into the open where it can be analyzed, interpreted, and that will hopefully shed light on how to change and alleviate mental distress that was caused by this buried material. It was posited that allowing the patients to discuss their past and intimate feelings would bring insight into the presenting problems, along with relief. While this form of "talk therapy" is common now, it was not as common in Freud's era, because those without financial resources (or those whose family lacked such resources) were often locked away in hospitals where little therapy was done (Kline, 1984). Freud believed indulgence in addictive substances was an escape from reality and a substitute for sexual pleasure; his focus was to look for deeper meanings from the blocked material in his clients' addiction. Still being considered a symptom of underlying problems, drug use in the post-war era was believed to be self-medication for feelings of low self-regard; therefore, psychoanalytically oriented therapists saw their role as providing affirmations (Matusow & Rosenblum, 2013). Psychoanalytic approaches for addiction still seek the problems that lurk beneath the addiction. Due to its origins that focused on sexuality, psychoanalytically based therapies have utility in the study of sex addiction.

Cognitive-behavioral therapy

Cognitive-behavioral therapy (CBT) is a combination of cognitive theory, which focuses on thought processes (particularly faulty ones), and behavioral therapy, which focuses on direct strategies put in place to create change. This form of therapy is a systematic and formulaic model of treatment and holds that maladaptive behaviors of thought and behavior, like functional ones, are learned. Through a process of correcting thought patterns (or cognitions) that are creating behavioral problems, a modification of behaviors will also occur, creating a reduction in the craving for or seeking out addictive sources, or other symptoms that are causing impairment.

Cognitive-behavioral therapy involves a highly structured therapeutic contract with a well-defined plan of specific goals, objectives, assignments, and techniques in its treatment programming such as:

- homework assignments
- consistent feedback
- thought records
- cost-benefit analyses
- negative thought-stopping exercises
- distraction techniques
- physical activity
- communication skill-building techniques
- relaxation exercises (Nichols and Schwartz, 2001).

There are several types and related methodologies of CBT, such as an older method known as rational-emotive behavior therapy (REBT) that emphasizes how activating events (A), often create an irrational belief (B) that eventually leads to a consequence (C). Clients are taught to focus on the irrational belief that is involved and are given plans to correct them. This is especially germane to addiction treatment since certain triggers lead to a return to the addiction source, and CBT therapists teach addicted persons skills to interpret and appropriately address bothersome cognitions, such as those that involve craving.

More recently, dialectical behavior therapy (DBT), was created as a form of treatment and is often used for people with personality disorders, eating disorders and depression, that encourages self-regulation of their responses to emotional triggers (Chapman 2006). It is also used in treatment for people with addictions due to this focus on self-regulation.

Another recent treatment associated with the tenets of CBT is acceptance and commitment therapy (ACT) in which clients are taught to recognize cognitive problems leading to distress, but rather than forcing a change in thoughts and situations, they are taught to accept the condition, often using mindfulness therapy techniques to accomplish this end (Dualdiagnosis.org, 2018).

Brief models of therapy

As the name implies, this type of therapy involves a short-term treatment philosophy that is focused and seeks rapid relief of symptoms. It is patient-focused and collaborative and strives to work on problems in the present, seeking ways to improve situations in the future. Time in therapy is rarely spent exploring past experiences. Brief models were created due to what was considered the impracticality and inefficacy of long-term treatment, especially when health management organizations (HMOs) started regulating the number and types of therapy sessions that were available for people with insurance plans. Since it relies so heavily on immediate problem resolution, it depends on client strengths and aspirations to guide treatment. Brief treatment can be beneficial because it focuses on quickly addressing problems and, since relapse is often a problem in addiction, exposure to treatment is important. And since it also prompts clients to envision a future without the problem behavior, it has utility with addiction problems.

Often used in family therapy models, solution-focused brief therapy, or simply solution-focused therapy, is one type of brief therapy and, as the name implies, emphasizes solutions to the problems encountered by patients. Outcomes are co-created by the therapist and client and therefore reduces a hierarchical structure that can be detrimental to therapy with addicted clients, especially those in court-mandated treatment.

Another type of brief therapy, narrative therapy, focuses on narratives, or personal stories, that allow clients to construct meaning and provide insight into their presenting problems. Clients are encouraged to observe their own "problem saturated stories" (White and Epston, 1990) and work toward formulating more productive outcomes. Metaphors are used extensively to address symbolic issues in a person's story. The use of metaphors in narrative therapy, and other short-term modalities, is based on the idea that people construct the world in ways that can be easily brought to consciousness through symbolic language. Rather than simply being symbolic language, however, metaphor, suggests Siegleman (1990), is an "elementary structure of thought" (p. 3). Through language, metaphors make the abstract concrete and can produce insights into a person's current situation. Metaphors are especially effective with children for whom many morality- and integrity-based stories are communicated, but since all adults were once children, most people have been exposed to various fables and fairy tales that can illuminate underlying issues. Basic metaphors involving journeys, paths, changing situations, and others require contemplation and one's own relationship to the metaphor (Siegelman 1990). Narratives can be beneficial in addiction treatment because all addicted persons have personal stories that helped created problems brought about by the addiction. It should be noted that narratives are a major component of twelve-step programs as each person's personal narrative is disclosed and becomes a part of the treatment process.

Family therapy

Family therapy, often called marriage and family therapy, developed in the 1950s and is a therapeutic model that seeks to include treatment of whole families (at least as many that will attend therapy sessions) through examining dysfunctional family patterns and seeking to improve relationships. In family therapy, the entire family is the "identified patient" rather than one single member. Therefore, the effects of inadequate family functioning on all members are addressed, and family patterns are explored. Better boundary maintenance, improved interpersonal communications, and specific individualized strategies are part of the treatment process in family therapy. Explored are both the family in which one was raised, to determine how problems are passed down from early experiences, and situations in the current family. Genograms, clinical family trees that reflect where problems might have originated in prior family relations, are often used in family therapy.

Psychodynamic, cognitive-behavioral, brief, and the other individual therapy models are used in family therapy, and it also has its own sub-modalities specific to family treatment such as structural therapy and Bowenian systems therapy. Structural family therapy is a type of family treatment that explores problems in family structure, such as when family boundaries are too rigid or too flexible, or if members form subsystems that are unhealthy. In this type of therapy, the therapist joins with the family in an active way and seeks to promote a more structured family environment (Nichols & Swartz, 2001).

Bowenian systems therapy, a popular form of family therapy, seeks to promote active differentiation in families, detriangulation, and stress reduction. Differentiation refers to the ability of people to grow and formulate their own personal identities apart from their family. Triangulation is a condition in which a person is pulled into a dyad (two-person group) in order to reduce tension; however, this can create more dysfunctions in dealing with problems, so detriangulation efforts are introduced by therapists. Stress develops in families, and specific strategies are incorporated into treatment planning to relieve this stress appropriately. (Nichols & Swartz, 2001). This form of treatment can be beneficial for families with addiction problems due to the high levels of stress that often result from addiction, and that can be complicated by faulty attempts by other family members in attempts to deal with the addiction. This is addressed in more detail in chapter six regarding families and addiction.

Group therapy

Group therapy is a common treatment model and takes place within a group setting rather than one-on-one with a therapist or with family members. It normally has a group leader (either a professional therapist or sometimes a non-clinician such as in twelve-step programs) who facilitates group discussion in certain topics or general ones, but which pertain to shared experiences of the group. Therapy groups come in different sizes, take place in different settings, and use different treatment modalities such as those listed in this section. Psychoeducation groups are a specific type of group that seeks to educate people about mental disorders and addictions rather than offer treatments for them and are often used in prevention programs.

Group treatment has certain goals that it seeks to achieve. These include:

- relieving symptoms

- building self-esteem

- building skills in relationships

- enhancing decision-making and problem reduction skills

- developing peer acceptance competencies (Dies, 2003).

Groups develop through different stages, which is important in determining their effectiveness. Brown (2013) presents this stage progression:

- the "forming, storming, norming and performing" stage, in which group members are involved in a complex process of interpreting the other members' thoughts and actions

- the conflict stage, in which frustration develops as members try to assert independence and individuality as trust issues emerge

- the cohesion stage, a period of bonding of group members and a relinquishing of the leader's role

- the termination stage, often a time of sadness, when members must use the skills learned in the group to function independently without the benefits of sharing experiences with the group (Brown, 2013).

Mindfulness approaches

Mindfulness therapy uses the teachings of Eastern philosophy to augment Western treatment approaches and has become very popular in recent years. Mindfulness promotes the acquisition of deep mental awareness, sustained attention, and memory that allows the person to focus on here and now experiences and to handle difficult situations that may arise in the future (Germer, 2013). Mindfulness uses meditation to help re-focus clients from negative life situations and problematic thoughts and assists in emotion regulation, improved cognitive functioning, more effective relationship skills, and enhanced emotional and physical well-being (Davis and Hayes, 2011). Mindfulness approaches are often used in conjunction with other models of therapy, such as dialectical behavioral therapy and acceptance and commitment therapy.

Mindfulness therapy can be useful in the treatment of addictions, and promising findings have been suggested for alcohol, marijuana, cocaine, and tobacco, and in eating disorders through the reduction of cravings. In addition, mindfulness therapy for addictive disorders combined with harm reduction techniques, is also producing potentially beneficial results (Shapiro & Carlson, 2017). It is assumed this approach will have similar benefits for persons with behavioral addictions.

Twelve-Step Models

Due to the popularity of twelve-step programs over the decades and their influence on the field of addiction studies, this section will be explored in-depth, beginning with its primary texts to give more background on the philosophy and treatment approach adopted by AA and other groups as well as the famous twelve steps that form the core of the program.

The original work *Alcoholics Anonymous* (also called the Big Book) was released in 1939. The lengthy subtitle to this venerated text is *The Story of How Many Thousands of Men and Women Have Recovered from Alcoholism*. Starting with a physician's assessment of the twelve steps called "The Doctor's Opinion" (presumably lending medical expertise to the philosophy by explaining the "theory of allergy" in which no amount of alcohol can be consumed without deleterious consequences) and moving to the story of AA's founding titled "Bill's Story," the book describes and details the Society's views on the consequences of addiction, the basic tenets of AA ideology, and the twelve-step program; the chapter is important because of its historical aspects and formative views. As the book went through revised editions, additions were made, such as information about the twelve steps and twelve traditions, and other personal stories were included.

One of the main books containing information about AA is *Twelve Steps and Twelve Traditions* (1952/1989) which describes AA philosophy as consisting of "a group of principles, spiritual in their nature, which if practiced as a way of life, can expel the obsession to drink and enable the sufferer to become happy and usefully whole" (p. 15). The book specifically states the principles were "borrowed mainly from the fields of religion and medicine" (p. 16), claiming that both clergy and physicians eagerly accepted the AA philosophy in their work with addicted persons. The book had sections for both the twelve steps and twelve traditions. Each of the twelve steps of AA will be provided with my brief explanation and narrative of each.

The Twelve Steps

1. We admitted we were powerless over alcohol—that our lives had become unmanageable.

   This step requires members to maintain a level of humility that can only be accepted by "hitting bottom," otherwise addicted people will continue to drink. This is the one step that can be "practiced with absolute perfection" (p. 68): the rest are ideals.

2. Came to believe that a Power greater than ourselves could restore us to sanity.

   Obviously, the issue of a higher Power introduced in this step clarifies the role of religion in convincing non-believers, questioners, or former believers to break the spell of alcoholism through religious belief. Sanity is defined as a "soundness of mind," but it was explained that no active alcoholic has this characteristic.

3. Made a decision to turn our will and our lives over to the care of God as we understood Him.

   The decision in step two affirmed that the higher Power in question relies on a subjective view. The authors state the decision to turn over their lives to this understanding is not different as AA members have already entrusted their protection and deliverance to the group itself. In step three is found the famous "serenity prayer": "God grant me the serenity to accept the things I cannot change, courage to change the things I can, and wisdom to know the difference. Thy will, not mine, be done (p. 41)."

4. Made a searching and fearless inventory of ourselves.

    An "inventory" is recommended here to locate blocked instincts and to find solutions. Instincts are natural but can be perverted in the areas of sex and overwork: these predate the inclusion of behaviors as addictions. This section, with its focus on the perversion of natural instincts and blocked drives, sounds much like tenets of Freudian psychoanalysis.

5. Admitted to God, to ourselves, and to another human being the exact nature of our wrongs.

    Considered a difficult step, this calls for admission to three entities (God, self, other) of one's bad behavior. Being free from isolation and having the gift of humility is a consequence of adhering to step five.

6. We were entirely ready to have God remove all these defects of character.

    Step six indicates God can and will forgive transgressions, but the alcoholic must first work toward sobriety. Perfection might not be wholly achievable, but all members should work toward a life of abstinence.

7. Humbly asked Him to remove our shortcomings.

    In what appears to be a request for salvation, alcoholics are asked to remove negative contexts through humility. As more is learned, especially in the stories of others, it will be healing not only for addiction but for other shortcomings as well.

8. Made a list of all persons we had harmed and became willing to make amends to them all.

    Creating a list of those harmed often requires dredging up old wounds and "will at first look like a purposeless and pointless piece of surgery" (p. 77). Through careful planning, the harm that was caused to others should be addressed. This stage simply asks for a willingness to make amends.

9. Made direct amends to such people wherever possible, except when to do so would injure them or others.

The actual process of making amends to those harmed is dependent on several factors such as timing, determining amounts of restitution (full and partial) due to the aggrieved, and the degree to which mending fences is possible, if at all. Discussions about recompense are many-faceted, but amends must be made without delay.

10. Continued to take personal inventory and when we were wrong promptly admitted it.

    Alcoholics are asked to keep a ledger (real or virtual) in which they keep spot checks on assets and liabilities. This requires a high level of insight, a skill hopefully developed in earlier steps.

11. Sought through prayer and meditation to improve our conscious contact with God as we understood Him, praying only for knowledge of His will for us and the power to carry that out.

    The use of prayer and meditation assist in the evolving process of self-examination and awareness. This step calls for members to stop resisting and recoiling from prayer, defined as "the raising of the heart and mind to God" (p. 102).

12. Having had a spiritual awakening as the result of these steps, we tried to carry this message to alcoholics and to practice these principles in all our affairs.

    The final step involves the experience of a spiritual awakening, a "gift of a new consciousness and being (p. 107) or a transformation from a sick path to one that has been restored. In *Twelve Steps and Twelve Traditions*, there is a discussion on the benefit to families with addiction and, of course, the idea of carrying the message to other addicted people and using the principles in everyday life are utilized in step twelve.

Twelve-step Lexicon

Another way of maintaining cohesion is through the many statements and slogans used by the group. Several of these are intriguing alliterations, beneficial acronyms, or quaint and folksy aphorisms. In addition to creating unity, these slogans and statements also shine a light on some of the ideas of AA and twelve-step movements. Examples can be found in the *AA to Z: Addictionary of the 12-step Culture* (Cavanaugh, 1998):

- "One Day at a Time"—probably the most well-known AA slogan, this statement implores members to take responsibility for sobriety on a day-to-day basis; also referred to as the "Twenty-Four-Hour-Plan"

- "Stinking Thinking"—another very popular slogan that refers to the irrational thinking, especially involving denial, that thwarts sobriety

- "Sick and Tired of Being Sick and Tired"—the feeling of malaise that precedes involvement in twelve-step programs

- "Easy Does It"—a popular statement that is basically a plea for patience in the recovery process

- "90 Meetings in 90 Days" (or "90 in 90")—a requirement for new members (often called pigeons) to attend a meeting every day for three months

- "Turn Over" (or "Turn it Over")—turning over problems that affect sobriety to a Higher Power

- "Yets"—experiences—such as divorce, loss of employment, and incarceration—that have not yet occurred due to drinking behavior, but that will occur if abstinence is not sought

- "Put a Plug in the Jug"—the idea that total abstinence is required

- "Nothing is So Bad a Drink Won't Make Worse"—a challenge to the idea that drinking is a suitable action when stressed or upset

An interesting idea that evolved though the 12-step movement was the idea of the "dry drunk syndrome," defined as "the period in time in which a person, though sober, behaves or feels if they're drinking" (Cavanaugh, 1998, p. 82). The dry drunk syndrome concept either accurately describes a condition related to addiction to simply extends the idea of addiction to new areas (similar to the idea of codependence, which will be discussed in more detail in chapter six), which in turn produces new areas which can apply twelve-step strategies.

Reward system

AA and other twelve-step organizations often use a "token" system in which rewards, normally in the form of "sobriety chips" or "coins" that signify periods of sobriety (such as receiving a one year chip at the person's first anniversary) and designated by a special color (for example, a one month chip is red, a six-month chip is dark blue, and the anniversary chip is bronze). Some groups use a white "slip chip" for members that relapse, with the notion they can regain a 24-hour chip (which is silver) when they have maintained that level of sobriety. AA has a wide variety of chips, medallions, key chains, etc. for members, in the hope that it will be a constant reminder of their goal to remain sober.

Twelve-step programs and Culture

Although most of this investigation has used sociological insights, the discipline of anthropology offers some additional cultural insights by showing how different patterns of action result from membership in this type through the power of symbolism. Antze (1987) notes that twelve-step programs seek to:

- totally reorder an addicted person's life

- create a new identity

- allow for alternative needs fulfillment

- congeal social solidarity

- promote conduct that encourages concepts of serenity (as in the Serenity Prayer), humility, forgiveness, surrender, and service—characteristics also associated with organized religion

Antze (1987) notes that due to AA's lack of a connection to medical knowledge, it could be better understood as a "folk system." He notes its religious connotations are like Durkheim's formula of "society as God" in which society springs from a single concept—that of a deity. AA is also totemic in that its single source is the avoidance of the addictive substance.

Challenges to Twelve-step Philosophy

As Barr (1999) notes, AA members are taught that any consumption of alcohol will lead to the "slippery slope of dependency and degradation" (p. 364); therefore, total abstinence is required. And that message has been communicated to the treatment field and to American society generally. These ideas, although they were common in the American landscape for decades, did not go unchallenged. Many people did not like the religious underpinnings—although twelve-step programs often claimed the Higher Power could refer to different interpretations of God and could include non-spiritual entities including the AA community itself (which, of course, elevates the group to deity status). In addition, the fact that many people who were processed in the court system are involuntarily placed by judges into twelve-step programs has been interpreted by some to be state coercion into spiritual activities. The idea of powerlessness has been an issue for some—the author of this book worked with adolescents who, at the peak of perceived youthful power, found it difficult to accept and admit powerlessness. Likewise, the idea of surrender seems antithetical to a competitive society that values a "fight to the end" stance against rival forces.

Twelve-step philosophy was seriously challenged by Wendy Kaminer in *I'm Dysfunctional, You're Dysfunctional: The Recovery Movement and Other Self-Help Fashions* (1993). Written as the self-help movement had hit its apex and was waning in its prominence in the addictions field, Kaminer noted that books on the subject were still bringing in million-dollar sales. In fact, it was not so much the actual treatment strategies she protested; it was "the ideology of the recovery movement and its effect on our culture" (p. 4). She makes this pronouncement with the understanding that many different groups make up "our culture" but that the self-help movement has had a collective series of consequences to ideology and action. And the movement created a growing and profitable industry based on the misery of others. The idea of victimhood, especially obvious in the codependency movement (examined soon in chapter six), was evident in twelve-step programs, and Kaminer observed: "someone else is always writing the script" (p. 13). And many of those had lucrative careers in the publication of these scripts, which often were not based on any scientific data. Combining religious, New Age, and (some would say) feminist elements, the movement grew in the 1980s and the 1990s, and the philosophy espoused became not only disseminated in books but on television (especially talk shows that featured celebrities) and in movies, eventually appearing to be reporting current scientific knowledge (though it often was not). Kaminer noted the broader implications of the self-help movement, claiming the focus on submission, surrender, and victimhood is more akin to the characteristics of a movement present in a totalitarian system than a democracy. The twelve-step movement promoted a group approach to problem-solving rather than the use of true personal inventories and personal intuition to create sober identities. The predictions in her book of a growing men's movement and of a push toward "resilience" in mental health treatment did become realities in mental health programs; this would be presented as the mythopoetic men's movements of the 1980s and 1990s which provided self-help activities focusing on men's issues, and treatment programs that focused on resilience, especially in therapeutic work with children .

Newer Treatment Models

Rational Recovery

Rational recovery (or just RR) is a movement that evolved in the 1990s that outright rejected the idea of addiction as a disease and chose instead to draw upon a method that goes by the clumsily named Addiction Voice Recognition Technique (AVRT) to maintain an addiction-free lifestyle (Trimpey, 1996). This technique posits there is an "addictive voice" that compels people to return to the use of addiction sources, however, this voice can be overpowered by the positive voices that are the essence of a person's true self, and that can promote an addiction-free lifestyle. RR refers to twelve-step programs as "slogan therapy" and recommends addicted persons avoid them. It provides a list of Don'ts and Do's that provide insight into the perspective:

- don't accept the label of addict as it invites stigma, and resist referrals to addiction treatment agencies that use the label

- don't admit to criminal behavior or "blackout" periods

- don't reveal personal information to databases or at groups or meetings

- do resist the idea of addiction as a loss of control

- do resist creating a moral inventory with a list of people harmed or actions to repair damages of the past

- do consider incarceration when given an alternative to attend diversion programs or court-mandated twelve-step programs

- do stop using addiction sources

- do read the book Rational Recovery (Trimpey, 1996), billed by the author as the "first book for America's post-treatment era" (p. 51) or use the supplemental materials on RR that are available for purchase

Trimpey's sound rejection of the "treatment gulag" of self-help movements provides an important critical "voice" that is needed in the addictions field. However, his proclamations denouncing the consumer-driven nature of the current field are dubious due to the commercialization of his own treatment product.

Harm Reduction Models

The ideology that promotes total and complete abstinence met a major challenge in the 1970s and 1980s with programs that introduced "harm reduction" strategies. These strategies had alternative goals for people who do not or cannot accept the strict adherence to total abstinence as demanded by twelve-step and other abstinence-based programs. The new philosophy of harm reduction instead seeks to lessen the harm created by the excessive use of substances or compulsive behavior (Marlatt & Witkiewitz, 2009).

Relapse, which is extremely common in the addiction process, should be monitored and controlled, with the expectation that relapse is a possibility in the harm reduction framework. Prochaska and DiClemente (1982) proposed a widely used five-stage change model of addiction in which addicted persons often proceed:

1. precontemplation—the addicted person has no intention of changing the using behavior

2. contemplation—the person considers discontinuing drug use

3. preparation—the person is motived to begin the needed changes

4. action stage—the person decides to make the change

5. maintenance—the person abstains from the addiction source

Total abstinence models are often unsuccessful for many people as they return to use at various points. And, as noted, harm reduction interventions assume that positive attempts at recovery are possible without complete abstinence (MacMaster, 2004). Since drug policy and most addiction perspectives stress zero tolerance, harm reduction runs counter to this orientation and is controversial for this reason (MacMaster, 2004).

Motivational Interviewing

Motivational interviewing is a relatively new treatment method, which merged with the brief therapy approach (Miller & Rollnick, 1991). By ensuring a safe environment for addicted clients, motivations for the use of addiction sources are explored with an expectation that changes will occur. The five-stage change model listed above (Prochaska and DiClemente, 1982) is often used as a guide for therapy.

Developed in the early 1980s, Motivational interviewing (or MI, or Motivation Enhancement Therapy) acknowledges the addicted person's ambivalence to treatment and, using a cognitive-behavioral framework, seeks change through the use of empathy, rationality, and support, and by using a non-moralistic approach. To be avoided are different "traps," which can threaten treatment and lead to non-compliance with goals. These traps are:

- the confrontation-denial trap in which the therapist assumes responsibility for the problem and the client rejects and denies it

- the expert trap in which the therapist assumes a non-collaborative stance

- the labeling trap in which labels create client resistance and hostility (Miller & Rollnick, 1991).

Contingency Management

Contingency management (CM) is another new treatment strategy based on operant conditioning concepts that provide rewards such as gift vouchers, prizes, and other incentives to clients who follow strict adherence to their meetings, medication schedules, and general behavioral goals to assist them in abstaining from addiction sources. The use of reinforcements by CM has been researched for decades and found to be effective for persons addicted to alcohol and other drugs (Higgins & Petry, 1999). Primarily used for substance use disorders, it also has shown promise for other mental distress problems, therefore presumably behavioral addictions as well.

Recent research suggests that both motivational interviewing and contingency management approaches are generally effective in helping clients achieve the goal of abstinence (Sayegh, Huey, Zara, and Jhaveri, 2017).

Prevention

There have been many initiatives and campaigns to help people, especially young people, avoid behaviors that can result in addiction; these include the D.A.R.E. (Drug Abuse Resistance Education) program, the Just Say No campaign, Scared Straight programs, and numerous others. In addition, there have been many ads, television commercials, and now social media campaigns that promote abstinence. Some have been successful, others have not, and still, others have produced mixed results. The motivation behind these programs is to provide psychoeducation to young people and their families to promote a lifestyle free of drug use.

Sanders (1998) developed a useful classification model for agencies and prevention programs that serve communities. This model can help determine levels of need for families requiring some type of intervention:

- level 1—low intervention strategies such as the provision of psychoeducation materials

- level 2—slightly more rigorous strategies that include the provision of self-help materials along with psychoeducation materials and minimal contact with service providers (non-mental health specialists)

- level 3—higher-level strategies that include hands-on skills training targeting specific areas of need

- level 4—provision of skills training with a broader focus to attend to multiple needs

- level 5—provision of intensive intervention to address multiple family problems

Freimuth (2008) also proposes a stage model: a simple but potentially useful "addiction continuum" that might have some utility in prevention strategies.

- recreation level—moderate, social, or experimental use; if the use of an addiction source becomes highly rewarding as an escape mechanism, problems can result

- at-risk level—more frequent use that does become so rewarding or escapist that addiction can become problematic if not curtailed

- problematic level—repetitive and problematic use of the addictive source; a pre-addiction stage

- dependence/fully addicted level—a heavy return to the addiction source due to limited alternatives for the reinforcement or escapism provided by that source; this is the most recognizable stage of addiction

Using the above model as a guide, prevention strategies can focus on the first three levels. People at the fourth level, full addiction, are probably too late for prevention strategies and in need of treatment.

Currently, most prevention programs focus on youth, though some are useful for all age groups. Most of the programs focus their efforts on thwarting substance use, and it will be interesting to see the results of prevention programs and strategies developed to combat Internet gaming and other forms of compulsive online activity.

Conclusion

The diagnosis of substance use disorders and behaviors that are now being considered behavioral addictions has a long and storied history and reveals the cultural understandings of addictions across time. It is, of course, the inclusion of addictions in the Diagnostic and Statistical Manual of Mental Disorders (DSM) and its revisions that move the issue of addiction into the mental health realm, and more generally, into the health care field which uses the medical model of diagnosis. While the field has focused more on the use of scientific data than in the past, it continues to cast a wider net, pulling more behaviors into the conceptualization of addiction and potentially resulting in "diagnostic inflation." The more recent inclusion of behavioral or process addictions, reveals the concern of some of the early anti-psychiatrists and even some current scholars that too many behaviors are becoming medicalized. At this point, the diagnosis of addiction is firmly entrenched in the medical scheme and likely to remain there until some other cultural understandings arise.

Much has changed since the early days when inebriated people were subjected to an array of torturous interventions such as being shackled, dunked, shocked, and incarcerated. Social controls had to be placed on colonists who arrived in a new land, a hostile environment that seemed to possess many addictive sources. A therapeutic subsystem emerged that moved the treatment of addicted persons to the medical arena. Different therapeutic models were adopted, including psychoanalysis, cognitive-behavioral models, brief models, family-based therapy, and mindfulness approaches. One of the most well-known strategies for addiction involves the twelve-step, self-help models of addictions treatment which include Alcoholics Anonymous, Narcotics Anonymous, Gambling Anonymous, Overeaters Anonymous, Al-Anon, Codependent's Anonymous, and many others; these strategies have been both beneficial and controversial and will likely continue into the near future. Group work has been a staple in addictions treatment, regardless of the underlying treatment modality, because of the social nature of addiction and its treatment.

Prevention efforts have been primarily, but not exclusively, directed at children and adolescents with the hope they will develop the rational thought processes that will prepare them for a life free of substance use, despite the challenges and temptations that exist in modern society. Psychoeducation in newer forms, such as provided in an online format, will likely continue to be a dominant media for prevention programs.

In the introductory quote, Woolfolk (1998) observes that psychotherapy is not only a scientific field of knowledge but a cultural manifestation, meaning that what society deems as a problem in need of a cure is bound by the knowledge that exists at that time and place. Similarly, Szasz (2010, p. 276) describes diagnosis in this way: "diagnoses are disease-names. Because diagnoses are social constructs, they vary from time to time, and from culture to culture." Prevention strategies are also grounded in our current understandings of what to prevent and how, and as more types of substances and behaviors are labeled addictions worthy of prevention efforts, they will likely expand quite quickly.

Chapter 6

Addiction and the Family

"...there is a concerted family *resistance* to discovering what is going on, and there are complicated stratagems to keep everyone in the dark, and in the dark they are in the dark."

(R.D. Laing, 1971 p. 77)

Families and Society

Although the term family is often used as if there was one type, it represents many different arrangements or structures. While the traditional nuclear family model, which is comprised of father, mother, and dependent biological children, is often the default position in discussions on families, many other types exist. Furthermore, although the binary distinction of functional versus dysfunctional is often used to describe families, it is more appropriate to view family functionality (how families function to achieve goals and meet the needs of the members) as existing on a continuum, or a range of experiences. Also, since not all families consistently function adequately, certain interventions can certainly make life better for many family members. This includes families who have addicted persons among their membership.

It is a social expectation of families to provide nurturance, support, and guidance to its members. It also has many tasks it must fulfill—securing an income, making sure children are in school, paying bills, maintaining the house and car, and other basics. In families where addiction exists, sometimes fulfillment of these necessary tasks becomes disorganized, and priorities get shuffled, requiring the family to focus more on the consequences of addiction. Ineffective adaptations are made, such as denying or concealing, blaming others, marking inappropriate boundaries, promoting dysfunctional roles, and creating and maintaining an unpredictable home life (Henderson, 2000).

Families reflect the value system of the society, or at a closer level, the community. If social value is placed on materialism, altruism, patriotism, or individualism, for example, it will be reproduced in how families socialize their members. As Coser (1964) explained, "relationships within the families and its pattern of life must be to some extent congruent with the demands that the community makes upon its members" (xiii). In general terms, two main considerations are made by families regarding child-rearing decisions—the life experiences of the parents, and the current value preferences of society (Hamachek, 1978).

Families and History

It is well beyond the scope of this work to investigate the history of the family. However, some observations since America's founding provides some foundational insights into families and addiction. In colonial America, most families were of the nuclear type—husband/father and wife/mother and dependent children. There were often two or three living children, even though the mother bore around six, attesting to the grim reality of child mortality. The family was the provider of education and religious training, as the external institutions of school and church had not been well formulated at the time or were not available due to proximity. Homes were often occupied by non-family members functioning as servants or other helpers. The father was the patriarch, decision-maker, and chief provider who did not relinquish inheritance until his death. Urbanization and industrialization would eventually erode this tightly knit structure as younger men moved out to create their own property (Brown, 2017).

In a rapidly industrializing territory, husbands were the primary breadwinners, valued for their earning potential, further solidifying the role as head of the family. Wives were valued for their domesticity and piety. The Victorian era was a period in which romantic love between couples became more important than marriage partnerships, the arrangement that was in place prior to this era (Brown, 2017). In working-class homes, which normally included minority families, women and children worked in occupations while middle- and upper-class women and children were supported by the patriarchs.

At the beginning of the twentieth century, the standard of living increased for many middle-class families. New inventions were created, which made housework easier, children began to relate to peers more than parents, and sexual restrictions loosened. In the mid-century, the Great Depression made life difficult financially, not only for those who were already poor and needing employment but also for those who experienced prosperity prior to the crash and who had savings to lose. Government programs helped many families during the New Deal era, and World War II created a need for greater manufacturing. Both men and women built the economic engine that created prosperity for many (Brown, 2017).

The 1950s are often considered the "golden era" for families, although this moniker is severely deficit since things were not "golden" for women, minorities, and other marginalized groups. The post-war economic boom allowed many families to move to suburbs and commute to cities for employment.

Homebuilding increased, and manufacturing boomed. More people were able to attend college, many on the GI Bill that covered tuition for military veterans. Many teenagers began to break away in the 1960s and 1970s from staid postwar conventions and questioned the differential treatment of people based on race, gender, and other factors. The feminist movement grew in the 1970s, questioning the foundations of traditional family life and generally supporting equality for women. The rebellion that fueled the growing youth counterculture movement also included the use of many psychoactive drugs.

In many ways, families look different today than in the past. Marriage is not necessarily required of people to be considered a family. Nor is the inclusion of children. Blended families and interracial and interethnic marriages are more common, and an acceptance of same-sex marriages would not have been conceived in earlier times. The point of this examination of families from a historical perspective is to illustrate the fluidity of the social grouping known as family. It is in this historical context that the issue of addiction can be examined in the context of family life. For example, a consideration of the rapid and immense popularity of the twelve-step movements examined in the backdrop of the cultural anxieties of the Depression-era 1930s provides some important insights. Also, the idea of a hippie drug counterculture is better understood with the backdrop of the turbulent 1960s with the Vietnam War and the executions of national leaders; these contributed to a generational divide within families. The popularity of the codependency movement of the 1980s and 1990s can be viewed in terms of conditions that created the feminist movement (although great differences exist in how this brand of feminism was promoted). And the current concerns of opioid addiction can be seen in how pharmaceutical companies, bent on making profits, continued to push drugs on the market despite the deleterious consequences to people seeking relief.

Systems Theory

Herbert Spencer, a social philosopher of the nineteenth century, posited an organismic view of society, in which society is viewed as a system of interrelated and interdependent parts that function much like a machine. The parts consist of social institutions such as the government, economy, family, education, and religion. The component parts in the natural world were perceived by Spencer as providing functions for the whole, however, in the social world, it is reversed, and the whole provides necessary functions for its parts (Olson, 1970). Spencer's organismic approach contains these features:

- the systems concept is applicable to human systems; the whole is more than the sum of its parts

- the whole creates the defining characteristic of the component parts; the parts can only be understood as indicative of the whole

- the parts are interdependent (Phillips, 1970).

Influenced by Spencer, sociologists would later analogize systems that exist in the social world with those in the natural environment. For example, it was pioneering French sociologist Emile Durkheim who conceived of a collective conscience (shared social values and morals by members of society) that functions to keep these parts operating in a cohesive fashion (Salerno, 2004). Later, sociologists would expound on this idea of perceiving societies as ecological systems in which the concepts of invasion, succession, and dominance, as found in plant and animal environments, are analogized to the behavior of people interacting in human environments.

Although many early formulations about systems focused on the positive characteristics of equilibrium, cohesion, solidarity, and interdependence, there are also negative characteristics in the tension that develops between systems. As systems evolve, they often do so in ways that evolve in different directions to achieve their goals (Timascheff, 1967). However, this is not entirely a negative thing as different systems must work through these conflicts in order to become more functional. Many theoretical models of systems theory have been developed over time, but a thorough investigation goes beyond the scope of this chapter. However, a general examination of systems from different levels will be examined, considering how they are related to the process of addiction.

The person most notable for work on systems theory was not a sociologist but Austrian biologist Ludwig von Bertalanffy, who, in the 1920s, created what he termed General System Theory (1968). This theoretical system significantly influenced a group of researchers in the budding field of family therapy after World War II, who integrated it into their work with families. The assumptions that guided this merger are:

- the whole is greater than the sum of its parts (the most basic feature of systems thought)

- the locus of family pathology can be found in the family system rather than individual members

- behavior is not linear but circular as many external forces create dynamic and repetitive behavioral patterns

- rules within families are created and often maintained despite different situations that call for changes (this is called the re-dundancy principle)

- behavior is guided by feedback (both positive and negative) that is intended to return the homeostatic balance (this circular communication is referred to as feedback loops)

- unclear or inappropriate communication patterns ("pathological communication") lead to family problems

- family members assume roles (Kantor & Lehr, 1975) such as the *mover* (initiator of some action), the *opposer* (who blocks the action), the *follower* (who aligns with the mover or opposer), and the *bystander* (who simply observes and refuses to get involved)

- families can be identified by their boundary composition (Kantor and Lehr, 1975): *open families* are democratic and mutually supportive; *random families* have few boundaries and are disengaged from each other, and *closed families* are enmeshed, or overly involved in each other's lives and are undifferentiated (Smith & Hamon 2012).

Systems have been described as "bundles of relations" (Rapaport, 1968). This term has contemporary meaning in that items such as books, Internet services, and insurance policies, are often "bundled," or placed together prior to sale. The idea is that these items, when placed together, are more beneficial (or functional) as a whole and create a more complete and desirable set (Steverson, 2018). A desirable society has been described as one in which most people actively contribute to the system and recognize common goals and promote changes that benefit the whole (Woo, 1997).

The proper functioning of a system's parts is of paramount importance and the ways in which the parts transfer information, called cybernetics, is a key factor in keeping the system stabilized (or destabilized); communication directs the flow of energy within the system and must be appropriately organized for the system to be functional. Feedback is also essential in order to help the system adapt and change as needed (Anderson & Carter, 1990).

Therefore, in summary, systems:

- exist as wholly separate entities with concrete and obvious boundaries

- are comprised of elements that interact with each other and that possess a consistent (rather than random) organizational structure

- possess a degree of stability and a means of controlling functions to achieve the goals (Stewart, Winborn, Burks, Johnson, & Engelkes, 1978).

Families as Systems

Anderson and Carter (1990) view the family system as a holon or a social entity that is both a part of a system as well as a whole. These scholars note how the family can be perceived as a dependent variable, which is a system that is influenced by external systems or as an independent variable that creates changes in other systems. For example, in the former case, economies in modern Western societies have fashioned families that are smaller and more mobile. In the latter case, family life creates changes in abortion laws in the government system. The distinction between dependent and independent variables is blurred when viewing the family as a holon: families are influenced by and, in turn, influence other systems.

Family members exchange action, products, and emotional activities based on their own calculated self-interest. This might seem overly egocentric, but often all parties can benefit from the exchange. On the other hand, exchanges are often unbalanced, and some members have more power than others, which can lead to a host of family problems. Often these imbalances are based on status in the family (parent/child), age (adult/child), sex and gender, disability status, and produced through tactics such as intimidation and violence, (physical, sexual, or emotional), manipulation, and other coercive means.

The idea that families are systems is a foundational idea of early manifestations of family therapy. Families are systems in that they are comprised of individual parts that constitute a whole and that when a change in one part occurs in the family, the other parts are affected as well. The idea of functionality is closely related in that it is expected that if the parts work together in an orderly fashion, a "healthy" family system will emerge. Therefore, actions that promote positive family functioning should be incorporated into family life. Examined later in this chapter will be the specific role of family therapy as it relates to addiction.

Family, of course, is only one type of system. Systems exist in the natural world in the form of solar, weather, and water systems, among many others. They exist in the social world as well in political, governmental, economic, and religious systems, among a vast assortment of meso- and micro-level human creations (see Steverson, 2018). A systems approach can be a useful tool in understanding how addiction has consequences for all members, not just those members with addictions.

A Systems Approach to Understanding Addiction in Families

Al-Anon and Adult Children of Addicts

The concept of Adult Children of Addicts, or as originally conceived, Adult Children of Alcoholics (ACA, and later ACOA) was conceived in the late 1970s and grew quickly during the 1980s and 1990s as a twelve-step based program that emerged from Al-Anon (Haaken, 1993). Al-Anon, as noted earlier, began as an organization that sought to assist people, primarily women, negatively affected by a substance-abusing spouse. Formed in 1951 by the wives of addicted persons, the organization sought to thwart the effects of alcohol and other drugs on couples and families. Previously, spouses of people in AA simply provided support and remained silent, but with the advent of Al-Anon, these spouses met and discussed the issues inherent in living day-to-day with an addicted spouse. Freudianism became the underpinnings of Al-Anon in the late 1960s as unconscious motives for abusing drugs was explored in more depth. As feminism developed in the early 1970s and a focus on women's issues became more prominent, patience and self-sacrifice became less of a focus than the personal issues of being an intimate partner of an addicted person (Haaken, 1993).

Described as "the ambivalent daughter of AA and Al-Anon" (Haaken, 1993, p. 336), the ACOA defined alcoholism as a family disease. Dysfunctional families became a buzzword, and a new concept—codependency—became a popular notion. This idea, with its origins in the Al-Anon concept of enabling, stressed that attempts by spouses and other significant others to control the behavior of addicted persons exacerbate the person's problems and place more burdens on the family system. A focus was on how the family lives of children of addicted parents affected their experiences as adults. The movement spawned much literature, and many writers jumped into this new cottage industry. In fact, the idea of adult children's experiences extended to various types of family dysfunctions. The idea of the codependency of addicted persons also became extended into new areas creating a movement characterized by "a progressive repackaging of watered-down psychological truths, with each book offering, like a new brand of breakfast cereal, less and less substance" (Haaken, 1993, p. 340). Wegscheider-Cruse (1989) also claims therapists and other professionals such as physicians, ministers, and school counselors can become enablers as well if they fall into the "family trap" of the dysfunctions caused by addiction.

One of the founders of the ACOA movement, psychologist Janet Woititz (1983), in a very small (slightly over 100 pages) but bestselling self-help book, described 13 traits of adult children raised in addicted families. Woititz claimed that these adult children:

1. do not have appropriate understandings of normality

2. have difficulty following through on various projects

3. tell lies when there is no apparent reason

4. are overly judgmental when it comes to themselves

5. find it hard to enjoy life

6. take themselves too seriously

7. have difficulty maintaining close relationships

8. overreact to situations outside of their control

9. continually need affirmation

10. perceive themselves as different

11. are either irresponsible or overly responsible

12. maintain loyalty, even when it is not deserved

13. are impulsive and must expend much energy in dealing with the consequences of that addiction-created trait

Claudia Black, another key player in the ACOA movement, provided some additional characteristics in a publication by Al-Anon (Black, 1984). Adult children, she added, have difficulty in trusting others and understanding the correct means to voice their feelings, feelings that often consist of fear, anger, sadness, and embarrassment. Twelve-step programs, she contends, are specifically well-suited for their ability to cope with these experiences.

Sharon Wegscheider-Cruse (1989) was another counselor who wrote a bestseller about the problems of "the alcoholic family" in this same vein. From her work with families, she identified a "supporting cast" to the addicted person's lead role in the family, whom she called the "dependent." The primary supporting cast member is the "enabler," often a spouse but who might also be parents or other family members whose consistent interventions such as lying, giving excuses, and providing alibis for the dependent simply allow the dependent's condition to continue unabated. Another role, that of the "hero" is often assumed by the firstborn child (having "charter membership in the family") and is characterized by attempts at being highly successful in various endeavors in order to correct the deficiencies created between the dependent and enabler; while the hero seems "together" this cast member absorbs the family stress and is miserable and perfectionistic. The "scapegoat" is often a child born after the hero, and due to the family stress, withdraws from the family, rebels, and brings disgrace upon it; this person is the "heavy" in the drama. Another player arrives late to the family drama that has been going on for some time—the "lost child"; like the scapegoat, this member withdraws from the family, however, in this role the player, usually a younger child, simply retreats from the family drama, preferring to exit the stage and become reclusive. The final role is supplied by the "mascot" who attempts to alleviate stress by introducing levity into the family situation; often the youngest child, the mascot is shielded from the secrets of the family's dysfunction and seeks to become the family clown in order to reduce stress (Wegscheider-Cruse, 1989). This typology of family members gained much traction during the period and extended into other areas of family dysfunction despite the fact there was little empirical evidence to support it.

Other family typologies were imagined as well, for example. Elkin (1984) designates the spouse of an addicted person, usually the wife, as a high achieving "co-alcoholic." An older child, identified by Elkin (usually the oldest daughter), as the mother's "apprentice" who learns the skills of enabling from the mother. The son is also an apprentice, this time of the alcoholic father; this apprentice becomes a "punk" who engages in anti-social behavior with other punks. Roles are also prescribed for younger children as well, which are also gender-segregated and that correspond with their same-sex parents. Even though sexism still exists in contemporary families, the strict placement of family members in these traditional roles makes this model, as with other models in the ACOA movement, problematic.

The Inner Child Concept

Another concept that emerged with the ACOA movement is the notion of the "inner child." This ambiguous concept represents the childhood version of a person harmed in the stressful environment of a dysfunctional, addicted family. In one conceptualization, the inner child represents a false self that is waiting to be revealed, appropriately tended to, and nurtured, allowing the true self to appear (Forbes, 1994). Similarly, Charles Whitfield, a medical doctor and another writer on this subject of the inner child, drew upon psychology and twelve-step philosophy. He described the inner child as a person's "real self," a self that has been stunted by growing up in a dysfunctional family (1987).

From a postmodern perspective, the concept reflects a merger of child and adult, a merger that is possible due to the notion of one person possessing more than one constructed self. From a basic, non-reflective perspective, it simply represents both problematic child development resulting from addicted families and the inverted roles of children and adults in these family environments (Forbes, 1994). It is the latter version that supplied the metaphorical analysis for the emerging ACOA movement.

Twelve-step programs were often used in inner-child schemas. Through "working the program" of twelve-step agendas, it was posited that adult children can integrate their inner children to the responsibilities of being an adult and maintaining adult relations (Forbes, 1994). In this model, the realities of adulthood must be countered with the reintegration of the child with the adult.

Codependence

The idea of codependence has been a staple in our understandings of addiction. It is defined by one of the developers of the concepts as a family disease "characterized by preoccupation with an extreme dependency or another person, activity, group, idea, or substance" (Wegscheider-Cruse, 1989, p. 243). This concept was a significant part of the overall ACOA movement and could be found in large quantities of self-help literature. Some writers began to use more scientific language and concepts such as contingencies, media of contact, and ecobehaviorism, and introduced different theories within the basic concepts of codependence and the ACOA schema. In addition, research agendas were constructed to provide explanatory representations for those concepts, not for lay readers but for professionals in the therapy field (see, for example, Ruben, 2001).

In addition to theorizing about the inner child, Whitfield (1991) also focused on the issue of codependence and described it as "any suffering or dysfunction that is associated with or results from focusing on the needs and behavior of others" (p. 3). This broad definition will be examined in this chapter's conclusion. He also describes it as a "disease of lost selfhood" (p. 3) in that people who are codependent lose themselves in the problems of others. He claims that of all the various types of addiction, the most common type is codependence, the "addiction to looking elsewhere" (p. 4)—to other people, things, or behaviors that are used to experience happiness, but that cause neglect of one's self. People become "wounded" in dysfunctional families due to addiction and must find appropriate ways of dealing with the effects of growing up wounded.

One addiction scholar (Forbes, 1994) attended Al-Anon and Codependents Anonymous meetings and found both advantages and disadvantages with the twelve-step formula used in these programs. The formalized steps offer a "moral alternative" to substances and other addiction sources which serve to re-socialize people needing help. In addition, the "shared language" with addicted others and the treatment community provides unity and belonging.

However, rigid conformity to group norms and rituals, while not forced, still stifles critical examination. In addition, the idea of codependence seems to continue an age-old tradition in the field of healing arts to blame women for the situations of others.

Family Therapy for Addiction

Family therapy focuses on how psychopathological symptoms that appear in one member of the family affects the other members of the family. According to the systems model, families are small social systems with component parts, and these parts coordinate in ways to accomplish some specific tasks or goals that affect not only the family but the larger society. The family, as a unit of the larger cultural system, is expected to function in ways that reflect larger social goals; these goals include, among others, primary socialization and social control. (Anderson & Carter, 1990). Family therapy developed in order to meet the needs of families and, by extension, society.

Family therapy emerged when a group of therapists and researchers were studying hospitalized people diagnosed with schizophrenia. They noticed that they behaved differently around their mothers and initially deduced it was the fault of the mother that the adult child was exhibiting psychotic symptoms. The researchers observed the interactions with family members and began to posit that psychosis was due to faulty communication patterns in which the parent's verbal statements were incongruent with the non-verbal cues that were given, causing confusion and anxiety in the patient. This idea, called the schizophrenogenic mother concept, of course, involved blaming the mother and was eventually dropped, but the belief that families are systems in which one member's behavior affects the others was retained. Families, as discussed earlier, were seen together in therapy, and there was a change in focus on the whole family being the patient. Family therapy was born from the idea that if dysfunctions begin in families, the whole family should be in treatment (Napier & Whitaker, 1978).

Psychiatrist R.D. Laing was a therapist that worked with families affected by schizophrenia. However, many of his observations regarding schizophrenic family systems are applicable to those families dealing with substance addictions. He noted how "the system perpetuates itself over generations; the young are introduced to the parts that the dead once played. Hence the drama continues. The dramatic structure abides, subject to transformations whose laws we have not yet formulated and whose existence we have barely begun to fathom" (p. 29). Laing noted the difficulty in families being able to "define the situation" (a sociological concept devised by G.H. Mead). In cases of family disorganization, including those families dealing with addictions, "no one in the situation knows what the situation is" (Laing, 1971, p. 31). It is difficult for family members actively engaged and emotionally invested in their problems to see the forest for the trees, which is why family therapy is important in creating a clearer picture of problems in families with addicted persons.

The growing influence of family therapy is the likely reason that the codependence movement, the ACOA movement, the inner child trend, and the concept of enabling became so popular. However, family therapy is based on family research, theories of the family, and the results of program evaluation. The fact that there was overlap is not surprising, and the codependency movement did have some components that were promising; certainly, the concept of enabling is an important one in many respects. But like many faddish movements that are based on assumptions rather than science, it was short-lived. Family therapy, on the other hand, has flourished for decades and will likely continue to do so.

Conclusion

Understanding the influence of and the reactions to family life is, of course, a very important part of the study of addiction. A systems approach is beneficial in examining the processes involving family addiction as it perceives the family as itself a system, in which the entire family often needs intervention rather than just individual members. It also effectively encompasses the interconnectivity and interrelatedness of the organizations associated with addiction and addicted persons.

Systems perspectives have influenced social thinkers, including sociologists, for a long time. Herbert Spencer and Emile Durkheim likened a system's construction to that of a machine or the human body; these systems possess interrelated parts that promote functionality or dysfunctionality. The systems approach has a good fit in the discipline of sociology as it allows people to view social phenomena from the personal level to the cultural, and it observes the interplay that exists between them.

Developing within the addictions field were the adult children of alcoholics (ACOA) and codependence movements, and the concepts of enabling and the inner child. The early family addictions literature was rooted firmly in twelve-step and other self-help models and had little scientific basis. These programs used pop psychology terms and concepts that, over time, began to appear as little more than psychobabble. Wegscheider-Cruse's (1989) definition of codependency, for example, describes a condition like addiction in which the addiction source can be another person, a group, an idea, or a substance. Addiction to other "people" sounds like love or at least infatuation, and since "groups" can describe two-person dyads to entire societies—there is much range here to be an addiction source. Additionally, an addiction to an "idea" is more ambiguous and creates a much larger range of possibilities, such as political, economic, or religious ideologies. And codependence to a "substance" was also proffered in this model—is that not a garden variety substance addiction? The incredible range of codependent objects means that, to some degree, everyone is codependent or has a good chance of becoming codependent. If people can be addicted to a broad range of behaviors and codependent to a broad range of behaviors, new possibilities open up for an expansive addiction industry, and one must wonder if that is the motivation behind this line of thought.

On the negative side, the many self-help books, workshops, "family reconstruction" programs, videos, television programs, and other forms of information about dysfunctional, addicted families that surfaced in the 1970s seemed to create a modern-day form of snake oil entrepreneurship. On the positive side, however, it brought attention to the effects of family life and the role of the family in formulating our behavior. And it certainly brought to light the consequences of dysfunctional behavior within families where addiction was a problem.

Family therapy is a form of mental health treatment that focuses on the entire family, or at least as many members that will come to therapy. It began as a research project with patients with schizophrenia and, upon observation, it was realized that all members of the family are affected by the thoughts, behaviors, roles, and rules of the family as a whole—much like parts of a system. Therefore, all members are treated as the patient. Its role in working with addicted persons has been and will continue to be paramount in addictions treatment programming.

Chapter 7

Addiction, Deviance, and the Criminal Justice System

"The addict in America suffers as much or more from the laws that brand his illness a crime as he does from the illness itself"

(Alfred R. Lindesmith, 1963 p. 33)

Contributions of the Sociology of Deviance to the Study of Addiction

A subfield of sociology known as the sociology of deviance has much to contribute to the study of addiction, as many acts related to substance and behavioral addiction are considered deviant behavior. There have been many contributions from sociological theory generally (these will be addressed in the next chapter), but the sociology of deviance has special relevance and is placed here in relation to the criminal justice aspects of addiction. Criminology is a discipline that also provides insights into this topic since many behaviors have been deemed by society as acts of criminality as well as deviance. The contributions of both groups will be observed in this chapter.

The sociology of deviance is a distinct subfield in sociology, closely related to the subfield of social problems. The concept under study, deviance, is not an easy one to define, however. Sociologist Kai Erickson noted decades ago that deviance seems to have "no natural boundaries" (1966, p. 5). Deviance is relative as it correlates to time and space—what is deviant in one period or place may not be in another, or to the same extent. One definition used to describe deviance is "the behavior that deviates from social norms and that elicits some type and degree of social sanction" (Steverson & Melvin, 2019). This definition considers the role of society in determining exactly what defines deviance and how to deal with it. Since the violation of social norms also involves behavior deemed criminal, or behavior so egregious it is codified into law, the discipline of criminology emerged as the study of the causes and consequences of criminal behavior and the social control measures implemented to deal with them; criminology is also a close cousin to the sociology of deviance. And since much behavior related to addiction and addiction sources is considered deviant and criminal, these elements are closely related in society.

Early American sociologists were concerned with social problems and the reform measures that would hopefully alleviate them. They conducted research on immigration, racial and ethnic populations, crime, poverty, juvenile delinquency, housing problems, and many other conditions, with the intention of applying knowledge from research findings directly to solve them. A group known as the University of Chicago sociologists, working and writing from the early to mid-twentieth century, founded this new practical approach to the field of social problems (Best, 2004). Social disorganization was the problem, and reorganization was the solution.

As Best (2004) writes, the term deviance entered the sociological literature in the early 1950s, and the primary concerns in the nascent subfield were:

- crime, and delinquency

- mental illness

- substance use and addiction

- sexual deviance

Goode and Ben-Yehuda (1994) describe two perspectives in which social problems are viewed by sociologists—objectivist and constructionist (or relativist). The former refers to an understanding of social problems as possessing objective, concrete, and realistic danger while the latter refers to a conceptualization of social problems as subjective, collectively defined, and "produced by specific sociocultural circumstances, groups and categories, social structures and societies, historical eras, individuals, and/or classes" (p. 51). In other words, a constructionist viewpoint uses a wider lens approach to social problems and considers a variety of factors before concluding a direct cause and effect relationship between variables and considers the possibility that outcomes of programs intended to assuage the problems are not as they are promoted.

Howard Becker (1973) focused on the labeling processes involved in the production of deviance. He proposed four categories of deviant behavior as a scheme to better understand the behavior:

- conforming behavior (non-deviant behavior)

- false accusations (behavior labeled deviant, which is not deviant)

- pure deviance (behavior labeled deviant and is deviant)

- secret deviance (behavior that is deviant but is not noticed)

As Holstein (2009) points out, however, Becker posited that for behavior to be considered deviant, it had to be labeled as such by someone—if it is secret and no knows, it can't be deviant.

With the introduction of Marshall Clinard's textbook *Sociology of Deviant Behavior* (1957) (which would be updated for decades), the subfield of the sociology of deviance was officially established. The subfield has grown and changed over the years, shifting focus on the etiology of deviant behavior from social disorganization, labeling, conflict, social control, strain, and recently, risk. Another contribution of the sociology of deviance was a concept known as moral panic theory.

Moral Panic Theory

Important to the sociology of deviance is what is termed *moral panic theory* as earlier proposed in the early 1970s by Cohen (2002) and further developed by Goode and Ben-Yehuda (1994) and a large host of scholars of the sociology of deviance. The idea of a moral panic basically states that throughout history, certain "explosions of fear and concern…about a specific threat…that were, in all likelihood, exaggerated or misplaced" developed (Goode & Ben-Yehuda, 1994). These events are normally (but not always) short-lived and vigorously promoted by media outlets and other groups that seek to resolve the problem or benefit from its ability to create some form of action. And they often involve fears related to addiction sources.

Cohen (2002) describes moral panics by these dialectic characteristics:

- they seem to be new (out of the blue) but also old (ancient evils)

- they are dangerous in themselves but also serve as a warning to society

- they are transparent (easily visible) but also opaque (there are deeply hidden associated problems)

- contain a group of people deemed deviant ("outsiders," "others," "deviants," and "scapegoats") referred to as *folk devils* and a group known *as moral entrepreneurs* seeking to maintain order by ousting them from society

Smelser (1962) describes panic as "a collective flight based on a hysterical belief" (p. 171). He defines a related term, craze, as "mobilization for action based on a positive wish-fulfillment belief" (p. 171). The action can consist of knee-jerk policy decisions without proper reflection and can have serious implications. While some of these drug panics have been short-lived, others, such as the crack cocaine scare, lasted for years and shaped social policy. Stronger words, such as "epidemic" when used in drug scares, add emphasis to its potential dangerousness by conjuring up images of plagues and the uncontrollable spread of disease (Jenkins 1994).

Moral panics have also been connected to living in a risk society. Miller (2006) describes moral panics as a process involving scapegoating of certain groups, the idea of risk, and the media as a "hinge between them." The concept of "at-risk youth," for example, reflects social attention to any cultural pattern that could affect our children negatively. The risk society concept refers to the fact that society has become increasingly complex and has generated a large variety of risks that can potentially disrupt the very fabric of society. To move this discussion to addiction-related panics—the fact that average citizens with a little knowledge of chemistry can easily combine substances from recipes effortlessly obtained on the Internet creates the level of concern needed for a panic; this is merely one example.

Marijuana, heroin, crack cocaine, methamphetamine, barbiturates, PCP, and club drugs have been presented to the public by those in power as major threats to the country's moral fiber. The current crisis of prescription medications will be furthered examined under the moral panic model due to its immediacy. While there is no claim here that the prescription opioid situation is fake or overblown, the model is a good example in which to examine the problem. This historical story has many *moral entrepreneurs*, who promote value judgments on different social acts and people (Cohen, 2002) *moral crusades*, the movements and campaigns associated with moral entrepreneurship (Gusfield, 1986), and *folk devils*, the people who are scapegoated in relation to the moral panic (Cohen, 2002). Drug dealers have, incidentally, been described as folk devils—as sketchy figures, often foreign and lurking in shadows providing free samples to hook unsuspecting strangers, especially children (so vulnerable to threatening situations), into a life of addiction, even though most dealers are actually friends or relatives (Ancrum, 2014).

To provide an example of how moral panics can unfold, Ben-Yehuda (1990) describes a moral panic in Israel in 1982 in which unreliable claims of drug use by half of the students in area high schools were reported. This report was immediately followed by a huge media campaign, conspiracy theories about school officials hiding information from the police, and involvement by policymakers to combat a "youth drug abuse panic" (p. 111). The effort was short-lived as the next month's military conflicts with Lebanon ended the panic as concerns shifted elsewhere.

Moral panics of various addiction sources in the United States will be examined next. They will be presented chronologically to reflect the social anxiety of these times in which these occurred. Throughout this book, history is used as a backdrop to provide a better understanding of the current manifestations of the problem of addiction.

Marijuana

Despite more acceptance today, marijuana has long been the subject of panics. Even though citizens were indifferent or apathetic to marijuana, and though laws again marijuana were lax or nonexistent prior to 1930, major concerns over the drug began in the 1930s (Goode and Ben-Yehuda, 1994). American newspapers and magazines broadcast fears of the "national menace" of the "killer weed," and a growing fear of marijuana dealers and users, or "outsiders" (Becker, 1973) developed. Movies such as the popular Reefer Madness depicted marijuana use as creating crazed behavior in users. The use of "drug scare films" shown to school children also provided unrealistic views of drugs and their effects (the author of this work was subjected to them in the late 1960s and early 1970s). The Federal Bureau of Narcotics gained much power during this period as a result (or concerted effort) regarding marijuana panic.

More recently, in the second decade of the 2000s, the concern over edible marijuana has been described as a moral panic due to special concerns over easy access by children to the drug in this form as well as the attribution of death and unsubstantiated claims associated with the edible form (Eversman, 2016). Changes in marijuana laws that are presently occurring across the country will likely produce fertile soil for new moral panics.

LSD

In the 1960s, the use of LSD, a powerful hallucinogenic, became emblematic of a moral panic. Resistance to the draft and the Vietnam War, racism, sexism, and other issues became the zeitgeist of that era. It also produced a "generation gap" between young and old and a time of experimentation with drugs by the younger generation, including a category of hallucinogenic substances that alter consciousness. LSD produced many false reports, including stories of youth starring at the sun until they became blind, running into automobiles, jumping from buildings, and generally going insane. According to Goode (2008), these stories promoted by the media created a moral panic because the drug was a threat to the work ethic of the white middle class, especially since there were so many LSD peddlers (folk devils *par excellence*), including some very famous ones such as Timothy Leary and Richard Alpert, trying to get their kids to "turn on, tune in, drop out" of the comfortable lifestyle of which the older generation was so protective.

Heroin

There were many narcotics scares in the twentieth century over the effects of heroin and many campaigns to prohibit it. A 1919 report sponsored by the Treasury Department singled out heroin and the "other fiend cocaine" (Musto 1973, p. 137) as being special concerns for males and females under age 20. Also, in the next decade, narcotics prohibition moral crusader Robert Hobson sought to eliminate the "narcotics menace" through radio broadcasts, print news, and even in school textbooks. In a 1927 radio program, Hobson called heroin addiction more incurable than leprosy and described people addicted to heroin "the living dead" who will commit any crime, including murder, to obtain the drug (Musto, 1973). Concerns over heroin continued to reappear over the decades, often in its association with crime.

In the 1990s, a new focus on heroin emerged. Represented by an emaciated and disheveled fashion style promoted by models and actors, "heroin chic" entered the American consciousness. Occurring along with the death of rock star Kurt Cobain, who died by suicide in 1994, but was known to be addicted to the drug. Numerous movies and news stories about heroin use contributed to a moral panic, not of a new drug, but one which by all reports had reemerged (Denham, 2008). The pale and gaunt models and actors who adopted the "heroin chic" appearance seemed to represent the living dead image promoted decades earlier by Hobson.

Crack cocaine

Crack cocaine provides another example of what has been considered a moral panic. Cocaine had been around for a long time, as discussed in chapter three, but a smokable form known as "crack" or "rock" arrived on the scene and created a strict distinction between the higher class predominantly white powder cocaine users and the inner-city minorities associated with the use of crack. Reports of crack destroying communities and families heated up to the point that President H.W. Bush promoted a campaign against the drug. Fears of the racially tinged images of "crack moms" and their children reported to be born addicted and to be feared as adults ("crack babies") provided a common message promoted in the media (Curra, 2014).

Methamphetamine

Armstrong (2007) describes a methamphetamine scare of the late 1990s and the first decade of the 2000s. Described in media outlets as a "new drug," methamphetamine was hardly new on the drug scene, but ongoing exaggeration about its use in rural America created a strong reaction and hence has been described as a moral panic. Known by the nicknames "meth," "ice," "crystal," "crank," and "speed," there was nothing exotic about it. Amphetamines have been used in many commonly prescribed drugs, including the drug Ritalin, used for attention deficit hyperactivity disorder (ADHD); incidentally, Ritalin has also received the label of moral panic, especially since children (the primary age group prescribed the drug) has often been concerns in moral panic situations (Miller & Leger, 2003). Methamphetamine is a drug produced in homemade "meth labs' which are often quite small, creating potential harm to families because of the toxic chemicals involved in their manufacture and for their potential for mishandling. The folk devil in this situation is the "chemical bogeyman" (Armstrong, 2007, p. 433) who cooks meth and creates an environmental threat in addition to addicting people. If crack cocaine was the fear in urban America, meth created fear in rural parts of the county but had the similar effect of directing attention away from the social-economic plight of rural Americans (Armstrong, 2007).

Weidner (2009) explained how media outlets, including local small-town newspapers in the Midwest, perpetuated the frightening claims of a meth crisis by using terms such as an epidemic, plague, or scourge and exaggerating the addictive nature of the drug and using lengthy articles to stress the urgency of the crisis.

In addition, the nickname "ice" which had special importance in creating concerns over methamphetamine, not only suggesting cold, hard fear ("chilling"), but also promoting such importance that it signified an ushering in of new era; many reports in magazines and newspapers in the late 1980s and early 1990s warned of a "new ice age." Additionally, its connection with crack cocaine in media reports added a new element of fear and concern, promoting the careers of politicians and government officials who vowed to fight it (Jenkins, 1994).

Barbiturates

A moral panic over barbiturate use was described by Rasmussen (2017) beginning around World War II. The drug had been used as a medication to induce sleep since the 1920s, but by the 1940s, its abuses (already known in medical circles) were broadcast via print media publications. These publications relayed the idea that seemingly benign sleeping pills were turning users into "drug fiends," akin to people addicted to heroin or cocaine. One journal article in the early 1950s purported that the poisonous effects of barbiturates had reached "alarming proportions" (Cramblett, 1953, p. 394). Their use represented a "triple threat" in that they were exposed as a serious threat to personal health through overdose, the potential for death (illuminated by several high-profile celebrity deaths of the period), and a threat to the social order. A common nickname for the pills was "goofballs" to illustrate the out-of-control behavior they caused and their potential for dependence, despite the fact they were a prescribed medication and therefore assumed to be safe. The social and economic changes brought about by the war created a sense of collective national anxiety, and association of the drugs with African American and Latinx citizens promoted racial fears and anxiety among whites (Rasmussen, 2017).

By 1944, public health officials began cracking down on barbiturates, and the Federal Drug Administration (FDA) decided to spend its limited funds on controlling them. The Hearst owned newspapers, who had earlier success in creating anti-marijuana sentiments, ran features of a wide range of "goofball" influenced panics, including murders, suicides, violence, and other forms of depravity, supposedly confirmed by official reports. The next several years saw clashes over the prescribing of barbiturates, eventually resulting in a loosening of the government's grip on their control. Consumption of barbiturates, however, remained high but was overtaken in the 1970s by the use of amphetamines (Rasmussen, 2017).

PCP

Phencyclidine (PCP) became a major cause of concern in the US in the late 1970s and into the 1980s. Known widely as "angel dust," PCP was previously used to dull pain for people undergoing surgery but rejected due to its uncomfortable physical side effects and hallucinogenic properties. Stories of graphic and brutal acts of injury such as a user gouging out his eyes spread rapidly. Stories in the medical journals also reflected this trend, such as the story of a person who smoked marijuana laced with the drug and followed voices to bite his arms, which he did, to the bone, apparently without any pain (Grove, 1979).

Club and designer drugs

Club drugs, also called designer drugs, were a major part of the rave dancing scene of the 1990s. The use of these drugs at dance clubs has been described by scholars as constituting a moral panic (Baldwin, Miller, Stogner, & Hach, 2012). Beginning in the United Kingdom and spreading throughout Europe and North America, young middle-class people comprising a subculture with distinct characteristics created concerns over their use of ecstasy, a derivative of methamphetamine. The young people, or "ravers" were described as out-of-control, sexually addicted cult members and anarchists that required government restrictions (including municipal) on their behavior in downtown areas, as occurred in Florida in the late 1990s.

Events in Toronto in 1996 also exemplified the reactions to club drug anxieties in which three people died in ecstasy-related incidents. The deaths led to a large municipal protocol that created difficult requirements to hold rave parties in town. The regulations were so intense they resulted in backlash from the ravers (Hier, 2002).

Moral Panics Involving Behavioral Addictions

It is unlikely that some of the conditions that have been defined as behavioral addictions, namely compulsive exercise, excessive shopping, problematic eating, or compulsive tanning, would ever result in a moral panic as they don't seem to constitute the same level of threat to society as substance addictions. Some of the others, such as Internet gamine and sexual compulsivity, are a different story and have an extensive history as causing social distress to the extent that some scholars have described them as constituting moral panics.

Internet Gaming

Gambling has certainly been a source of concern at different places and times in history. However, it has been around for a very long time and has gained some degree of acceptance. This is evidenced by the fact that some cities, such as Las Vegas and Reno, Nevada, have developed around gambling. Therefore, gambling probably does not fit as well in the moral panic model of deviance. However, its technological counterpart, Internet gaming, has been suggested by many scholars to be a better fit. Online gaming can be seen in connection with moral panics as they continue to surface when there are growing concerns, especially concerning new and evolving forms of delinquency.

The use of pinball machines was a precursor to Internet games and, due to concerns of the corruption of youth, were destroyed after mass seizures of the police in a highly publicized way in the 1940s. Video games grew in popularity in the 1970s, and arcades were frequented by young people and working-class immigrants, creating rumors such as the video game's connection to gambling and kidnapping for human trafficking. By the 1980s, politicians entered the fray as moral crusaders, and even the nation's surgeon general warned of children getting hooked on gaming.

Video game machines gave way to personal computers, allowing games to be played at home instead of arcades, but the fears of their danger did not subside. In an era colored by 1999's Columbine School Shootings, concerns over the displacement of violent game activity to real-life continued to grow, not to mention concerns of childhood obesity resulting from the lack of engagement by young people in any activity other than gaming (Walker, 2014). Currently, Internet games contain themes of violence, warfare, and other forms of deviant conduct, promoted by a highly successful entertainment industry (Rodgers, 2014) and have long been at odds with many concerned citizens. Obviously, possible addiction to this type of entertainment has created enough anxiety to warrant consideration for inclusion in the next DSM.

In China, concerns over Internet gaming addiction is especially pronounced. Though media depictions anxieties have increased, in fact, these depictions possibly resulted in the premature designation of the activity as addiction. China has long sought to maintain control over its citizens through the promotion of a morally intact society (Szablewics, 2010). The growing use of online activity, especially among youth, has been compared by the Chinese government to abuse of opium, presenting a powerful cultural image. The stigma of mental illness in the country has created a unique situation in which the moral panic of gaming has now gained a deviant and devalued status. Moral panics then, "while sharing many attributes, actors, and stages across time, are ultimately unique to the cultures from which they spring forth" (Szablewics, 2010, p. 465).

Sexual Compulsion

Concerns over sexually compulsive people, or "sex fiends," "degenerate," and "sexual psychopaths" preying on people, especially children, created three major waves in the United States (Jenkins 1998). The first of these happened between 1935-1940 when high profile sexually-oriented murders gained national attention. Police agencies reacted by increasing arrests of lower-level sexual activity that had previously been ignored—this furthered the impression a sex crime wave was underway. The sex crime panic peaked again in the period 1947-1950 as sensational sex crimes once again raised national attention, promoted by news articles, movies, and films, although the sexual nature of the crimes was muted by censorship activity of the era, gruesome murders portrayed an implicit sex motivation. The FBI, under the leadership of J. Edgar Hoover, also became involved to boost their "law and order" image. The third wave of 1948-1952 introduced the notion of the "sexual psychopath" or "sex fiend." The panic made its way into psychiatric journals and was reinforced by the growing influence of psychoanalysis, which posited sexual psychopathy was driven by the motive of satisfying intractable instinctual drives (Jenkins, 1998).

A major assumption by law enforcement and psychiatry was that small seemingly minor deviations would emerge as full-blown sexual compulsions. This view persisted despite contradictory positions taken by people such as sociologist and criminologist Edwin Sutherland, who by this time had already made an assessment of the situation, explained: "a community is thrown into panic by a few serious sex crimes, which are given nationwide publicity; the community acts in an agitated manner, and all sorts of proposals are made; a committee is then appointed to study the facts and to make recommendations" (Sutherland, 1950). These steps occurred prior to the creation of sex offender laws.

Caught up in this furor over sexual deviance were gay people who became targets of "sexual degeneracy." Even one liberal-minded (for the 1950s) psychiatrist referred to gay people as "normal perverts" (Jenkins, 1998). A possible reason for this type of panic could be found in the era in which it emerged. World War II and the Korean War pulled many men into military service, creating family disruption and a source of concern regarding the women and children left at home. As fears spread and media coverage expanded, police agencies and lawmakers certainly had to respond to these fears. The panic also opened new avenues for the growing field of psychiatry (Jenkins, 1998).

Hoarding

Hoarding has been described as creating a unique moral panic, one described as an "object panic" (Herring, 2014). While hoarding is not a new phenomenon, it has evolved from early twentieth century understandings of the condition as "sanitary deviance" (referring to an attachment to unclean things) to a disorder formally designated in the DSM. The first major sensational case, which appeared decades before the TV show The Hoarders, was in 1947 in which over 100 tons of garbage was found in the New York home of the Collyer brothers, a lawyer and concert pianist who were found dead in their home. It took weeks to find the second brother among the accumulated materials in the house. The case of hoarding metaphorically represents social disorder and those who hoard materials create an image of folk devils of an interesting type; people who feel compelled to live in unsafe environments, despite the negative physical and social consequences of this behavior.

A Final Word on Moral Panics

Moral panic theory has been criticized, and its usefulness has come into question on several fronts, including its suggestion that irrational behavior results without contemplation of the time and effort it took to construct the problem. In their challenge of the LSD threat in the 1960s, Cornwell & Linders (2002) explain that people facing emergent threats seek clarity and factual information about the problem through debate and deliberation. Another challenge has been that panic is not only generated by a frightened public but by actions taken by policymakers and practitioners with an agenda as in the case of concerns of heroin overdoses in Australia in the 1990s that were overblown by officials, though in this case, the researcher maintains the situation could still be considered a moral panic, despite the different impetus (Zajdow, 2008). Flinders and Wood (2015) challenge the moral panic thesis by arguing a mirror

approach sometimes exists ("moral euphoria") in which folk devils were originally viewed as "folk heroes," often disgraced politicians.

However, despite these challenges, the analysis of how changing notions of
addiction (and related "drug scares") can be perceived as new risks and can
add to social anxiety is a key argument made in this book. Concerns such as
these heighten feelings of fear and contribute to dread in an already frightening world and can feedback into the system.

The Criminal Justice System

The criminal justice system is closely connected to the addiction field in many
ways. Three major components—the police, the courts, and corrections—
make up the criminal justice system, and each has close connections with
substance and behavioral addictions. Each of these system components will
now be considered.

The Police

The police constitute the entry point in the criminal justice system. The police, or law enforcement agencies, are responsible for enforcing laws, maintaining order, and ensuring public safety through the prevention, detection,
investigation of criminal behavior, and the arrest of citizens suspected of a
crime (BJS, n.d.). There is much discretion in the police function and a significant amount of contact between police and persons with addiction.

The current policing philosophy involves a community-based approach in
which officers actively engage the communities in which they work in collaborative efforts with citizens. Officers, therefore, have much knowledge
about the people in their areas and armed with this knowledge can inter-
vene with a greater degree understanding of the people, the community,
and its problems. If addiction to a certain drug is a problem, experienced
officers will have some degree of familiarity with the addictive process as
well as possible resources in the area. This approach is more practical than
in an era before community-based approaches when police remained removed from extensive citizen contact.

Johns Hopkins University recently sponsored collaboration between police
and public safety to establish a best practices program for police agencies in
their dealings with the opioid crisis. That collaboration created a list of standards of care involving these strategies:

- promoting, through research and data-informed practice, a
  protocol to reduce overdose-related deaths

- equipping and training officers on the use of naloxone to impede overdoses

- providing education to communities regarding the consequences of substance use and addiction

- providing training to officers on how to refer addicted persons to treatment programs

- providing access to "on-demand" treatment services for those in need of such services

- advocating for addicted persons in the correctional system (institutional or community)

- preventing outbreaks of HIV and hepatitis by working with public health agencies regarding syringe service programs

- preventing fentanyl overdose through training on early detection

- advocating innovative, collaborative programs between the police, public health agencies, and the community on opioid-related issues

- establishing "good Samaritan laws" to allow providers of emergency care consideration when working in good faith to assist those in need (Johns Hopkins University Bloomberg School of Public Health, 2018).

Courts

Criminal courts are responsible for hearing cases that involve some degree of criminal, as opposed to civil, activity. The court system in the U.S. is a dual system with Federal courts and a large variety of courts that exist at the State level. The system is adversarial in that one side, the prosecution, represents the state and seeks to prosecute a defendant while the other side, the defense, seeks exoneration; another key figure, the judge, is impartial and hands down the sentence. Juries are also often involved in the process and deliberate the cases before them, and witnesses testify to information to which they are privy. The more serious offenses are classified as felonies, and those determined to be less severe and that warrant shorter periods of punishment are classified as misdemeanors; drug charges fall into both categories based on the type of drug offense and sometimes on the amount of the drug possessed. Almost half of the people in jails and prisons admit they are incarcerated due to offenses committed while intoxicated (Lab et al., 2016).

Sentences handed down by criminal courts can have either a retributive or restorative philosophy. In the former case, punishment is applied for the sake of maintaining justice—criminal offenders receive their sentences to the satisfaction of the law. The latter approach, the restorative philosophy, occurs when offenders are made aware of harms they have caused, and attempts are made to restore the life situations of victims, the community, and the offenders, using local resources and services. This type of justice is related to the idea of reintegration, reflecting the idea that after offenders "pay their debt to society," they should be provided services that will assist them in successfully readjusting to life without correctional control and remaining crime and addiction free.

Drug courts were created in the 1990s to handle the specific problems that exist with addicted persons. They have docket programs that involve drug-related crimes for both adult and juvenile drug offenders, and parents with addiction problems who have pending child welfare cases. There are currently over 3.000 drug courts in the country, most targeting adult cases. These courts are meant to be non-adversarial and have a treatment team of court personnel, treatment providers, and community corrections representatives. Families and community members are encouraged to be involved in the drug court process as well (National Institute of Justice, 2018). The following are common components of drug court programs:

- screening for risk, needs, and responsibility

- judicial interaction

- monitoring through supervision and drug testing

- enforcement of graduated sanctions and incentives

- availability of treatment and rehabilitative measures (NIJ, 2018).

Formed in part due to the punitive drug sentences that caused jails and prisons to overflow with sentenced offenders (Tiger, 2011), drug courts have generally been successful, producing lower recidivism levels than those not processed through these courts. However, the fact that defendants in these cases entered the program voluntarily does not provide a definitive verification as to their effectiveness (Arnold et al., 2000). Similarly, acknowledging the ambiguous evaluation methods conducted on drug courts, a systematic review of the effectiveness of these programs found them to be generally effective in reducing drug use and other criminal behavior (Wilson, Mitchell, & MacKenzie, 2006).

Correctional System

The final component of the criminal justice system is corrections, which is comprised of the jails, prisons, parole, and probation systems, as well as the many diversion programs that were instituted to redirect offenders from incarceration.

While the primary purpose of correctional institutions of all types is the protection of the public, all the correctional programs mentioned—jails, prisons, parole, probation, and incarceration diversion programs—normally have addiction treatment and prevention components. Clinical diagnostic assessments, to the extent they are provided, are typically performed in external mental health programs.

Local jails are run by country or municipal governments and normally house people who are awaiting court but do not have options for bail. However, they also are used to hold offenders who were given incarceration sentences, normally those that are short term or have extenuating circumstances regarding their convictions.

Prisons normally house people after they have been convicted and given a sentence of incarceration. Prisons are run by the federal government, states, and recently, private corrections corporations. Prisons have different levels of security and sometimes house special populations, but offenders with addiction problems are usually housed along with general populations. Prisons do often provide treatment services for addicted persons to varying degrees and types such as group meetings, (twelve-step model or other types), individual counseling, and other forms.

Prisons, and sometimes jails, are referred to as institutional correctional systems since the correctional process is systematic and bureaucratized in an incarceration setting rather than allowing people to remain free in communities. This is different from other forms of correction that allow offenders to remain in the community if they are willing and able to abide by conditions of parole or probation.

Parole refers to the community supervision by parole officers of offenders who have been granted early release from their incarcerated sentences. Parolees are normally required to maintain stable residence and employment and to abide by all conditions of their parole, specifically to remain crime-free and to refrain from the use of intoxicants, among other conditions. They are subjected to supervision at home, at work, or in other designated places to ensure compliance with their parole. Since parolees have been incarcerated prior to being released on parole supervision, they have often already received some addictions counseling. However, many parole agencies continue to require attendance at out-patient or day treatment programs that deal with substance use. Parole officers are often involved in case management activities in ensuring the people under their supervision receive the treatment needed to keep them from returning to prison or jail. Since parole is offered to offenders as a reward (early release from incarceration), it is often referred to as a back-door option and often involves reintegration back into communities.

Probation refers to community supervision of people who were given probation as an alternative to incarceration. Thus, this type of supervision is referred to as a front-door option. Like parolees, probationers are required to maintain stable residence and employment, to abide by all conditions of their probation, and are supervised by probation officers to ensure compliance. Some probation agencies have intensive probation programs that supervise offenders' behavior more thoroughly. Many probationers are addicted persons or at least have some involvement with substances of abuse. Like parolees, probationers are monitored to ensure attendance at all programs directed by the court. Probation and parole are often referred to as community corrections as the offenders can remain in the community if supervision requirements are met.

Diversion programs in the correctional system are intended to provide more intensive services for certain correctional populations. Some diversion programs are residential, and others are community-based; these include community corrections diversion or detention programs, day reporting programs, "shock incarceration" programs (short periods of incarceration intended to scare young offenders), quasi-military "boot camp" programs, and other novel diversion schemes. Many of these programs offer substance abuse counseling.

Juvenile Justice System

In addition to the adult criminal justice system, there exists a juvenile justice system that differs in several ways from its adult counterpart. Coming into existence at the dawn of the twentieth century in the U.S. under the spirit of reform by a group often referred to as the "child savers" (Pratt, 1969), the juvenile justice system was created to protect impressionable youth from the corrupting influences of incarcerated adults. However, this system was not fully embraced until the 1930s; therefore, juvenile justice is a recent innovation in the history of criminal justice. There are several differences from the adult system: the age grouping in this system is normally under 18, though this varies in different jurisdictions; there is a rehabilitative rather than retributive focus; hearings rather than trials are held, and delinquency rather than crime is the focus. The concept of at-risk youth reflects society's need to redirect impressionable and hopefully malleable youth to alternative healthy lifestyles that will dissuade them from crime and addiction. The juvenile justice system, however, appears to be mirroring the adult system as concerns over crimes by youth has increased since the late 1960s, requiring some scholars to call for "preventative justice" for juveniles (Slobogin & Fondacaro, 2011).

The Revolving Door

Although the criminal justice system is a social control system set up to keep people from committing criminal acts, many get caught in a so-called "revolving door" process, which often keeps people reentering the system. Many addicted people are involved in this process due to the nature of addiction, and when they are released from incarceration, they reenter the communities which offer the same temptations to use addictive substances.

Describing concerns over this situation in the 1960s as "the cycle of public intoxication, arrest, trial, incarceration and release that dominates the life of the skid row alcoholic" (Giffin, 1966, p. 154), sociologists and criminologists were concerned about addicted residents of areas that had few occupational opportunities and that were rife with taverns, houses of prostitution, and other "pulls" that helped maintain their situation. As two scholars noted, incarceration by homeless addicts does not have the effect of diminishing status "since Skid Row residents regard a month in jail (especially during the winter) as a good way to recuperate from the effects of cheap liquor, poor food, and haphazard sleeping arrangements" (Lovald & Stubb, 1968).

The rehabilitative ideal came under attack, though some scholars were trying to keep it alive, insisting that addicted persons do indeed benefit from treatment strategies. The punitive approach gained momentum when the results from a research article by sociologist Robert Martinson called "What Works? Questions and Answers about Prison Reform" (1974) led people to the conclusion that "Nothing Works"—that rehabilitative methods do not work for incarcerated people. A series of retributive/punitive strategies were put in place beginning in the 1970s to deal with the serious overcrowding problem, which was, in part, a consequence of the growing drug problem. These measures included mandatory minimum sentences, treatment sentencing alternatives, and with a variety of intervention programs. Although these strategies slowed the revolving door somewhat, specific rehabilitative programs show more progress (Warner & Kramer, 2009).

As mentioned earlier, the issue of addictions treatment that is mandated by the court system has long been a concern among those in the addictions field as well as interested observers. The NIDA reports that legally mandated treatment as a result of parole, probation, or pre-trial release has good or better outcomes than those who enter treatment voluntarily. Mandated people remain in treatment programs longer and have better attendance in these programs (NIDA, 2014).

Conclusion

Many of the founding studies in the sociology of deviance were focused on drugs and addiction as it "provides a vivid illustration of the contested nature of what constitutes deviant behavior" (Wincup, 2014, p. 107). If a serious and critical look is taken at the types of behavior considered deviant, a clearer picture will emerge of the subject of addiction. Dangerous drugs and addictive behavior fuel fears of a disrupted society, making it less predictable and more frightening. As illustrated in the infamous 1938 "War of the Worlds" radio broadcast in which a fictional story about alien life forms landing in America caused people to react as if extraterrestrial aliens were, in fact, landing on earth, it is clear that fear motivates people to do dramatic things.

This discussion on moral panic is not to suggest that all responses to drug and addiction-related crises are fake or without basis. In fact, the utility of the moral panic framework was questioned by some scholars. In examining the prohibition response of the hallucinogen LSD in the 1960s, Cornwell & Linders (2002) describe how the focus on "panic" in moral panic theory undermines the efforts of key players in dealing with the societal concerns over addictive drugs. Using research data from disaster situations as a conceptual model, they explain how people in hazardous situations (including concerns over drugs) often act in rational ways to combat problems rather than just haphazardly reacting to them. The moral panic construction is beneficial, however, in fully examining the societal reaction to things that become framed as a crisis, epidemic, or plague. The world has a long history with phenomena that could be considered moral panics. The model is beneficial but not complete in explaining the current opioid crisis, but it does beg the question: if racial minorities and the underclass constitute the folk devils in this current situation, do racial majorities and those in the upper classes comprise folk *angels*?

The criminal justice system, comprised of police agencies, the courts, and corrections, has long sought to deal with the problems of addressing addictions. A separate justice system has been created for younger substance abusers, often considered at-risk as it is felt that aspects of human development should be considered in their treatment, along with the hope that they can be deterred from further use. The concerns over a "revolving door" in which recidivism and relapse lead to a continuous cycle through the criminal justice system prompted some agencies to adopt a retributive philosophy that punishes addicted persons in the criminal justice system. Others believe a more rehabilitative approach should be taken in which treatment, including that which is court-mandated, is a better philosophy.

Chapter 8

The Sociological Perspective

"A theory is a guide to what to look at, what to ignore, in any type of inquiry. By directing inquiry, and by focusing on a set of data relevant to the theory while deliberately neglecting others, a theory acts like a searchlight in illuminating one area while leaving another in darkness".

(Lewis Coser, 1981 p. 170)

Approaches to the Study of Addiction

The concept of addiction is multi-faceted with medical, psychological, criminological, philosophical, historical, and legal understandings and implications; this disciplinary variety reveals the complexity of the concept. Medical approaches to addiction view the concept as a problem that involves brain physiology, one in which the general characteristics approximate those of medical conditions and illness and in which remedy is sought through a series of interventions and treatments that conform equivalently to other medical interventions. In short, addiction is seen as a brain disease that requires a medically oriented treatment.

Psychological approaches focus on how cognitions, learning experiences, and various mental states apply to addiction. The structure of the brain is also a focus of the psychological study of addiction and how activation of reward centers in the brain perpetuates the action that contributes to what is defined as addiction. Since all behavior is learned, psychological positions also observe the role of social learning and how it starts and perpetuates addictive behavior.

Criminological perspectives, as described in depth in the previous chapter, focus on issues surrounding the fact that many behaviors involving addiction are defined as deviant and, in many cases, criminal. Criminality is involved in not only substance-related addictions but in some behavioral addictions involving sexuality and, in some cases, gambling. Even hoarding, commonly associated with addiction, sometimes involves cases with violations of housing codes or other ordinances. Criminality is also involved if pyromania and kleptomania become designated as addictions.

There are, of course, additional areas such as those involving spiritual, philosophical, economic, and political areas that have an interest in addiction and addiction behavior. It is beyond the scope of this book to address these areas, but they are relevant to understandings of addiction. Since so many of our academic disciplines and treatment considerations focus on addiction, its importance to society is affirmed.

Sociological understandings have long-range consequences, not only in the addictions field but on society generally. Sociology has made its contributions to understandings of addiction through its theoretical assertions, its research findings, and the practical applications which, in return, provide new understandings to be theorized about and researched. Through this process, understandings of addiction become clarified.

The Sociological Imagination

Sociology is the study of groups, group behavior, the relationships that exist between humans, and the relationship of individual people to the greater society. It studies all forms of social phenomena, including the focus of this work, addiction. The sociological imagination is a tool envisioned by sociologist C. Wright Mills (1959) that is used to make the mental connections between people's individual *troubles* and larger societal *issues*. It prompts the user to see how problems at the micro-level can be understood at the macro-level, where problems can be better addressed. As Mills notes, "the sociological imagination enables its possessor to understand the larger historical scene in terms of its meaning for the inner life and the external career of a variety of individuals" (p. 5). In this context, career refers to a trajectory that one's life takes, which can include paths to addiction.

In this work, the sociological imagination is used to understand the inner life of those addicted as it relates to the external conditions of society, rather than focusing only on an individual's addiction to a substance or behavior. True understanding can be made if it can be understood why society is addicted to drugs or behaviors. Perhaps policies enacted on a larger social level will alleviate problems at the individual level. Using our imaginations requires mental activity, but it is only through this mental activity that change can occur (Mills, 1959).

Sociological Theory

Sociology has a rich history of explaining social phenomena from different levels of analysis. Sociological theories of addiction from the macro-level understandings utilize a cultural perspective and seek to understand the large-scale patterns and structures that define addiction. Theories at the meso-level focus on how addiction impacts communities and small groups. Micro-level theories emphasize personal involvement with addiction sources and the interactions that occur between people in small groups. All three are important in examining the concept of addiction.

The following are but a very small number of sociological theories but were selected for review because of their utility in understanding addiction and addiction-related behaviors.

Theoretical Perspectives

Theories of Social Disorganization

Social disorganization theories consist of macro-level approaches that focus on how various social phenomena can cause disruption in the social order. These disruptions create instability that renders social institutions unable to perform two of their core functions: the maintenance of order and the assurance of the safety of its citizens. The resulting condition is a state of instability, a breakdown of the norms, disorganization of social institutions, and a gap between socially desirable goals and the opportunities to achieve them (Osco, 2003/2004). This condition, developed by founding sociologist Emile Durkheim as "anomie," is a major component of structural-functionalist theories in sociology and one that will inform the perspective taken in this section on social disorganization.

Often referred to simply as functionalism, this theoretical perspective has several main characteristics: it emphasizes the functions and interdependency of social institutions (such as the family, government, economy, religion, and education), the evolutionary nature of social organization; and the role that cohesion and social solidarity play in keeping society "healthy" (note the medical parallel here). The perspective analogizes society as an organism, a system of parts dedicated to maintaining the operation of a social system, as examined in chapter six. When the institutions fail to perform their functions adequately, social problems occur, requiring special attention to address the maladies. Often the government is the arbiter in matters dealing with social concerns involving addiction (through laws and policy initiatives), through certainly the other institutions—family, religion, the economy, and the educational system—all have interests in this area and all seek to address addiction in different ways.

The use, and especially abuse, of alcohol and other drugs and the addictive processes they can create in individuals, endangers the whole society. This is likewise true of conditions labeled behavioral addictions such as gambling and Internet gaming. Moral panics addressed in the previous chapter describe panic reactions experienced by large numbers of people who believe their established way of life is being threatened. Social disorganization theorists examine the ways in which human behaviors such as drug use and addictions tear at the fabric of society, or as social disorganization theorists might put, create states of anomie.

One scholar (Dyer, 2003/2004) believes Durkheim would see our current drug use problem as resulting from the modern-day sense of loneliness and powerlessness with no "guideposts" to follow. The euphoria once offered by religion, it is often believed, is now replaced by the euphoria provided by drug use. That, coupled with the sense of community and camaraderie offered by drug subcultures, provides a function as a substitute for addicted persons.

At times, society's institutions do not allow for individuals to meet the goals and aspirations that they have been encouraged to achieve. This creates a state of "internalized" anomie. Robert K. Merton, an American functionalist sociologist, created a popular model that was an extension of Durkheim's anomie perspective in his "strain theory" (Merton, 1938). If people have opportunities to achieve commonly desired cultural goals, they will conform to social norms, thereby contributing to social stability. However, if people do not have this opportunity to achieve the "American dream," they often adapt by resorting to deviant acts, which could certainly involve the potential for money gained from drug sales, as an example. They could follow norms without any desire for material gain, or they could simply "drop out" of society, a path followed by many addicted people; in this "retreatist" category, Merton assigned several social types, including "chronic drunkards and drug addicts" (Merton, 1938, p. 677). In the last category, people can reject both the prevailing social goals and the means to achieve them, resulting in rebellion.

To correct some of the problems created by social disorganization and anomie at the societal level, theorists of this persuasion would advocate the creation and enforcement of clearly defined and equitable policies and a just opportunity structure. At the community level, grassroots projects can provide recreational activities that do not involve drug use. At the individual level, confusion regarding rule obeyance and strain are normal occurrences but can be allayed in a manner that does not involve the use of addictive sources (Shaw, 2002); adequate socialization by the family can assist in this objective.

Risk Society Theories

Conditions of unease, distress, and malaise found their way into the thought of scholars who would focus their attention on risks. Conditions of social disorder and disorganization are indicative of a "risk society" described as a current condition in which major risk factors must be adequately managed, or anomic conditions will occur. In earlier times, risks were more visible and able to be addressed through social policies. However, today's dangers, such as invisible pollutants or the risks of medical "advancements" with unknown consequences, are less detectable until a full-blown crisis has occurred. The risk society thesis has a symbiotic relationship with social disorganization theory. Life in contemporary society is becoming increasingly fast-paced and complex, and people are becoming more reliant on scientific advancements. As Shaw (2002) notes, "belief in science and reliance on medicine support a widely spread perception of and a deeply felt sentiment toward substance as the ultimate cure for ailments, diseases, and problems, from physical, psychological, emotional, and personal, to social" (23). Sociologist Max Weber (1930/2003) called this process *rationalization* and concluded that an excess of rationalization would result in what he metaphorically called *the iron cage*, the trap that occurs in rapidly advancing Western society that promotes an excessive emphasis on efficiency and control. Certainly, the current concerns over prescription opioids can be represented by this analogy, as a focus on curing illness through new medications has resulted in an addiction problem in our society.

It is certainly true that addictive substance use and addictive behaviors are not new; however, it is important to consider how often new or modified drugs appear on the scene and how they affect social life. As can be recalled from the last chapter, much moral panic has been generated over the past several decades involving substances—marijuana in the 1930s, barbiturates in the 1940s, LSD in the 1960s, PCP in the 1970s, crack cocaine in the 1980s, club drugs and methamphetamine in the 1990s, and prescription opioids in the current period. Observation of these panics illustrates the influence of drugs on society at different intervals at the macro-level of analysis.

In addition to the macro-levels of risk, risk also occurs at the meso-level as well. Risk is inherent in communities that fall prey to the consequences of addiction sources, in this case, primarily substance addiction. When communities experience high levels of addiction in its residents, this creates social disorganization that, in turn, promotes addiction in individuals. Gangs and other subcultural and countercultural groups often form in neighborhoods where cohesion and opportunities are lacking.

And of course, there is the micro-level issue of risk regarding addiction. In substance addiction, risks exist to a person in the form of loss of one's dignity, sense of self, health, and even life. Then there is the loss of significant relationships, employment, residence, and various opportunities. The same consequences often exist in behavioral addictions as well, and, as discussed earlier, gambling and gaming have risk as their defining characteristics.

Conflict Theories

In sociology, conflict theory has a special place in defining the discipline as one which welcomes a challenge to traditional models of thinking, as well as an embrace of social action. Conflict theory emphasizes the role of social discord and social inequality in society, and conflict sociologists place the conflict of money, status, and power at the core of their analysis (Vold, Bernard, and Snipes, 2002). These three issues are certainly a part of the long-running social conflict that results from addiction. Shaw (2002) observes "substance abuse is a phenomenon of conflict" (p. 57), but he also notes that substances of abuse are neutral objects and have no effects at all until they come into contact with people. But they have certainly been a major source of concern, and much contention, in society.

There are different types of conflict theory—those that:

- focus on the idea that laws and rules are employed by social elites and governmental powers to maintain control over the mass of less powerful citizens

- emphasize deviance and crime are a result of in-fighting among various groups

- those of more recent origin that note the role of discriminant factors such as race, gender, sexual identity, age, and others in the treatment of people by social control agents in the criminal justice system (Shaw, 2002).

The first two approaches, drawing on a Marxist ideology, assume that definitions of lawful and unlawful behavior, including those that involve substances and behaviors, are created and maintained by those in power, or according to Quinney (1974), "contrary to popular belief, law is a tool of the ruling class" (p. 52). Therefore the "war on drugs" is a continuing national drug policy meant to maintain control over basic citizens and the recreation provided by drugs. And behavior defined as deviant, including individual drug use, gambling, or any other activity designated as deviance, is subject to sanctions by the government. As and Marx noted, a host of strategies are used by those in power to keep citizens complacent; religion, as he famously stated, is the "opiate of the masses" by keeping them in states of euphoria and apathy.

Race has certainly played a large part in the treatment of addiction by society. As in the case of the moral panics, for example, it can be seen how race is a factor in how certain drug scares became "scarier" when racial stereotypes were employed. Also, during the moral panic of the 1980s, the fact that crack cocaine, used more by racial minorities, had higher penalties than powder cocaine, primarily used by middle- and upper-class whites became a focal point of conflict theorists.

Sex and gender are also subsumed under this category, and feminist theory responded as women were not being represented in scholarly discussions on deviance and criminality until a few decades ago (Vold, Bernard, and Snipes, 2002), discussions which, of course, include addiction. Challenges to the hypermasculinity of the criminal justice system were also promoted by feminist theorists.

Symbolic Interactionism

Symbolic interactionism is a micro-level theoretical perspective that examines the relationship between individuals and their environment and how meaning is created in the interaction processes between people. It is a form of social psychology in that it is a bridge between individuals and society. It is a distinctly American sociological theory and one of the major theoretical perspectives in the discipline. Developed primarily by George Herbert Mead of the University of Chicago (known for its distinct theoretical and research-based sociology at the Chicago School of Sociology) and solidified by Herbert Blumer, symbolic interactionism, also referred to simply as interactionism, seeks to understand how the "self" is created in interaction with other people and how one's significant others and reference groups help create individual identity. The theory pays special attention to small group dynamics to better understand social phenomena, and it evolved to explain the causes and effects of labeling, social stigma, and how people manage impressions of themselves around others. The theory has produced some concepts valuable to understanding addiction, including:

- generalized other-when the collective standards of a community are inculcated into a sense of self (which could prevent people from turning to addiction sources)

- the Thomas theorem-the idea that if many people believe something is real (even if it is fake or false), it still has consequences (which could involve the idea of addiction as having a natural fit in the medical or twelve-step models)

- self-fulfilling prophecy-when people believe something about themselves due to the influence of others, and they act on these expectations (in which people can internalize the image of themselves as addicted persons)

- role taking-attempts to understand things from another's position (as in attempts to understand the role of addiction in others' lives)

- significant symbol-a symbol whose meaning is shared by the one who communicates it and those who receive it (which could include the lingo shared by addicted persons or other symbols such as marijuana leaf designs on clothing)

- total institutions-facilities in which institutional staff strictly isolate and control the actions of those in their care, who are there to receive some type of resocialization (in which mental health and substance abuse residential treatment programs could be considered)

Regarding addiction and the use of addiction sources, there is a rich history in symbolic interactionism. The Chicago School sought to understand many social ills in a rapidly urbanizing and industrializing period in American history (the turn of the twentieth century). There were many challenges in this new urban landscape, and the use of alcohol and other drugs was common. The ideas of one scholar, Alfred Lindesmith, trained in the Chicago School, requires special attention in this investigation of symbolic interactionism. Lindesmith was a sociologist who took a special interest in addiction and has been described as the father of the sociology of addiction (Weinberg, 2011).

Lindesmith's view was that the misery produced by withdrawal symptoms of opiates leads to addiction. Addicted persons then developed an identity as "addict" that kept them in the cycle of drug use. His studies of the lived experiences of addicted persons led him to the conclusion that "addiction begins when a person suffering from withdrawal symptoms realizes that a dose of the drug will dissipate all his discomfort and misery" (Lindesmith, 1938, p. 599). It is at this point that this "almost magical relief" (p. 599) becomes a necessity, and the person is actively becoming addicted. Once "hooked" the person is "forever after classified by himself as well as other addicts as belonging to the in-group, as an addict, a 'user' or 'junker' regardless of whether he is using the drug at the moment or not" (p. 600). Lindesmith also made other observations about those addicted to heroin: they developed a self-concept of "addict," they had normal intellectual ability, they were not excessively violent or sexual, they came from all racial and ethnic backgrounds, many used the drug to feel "normal" rather than seek euphoric experiences, they did not agree with prohibition efforts, and they were part of a subculture in which hedonistic drug use was greatly exaggerated (Keys & Galliher, 2000). While the perspectives on heroin and other drug use have changed with the times, Lindesmith's work constitutes a basis upon which many current investigations can build.

This idea of withdrawal aversion ran counter to the prevalent idea that it was the drug's euphoric properties that created addiction and the need to engage in criminal activity to support the person's habit. This latter view was actively promoted by Federal Bureau of Narcotics director Harry Anslinger and other law enforcement bureaucrats of the early to mid-1900s who sought aggressive, punitive action against addicted persons through the creation of a narrative of the junkie as an outsider and criminal, relying on racism and ethnocentrism to support the narrative. Lindesmith and Anslinger had a long and contentious relationship as Lindesmith had created an alternative theory that contradicted the bureau's account. Lindesmith remained involved in advocacy that sought to portray addicted persons, not as psychopaths or criminals, but people with a medical problem needing assistance. Lindesmith's challenge to Federal law enforcement philosophy at this time could have resulted in losing his professorship but his noncombative style (which was quite different from many other public intellectuals at the time) and noted expertise in the addictions field allowed him to continue his row with the law enforcement establishment and political environment, even in the era of J. Edgar Hoover and Joseph McCarthy, in which "subversives" were actively sought and punished (Keys & Galliher, 2000).

Since the discussion of addiction in the addictions field has currently extended into behaviors, it would be appropriate to discuss how they fit into this model. Weinberg (2011) posits that these behavioral addictions fail to produce the major withdrawal symptoms, which were a major focus of Lindesmith's model. For example, anorexia nervosa has been investigated in its relationship to addiction in that starvation can potentially create an experience similar to a "runner's high" (Brumberg, 1984, Brumberg, 2000), however since people with this condition do not develop withdrawal symptoms, its relation to this model is questionable.

Gusfield (1986), another scholar with roots in the Chicago School, explores from a symbolic interactionist perspective how contemporary modern life has been dictated by labor, and an important factor involves time. Time was a social creation that broke up social life into structured categories such as seconds, minutes, hours, days, weeks, and so on. The week was separated from the weekend due to the expectation that workers labor during the workweek and are allowed leisure time (the opposite) for the weekend, creating a rhythm that is culturally understood and generally conformed to. Drinking alcohol is a symbolic gesture and is primarily expected to occur on weekends, as a leisurely activity. In contrast, the use of another beverage, coffee, provides a symbolic cue for the beginning of work activity. While alcohol has a long history of concern with many social controls connected to its use, at times, a "cultural remission" takes place when these standards and prohibitions are relaxed to some degree. Parties in which alcohol is available creates a type of ritual as do traditional meals served with alcohol. The familiar "happy hour" provides a designated time and space to allow for alcohol consumption, and its festive character resembles ritualistic behavior. Drinking alcohol and consuming other drugs is a symbolic act, with many rituals to symbolize its importance in our culture. Time and environment are also factors in behavioral addictions as well, and influences when certain activities, such as eating, exercise, or sex, are to occur.

The issues of "set" and "setting" are related to symbolic interactionism and refers to how drug effects are fashioned by users' social environments: the "set" (or mindset) refers to a person's individual, personal, and cognitive characteristics and "setting" refers to the social and cultural environments in which drugs are used. These factors, which have a long history in addiction studies, can be an important component in psychoeducation and prevention training programs (Hartogsohn, 2017). Zinberg (1984), in his study of American heroin users after the Vietnam war, added the concept of "drug" to set and setting to include the type of drug and the form of its ingestion; his findings that many veterans who used the drug during the war to combat boredom basically ceased its use upon returning home, presenting a challenge to the physiological effects of addiction and the bio-medical model. Although the above analysis includes only substances of abuse, certainly other sources of abuse that involve behaviors can be included as well.

Labeling theory also has a long history in sociology. In this perspective, the focus is not on the offender but on the label that is applied to the person's behavior. Labeling theory is also known as the societal reaction perspective as it explores the reactions of others to the behavior of the person so labeled. A negative label once affixed to a person can change the course of a person's life; in essence, a self-fulfilling prophecy can develop that will perpetuate the behavior. The label often results in stigma, defined by Erving Goffman (1963) as a disqualifying "mark" that gives off a negative impression to others and creates a "spoiled identity" in the stigmatized. Addicted persons consistently get labeled and stigmatized, as evidenced by a large number of derogatory names provided to them. The notion is that they have been improperly socialized and are in need of resocialization; this resocialization process is completed at inpatient treatment programs, termed total institutions by Goffman (1961).

Rational Choice Theory

Rational choice theories posit that people behave in ways that are in their best interest after deliberately weighing the costs versus rewards of their actions. Rational choice theories have a very long history, reflecting eighteenth-century philosophy that sees people as rational actors that work in their own self-interest. *Ratio*, in Latin, refers to reason, and choice expresses the notion that human beings can make a reasoned selection considering possible alternatives; in addition, the term rational implies the actor makes an individualized choice (Scholtz, 2015).

This theory, as evolved from classical criminological theory, promotes the idea that the government is compelled to react in ways that suppress or deter behavior considered against the needs of the whole. Different types of deviance are assumed to have different motivations (Vold, Bernard, and Snipes, 2002); therefore, motivations for the use of addiction sources would be to:

- activate the reward centers of the brain

- relieve pain

- escape unpleasant feelings

- join others in a social environment (often away from disapproving others)

- expand consciousness

- rebel against authority

- win money (or other material goods)

- increase esteem among peers

Becker and Murphy (1988) proposed a theory of rational addiction, complete with mathematical formulations, that observes how addictive behavior seems antithetical to rationality but is instead based on the understanding that the use of certain substances or behaviors (their model takes into account behavioral addictions) comes with the possibility of addiction, and that understanding is figured into the decision to use the substance or perform the activity.

Rational choice theory has been used in various disciplines, including economics, as consumers make choices based on a variety of factors, and examining these motivations provides a greater understanding of social behavior. This is true regarding choices involving a specific substance of use—people often speak of a "drug of choice" among many possibilities. There are also preferences in types or styles of the administration of the drug, through smoking, drinking, inhaling, injecting, etc. (if those choices are available for that drug). Of course, there are choices to be made in forms of the drug, such as powder cocaine vs. crack cocaine; different varieties of the drug, such as different strains of marijuana; and different amounts and times of consumption. In addition, there are numerous addiction treatment types and providers available to people when it has been determined (another choice) that treatment is warranted. In the case of the intervention model, family members and friends are required to make a choice to refuse to offer support to addicted persons in return for them choosing to accept treatment. In cases of mandated treatment, the element of choice is removed, forcing the person to accept an action without the element of choice.

Obviously, rational choice theory has some contradictions with a major force in current addictions philosophy—the idea that addiction is a disease rather than a choice. The disease concept of addiction and the twelve-step model assumes that the use of addiction sources, substance or behavioral, sets in motion a process that is beyond the control of the addicted person. If, however, addiction is the result of choice, the personal responsibility philosophy becomes the primary means of understanding addiction. And the treatment of choice would involve interventions such as rational recovery and harm reduction approaches as the role of individual choice and free will come into play more prominently in these modalities. If there is a gene that contributes to the chances of a person becoming addicted to a substance or process (as some scholars believe), the idea of rational choice seems less plausible. However, there still must be a choice to begin experimentation with a substance or behavior.

Lifestyle Theory

Lifestyle theory has been offered as an alternative to the traditional concept of addiction (Walters, 1999). With its roots in Adlerian psychology in explaining the role of environment in shaping personality (Giorgi, 2012), this theory stresses four major themes that separate it from the traditional model of addiction:

- it focuses on the interaction of people, including both internal agency and adaptation to the environment

- it emphasizes the labeling of the lifestyle rather than the person

- it rejects the issue of personal choice regarding the situations that created addiction but accept it in the role of seeking help

- it uses a spectrum, or continuum, model to explain levels of addiction, rather than the traditional binary scheme (addicted vs. not addicted) (Walters, 1999).

Classifying a condition in a certain way can have major ramifications (Giorgi, 2012). If addiction is accepted as a disease, it requires medical treatment. If, however, it is classified as a lifestyle that has consequences other than those involving addiction (for example, other health problems such as the potential for heart attack, stroke, or HIV) it is a social problem with many environmental and external factors and a wider range of potential policy implications.

Koop (2008) introduces concepts of sociologists Bourdieu and Wacquant (1992) to augment the lifestyle thesis. These scholars explain the concept of *habitus* as how people understanding the world through:

- their socialization experiences

- an adaptation to their surroundings

- their personal social circumstances

- the way they manage these circumstances

The different people, groups, and institutions with whom there is a struggle over resources, is termed a *field*. Since the statuses are different between the players in the field, how a person understands their position is crucial to developing a sense of self and how they adapt and create lifestyles, which in turn reproduces itself (Koop, 2008). This approach to lifestyles is important in understanding addiction and redirects policy strategies from simplistic notions that suggest addiction is only a matter of will power or the total dependence on an addiction source.

Social Learning Theory

Social learning theories refer to sociological perspectives that emphasize the role of learning, adapting, and becoming socialized into human environments. The sociology of deviance and criminology, borrowing from social psychology, have contributed to our understanding of how group processes influence individual decision-making, such as the decision to initially become involved with addiction sources, or peers that use them. This, of course, to some extent, challenges rational choice theory to the extent it focuses on the role of others in our choices. The social forces that encourage individual behavior, such as the use of alcohol and other drugs, or to engage in addictive activities, is the focus of this theory.

Though he was a pioneer in symbolic interactionism and labeling theory, Howard Becker (1973) is also famed for his work in social learning theory in illuminating the process in which people learn how to use drugs and how to interpret the effects created by them. Becker, trained in the Chicago School method of research design, was highly influenced by the work of Lindesmith and used his analytic inductive method to study jazz musicians (the "outsiders") in the mid-twentieth century. Doing this research was easy for Becker since he was a jazz pianist who spent time playing with the musicians (and using drugs with them) outside his academic work (Muller, 2014). It seems he, himself, was an outsider.

Differential association is a theoretical approach Edwin Sutherland described in a textbook called *Criminology* (1924) that explains how people (often juveniles) adopt deviant behaviors by learning the deviant acts from others in peer groups. Sutherland, also trained in the Chicago School, continued to update the text over the years and, in the process, developed a theory that maintains that through close associations with antisocial people, offenders develop a definition that supports the violation of laws over conformity to them. Therefore, people learn from others to use addictive substances through their level of involvement and identification with the group members (who become reference groups). This theory has become one of the most dominant in the study of deviant behavior and crime and is quite applicable to the field of addiction.

Subculture Theories

Subculture theories are those that attempt to explain behavior substance use or addictive behaviors within the context of group behavior in which people coalesce around certain common interests. A subculture is defined as a part of the larger culture, but that has its own unique characteristics and a well-defined structure consisting of norms, values, beliefs, and rituals that form the social core of the groups (Shaw, 2002). Camaraderie, solidarity, inclusion, and increased knowledge and skills are reasons people become involved with subcultures. The term often refers to groups that, in some ways, deviate from the greater society, but this is not always negative. A type of subculture known as a counterculture, however, actively opposes some of the core elements of society. The concept of the *reference group* is important in understanding involvement in subcultures; a reference group is a group in which a person uses as a guide to formulate their own self-identity. *Normative functions* of reference groups exist to enforce the general belief systems of the group while *comparative functions* stress the differences between the group and other groups in society. The normative functions revolve around the core issues of a lifestyle of addiction while the comparison functions emphasize the differences with the non-substance using parts of society—an example of this is the hippie subculture (often considered a counterculture) of which a certain appearance and lifestyle (which frequently included relaxed attitudes about drugs) also had the comparative function of creating a marked difference between them and the "straights" or people of the "establishment," who were concerned over the use of drugs in society.

Whether the substance-using subcultural group is a street gang, motorcycle gang, or people who regularly meet to consume alcohol or other drugs for recreation, there still exists a structure. As with social learning theories, the group members learn new techniques, establish preferences, and learn about the consequences of certain aspects of use and addictive responses. The club drug phenomenon mentioned earlier, for example, represents how the ravers developed special strategies for its members, including the dissemination of information via social media to ensure the members did not overdose or get ill from the mixture of dancing and drug use.

In this theoretical approach, it is important to differentiate between two types of culture—non-material and material. The *non-material culture* of substance use subcultures consists of a series of beliefs, norms, values, and rituals that revolve around the addictive source. Often the use of substances or behaviors is buttressed by a philosophy that glorifies the use of the addictive source or justifies its existence in relation to the outside world. The non-material elements often include common parlance (or language), and a connection between substance use as a form of freedom as well as a form of defiance which also emotes activities that "embody the spirit of use" (Shaw, 2002, p. 228). The *material culture* of these groups is tangible and is often represented by the "tools" employed—bottles, pipes, needles, inhaling devices, etc. and contains meaning about the philosophy that sustains the cultural beliefs of the group. It is also represented by symbols, such as a cannabis plant or mushroom image in which users identify, and musical forms, such as psychedelic music enjoyed by those groups that are involved with hallucinogenic drugs.

The special argot, or language, used by subcultures, is understood within the group but less with the greater society is of special note and will be addressed here in more detail. William Burroughs, in *Junky: The Definitive Text of "Junk"* (1953/2003), exposed the public to a host of street-level drug terms and even included a glossary of terms so the readers would understand this seemingly foreign terminology. Some terms used in substance use subcultures have fallen out of use and are alien to modern ears while other terms have stood the test of time and are commonly identified today. In the *Junky* glossary (pp. 151-156), for example, Burroughs uses many currently used terms such as "weed," "grass," and "pot" for marijuana but he also uses these terms for the same substance: "tea." "grefa" and "muggles." Other recognizable terms are "coke" for cocaine, but less familiar are other terms he uses: "charge" and "charley." When Burroughs speaks of "writing" or "making a croaker for a script," he is referring to asking a doctor to prescribe "junk," or narcotics. A "hog" is "anyone who uses more junk than you do." And "burned down" refers to when a restaurant gets raided by the police because it is frequented too often by "junkies as meeting-places."

Recovery groups can be also be understood as subcultures. These groups certainly act like reference groups for many people and, as noted in other parts of the book, the twelve-step movements have created a highly specialized set of rules and rituals, as well as an extremely well-developed argot (it can be recalled that twelve-step programs were referred to by one critic as "slogan therapy"). These programs even have a defined philosophy with steps for all followers to the point it has been described by critics as having cult-like aspects, with a built-in analogy with deviant subcultural groups.

Control Theories

Travis Hirschi (1969) proposed that since all people deviate from social norms to some extent, perhaps it is more important to examine the factors (social bonds) that thwart people from committing acts that violate those norms. In his original control theory, he posited that four factors, or social controls—attachment, commitment, involvement, and belief—exist to promote conformity to prosocial behavior, thus rejecting antisocial activity. The implications for the addictions field in Hirschi's original theoretical formulation is that if people maintain primarily social contacts with non-substance users, in other words, if people have attachments with non-addicted persons, they will be less likely to become involved with substance use themselves. If they are committed to maintaining a drug-free lifestyle, they have an investment in doing so and will also be less likely to become addicted to substances or behaviors. Similarly, if people are involved with prosocial activities, they are less likely to become involved with the lifestyles that promote addiction. The controlling influence of belief refers to the fact that a person has successfully inculcated the norms of society into their way of understanding and being in the world, therefore rejecting a lifestyle that includes addictive substances or behaviors.

Gottfredson and Hirschi's (1990) alteration of the original control/social bond theory differed by focusing on one controlling element instead of four. The theory claims that early childhood socialization determines the course of a person's ability to make accurate decisions by conforming to social norms. People not socialized in ways to develop appropriate self-control will seek immediate gratification through risky and impulsive activity, especially in the form of *analogous behaviors*, often experienced in adolescence, that include alcohol and other drug use, smoking, gambling, and driving while intoxicated. Risky and impulsive behavior has often been used to describe the behavior of addicted persons, especially by those who believe that addiction-related experiences are the result of poor decision-making. This idea also supports the codependency movement's position that the problems that lead people to assume certain dysfunctional roles begin in and are cultivated in the family. Since early socialization is of profound importance in this theory, self-control explanations offer a series of recommendations including close supervision of young people, curfews, the use of school uniforms, and truancy programs, which are deemed as more important than punitive, rehabilitative, deterrent or increased policing strategies (Hirschi & Gottfredson, 2001).

Social Constructionist and Postmodern Theories

Social constructionism has its roots in symbolic interactionism and the philosophical concept of phenomenology. It seeks to understand common everyday life experiences and how social phenomena that seem to be "natural" are, in fact, based on social constructions. Social constructionism has been a major focus in sociology since the 1960s. In *The Social Construction of Reality*, Berger and Luckmann (1966) described how understandings of reality, although they differ with individuals, are often negotiated to a commonly accepted reality. Social constructionists seek to discover the sources of this collective reality and potentially uncover alternative explanations.

Social constructionist theories have offered much to the field of addiction as it forces an understanding of the fact that all social phenomena have been constructed in some way. The idea of addiction has been constructed in different ways, such as a moral failing, mental illness, disease, deviance, crime, etc. Since reality is malleable and differs according to time and space, the idea of the social construction of addiction is more accessible. The reality of addicted persons has also been constructed in various ways, normally negative; as scholars note, they are often "othered," "stigmatized," and labeled as useless outsiders (Singer & Page, 2014). And, it has been discussed at different points in this text how moral panics how been constructed by moral entrepreneurs at different times in our history.

Fraser, Moore, and Keane (2014) explain the most prominent source of knowledge regarding addiction, as with many other types of human activity, is sourced from the field of medicine. It is also framed with technology that reinforces its claims to legitimacy in this field. As noted in the introductory chapter, terms such as relapse, recovery, symptoms, and especially the concept of addiction as a disease or brain disorder, firmly establish medical knowledge as the only viable source applicable to the field. However, the medical model itself is based on cultural assumptions. Noting medicine's role in "treating" addiction, Fraser, Moore, and Keane (2014) suggest that "culturally specific ideals such as self-control and autonomy inevitably involve normative judgments about how to live and how to prioritize pleasures" (p. 28). The use of the terms "normative judgments" and "pleasures" here is instructive as it shows that people make individual choices about obtaining gratifying sensations but within the value-laden constraints of society.

When new and ambiguous symptoms arise in society, medical knowledge draws upon cultural assumptions to determine how to address them. Shorter (1992) refers to these cultural repositories as "symptom pools," again suggesting medical knowledge is not derived specifically from scientific discovery but also from a source deeply rooted in culture. Horwitz (2013) sees the anxiety produced from a rapidly evolving society as contributing to the symptoms. The notion of symptom pools reflects a constructionist element in that cultures address anxiety in very different ways and draw from their own cultural understandings rather than some universal pool of information from medicine and science. "Culture bound syndromes" is a term used to express conditions that are influenced by common and medico-scientific assumptions that exist in various places. An understanding that treatment protocols should at least acknowledge distress causing symptoms from a culturally-based standpoint has even been included in the DSM-5, and it is hoped this will continue in subsequent editions of the manual.

Postmodern theories represent several different ideologies that seek to understand contemporary society; however, they are generally characterized by an understanding of the rapidly changing social conditions that have occurred since the industrial period (the modern era). The current postmodern era has a host of new risks (as explained in risk society theories) fashioned by new patterns of globalization, the expansion of scientific knowledge, and changes to the basic social institutions must be critically analyzed and addressed. Like social constructionism, these theories deconstruct current understandings to explore meanings that lie underneath common conceptions.

Michel Foucault determined the need to investigate the history of any subject in getting a clearer understanding of that subject; he termed this method of investigation, *archaeology*. He also stated the necessity of being continually aware of the power relations revealed in this analogy; this he called *genealogy*. His concept of the *episteme* is especially beneficial, which looks at how knowledge is constructed at given places and times in history. These concepts allowed him to study mental distress (1960), medical clinics (1963), and other aspects of life using the benefits of history to better understand these institutions. Addiction has been understood very differently over our history, which has resulted in changes in the way it is viewed. The ongoing discussion of moral panics, for example, represents these changes, and it is hoped some current understandings can be derived from them. The reader will notice that history provides a major component of this book.

David Forbes (1994) is an addictions scholar who represents a postmodern sociological philosophy. Addiction, he argues, is not a medical term but a cultural signifier. Looking beyond the physiological aspects of addiction, different people may experience what is collectively known as addiction, but the meanings attached to their desires and distress of substances and processes come from society. This view allows for the deconstruction of narratives of addiction as well as a greater understanding of the concept. Since addiction is subsumed under the medical model, and since the knowledge is created by the medical establishment, the medical field defines the concept. However, medical knowledge develops within cultures and a critical review that deconstructs this knowledge is needed (Forbes, 1994); in other words, a genealogical approach would be instructive in this situation.

Dislocation Theory

A newer theory has been offered by Alexander (2000, 2008, 2012), which has elements of both functionalist and conflict theories and focuses on how factors brought about by economic conditions, specifically free-market capitalism, relate to addition. Dislocation theory posits that aggressive competition, wealth production, expansion of markets, and other factors create a dislocation of people from the basic social institutions such as family, community, and religious organizations that have traditionally provided adequate levels of social integration. Dislocated people are at risk of depression, anxiety, and boredom and turn to substitutes such as maladaptive behavior involving addictive substances or compulsive behaviors, which in turn feeds back into an already dislocation-inducing system.

Historically, the focus has been placed on problems that can be found in the individual, such as the deviance and disease conceptions that label the addicted person as criminal and addict. The dislocation approach places emphasis on society—how the pervasive quality of the capitalist system is a key (but not only) contributor—rather than the individual. This theory incorporates a socio-historical approach and has been criticized for methodological problems in research concerns (Roizen, 2012)., but is one that should be at least considered by those who adopt a medical model approach to addiction. Even though the theory's founder is a psychiatrist rather than a sociologist, Alexander's theory is an example of the use of the sociological imagination (Mills, 1959) to explain understandings of personal troubles (in this case an individual's addiction) by analyzing them in terms of greater social issues (an economic system that contributes to addiction).

Alexander's recommended solution is not to engage in revolutionary activity to overthrow capitalistic society but to focus on advocacy to redirect energy and funding toward programs and treatment protocols that thwart dislocation, removing addiction at its root level. Strategies to reinforce traditional means of integration and cohesion so that people will not turn to addictive substances will eliminate the need for substitutes for community integration. Therefore, the grand theory and its focus on social integration and cohesion are characteristic of functionalist approaches, also possess an awareness of the effects of inequalities combined with a push for advocacy and change, attributed to conflict approaches. Some will see this approach as utopian because a paradigm shift of this type would be exceptionally challenging;

however, Alexander argues the current strategies to address addiction have failed in an exceptional manner.

Conclusion

This analysis has included several theoretical perspectives from sociological approaches to understanding addiction in its various forms. The use of sociological theory and the sociological imagination inform how what seems to be individual behavior is often governed by social influences. Understandings of the concept of addiction come from medical, psychological, and criminological understandings, as well as political, spiritual, philosophical, and legal knowledge. Addiction also has social understandings as well, and the sociological perspective as the focus of this book should be obvious by now. This is, of course, not to state the other disciplinary contributions are not important, but those are areas best explored in other sources.

In this chapter, certain theoretical positions in sociology were reviewed in their relation to addiction: social disorganization theories, conflict theory, symbolic interactionism, rational choice theory, lifestyle theory, social learning theory, subculture theory, and social constructionist/postmodern theories. Theories of social disorganization and risk emphasize how social problems are created when society's rules break down, creating a form of chaos called anomie; obviously, addiction sources have added to concerns of social breakdown. Challenges to current understandings of addiction come in the form of conflict theory, which takes note of how ideas about addiction and other forms of deviance are created and maintained by those in power. Symbolic interactionism is a micro-level theory that focuses on how the individual use of drugs or the performance of addictive behaviors has social influences and consequences such as labeling and stigma.

The reasons why certain substances or activities are selected (or rejected) by individuals, why some substances are regulated for use by certain groups, and why particular substances are allowed by authorities, are all issues examined by rational choice theory. Related to rational choice theory is lifestyle theory which stresses the interaction between people and their environments; environmental adaptation is a key factor, but when the adaptation in the form of one's lifestyle becomes problematic (such as when addiction occurs), the focus is on the lifestyle, not the person.

Social learning theories such as differential association acknowledge the role of peer influence in behavior considered deviant, including behavior involving addiction sources. Subculture theories also consider the influence of peers in an individual activity and observe how common language and other cultural elements reinforce cohesion and maintain subcultural activity, which sometimes includes drugs or other addiction sources. Twelve-step programs attempt to create their own subculture, one that stresses abstinence from addictive sources.

Control theories such as one created by Travis Hirschi posit how the four social controls of attachment, commitment, involvement, and belief exist to keep people from engaging in deviant behavior. The theory was modified to focus on self-control; the idea of self-control has long been a consideration in the addictions field and challenges the medical model and twelve-step philosophy.

Social constructionist theories view how understandings of social phenomena, such as addiction, have been created through human deliberation and, over time, become taken for granted. Relatedly, postmodern theories view society as evolving through phases, and the current phase, the post-modern period, offers a series of threats and challenges due to changing technology, such as the technology that creates new and intransigent drug concerns. In both theoretical formulations, meanings that exist beneath the surface are explored, deconstructed, and challenged, to uncover truths hidden beneath traditional social explanations. Finally, a newer theory known as dislocation theory attempts to explain how living in contemporary capitalist society creates conditions for addictive behaviors unless the society has substitutes that are obtained from bonds to various communities.

Chapter 9

Strategies for Advocacy
in the Addictions Field

"If we know our society produces the need for psychotherapy as surely as it produces racism… (we) should perhaps speak to the humblest voter and taxpayer, and to the decision-making elite…If words…do not catch attention, then perhaps political action, lobbying, mass resignation, or other deeds of dissent and proposal might."

(Sidney M. Jourard, 1971 p. 130)

Advocacy Defined

The term advocacy is normally understood as the representation of a group that lacks the power to be heard by people who could potentially help them improve their conditions. A more comprehensive definition of advocacy is "the process of identifying with and representing a person's views and concerns, in order to secure enhanced rights and entitlements, undertaken by someone who has little or no conflict of interest" (Henderson & Pochin 2001, p.1-2, cited in Newbigging et al., 2015). It requires advocates to communicate the needs of a group to those who can potentially improve their lives. Therefore, adequate communication in promoting awareness of a cause to those in power is paramount. There are many individuals and organizations that provide advocacy for others, including people who are suffering from various mental health conditions (including addiction).

Referring specifically to advocacy for addicted persons, Taleff (1999) describes advocacy as "the action of the person or organization that pleads, recommends, or supports an argument, cause, or policy which contains…elements of counseling, politics and passion" (p. 121). Counseling is a familiar function for people who work in the addictions field, politics provides the battleground for legislative action, and passion is the motivation that fuels change.

The World Health Organization (WHO), a global organization that advocates for many groups with the hope of improving their situations, reducing discrimination, and decreasing stigma. In referring to mental health advocacy generally, but which also includes addictions advocacy, WHO suggests that groups providing advocacy should:

- promote awareness

- disseminate information

- provide education and training

- provide counseling and mutual aid

- mediate, support, and denounce (WHO, 2003).

There are many types of advocacy, as described by Newbigging et al. (2015), and while there is some overlap between these types, they provide a useful means of examining advocacy. These types are:

- collective advocacy—people championing a cause either individually or as a group

- community advocacy—collective advocacy for specific groups

- professional advocacy—people in a professional capacity advocating for those to whom they provide services

- peer advocacy—people with similar circumstances supporting a cause

- legal advocacy—legal representation on causes of concern (illustrating the original use of the term advocacy as meaning "legal counsel")

- citizen advocacy—long term, unpaid collaboration for vulnerable people

- non-instructed advocacy—people advocating for those who lack the power to be heard

- self-advocacy—people with a cause advocating for themselves

Goals for Advocacy Programs

At the individual level, advocacy programs provide support for addicted persons. At the societal level, they can assist in bringing attention to related situations such as dangerous social environments, housing problems, and educational barriers. Sub-units of advocacy programs can be formed to address each of these issues to improve the lives of many people and become a preventative factor for future addiction problems (Taleff, 1999).

Describing a community-based program in Pennsylvania, Taleff (1999) provides the following strategic goals in advocating for addicted persons:

- efforts to reduce stigma

- community volunteer utilization

- drug-free events to communities

- evaluation of treatment programming

- educating addicted persons in legislative and policy matters

Social Justice and Advocacy

Social justice is a term with imprecise definitions and, in a country divided on political grounds, has become controversial. Moving from political ramifications and to its progressive roots and in an advocacy framework, it refers to the rights of all people to effectively be heard on the issues important to society. Certainly, the advocacy and promotion of ideals that encourage policies that promote better mental health by citizens is a worthy goal. Advocacy in social justice "can give a voice to those who may be unable to protect themselves, mobilize communities for a cause, improve public services, and hold elected officials accountable" (Marshall-Lee, 2019, p. 1). In a discussion on advocacy by counseling psychologists, Goodman et al. (2004) describe the work of social justice advocates as "scholarship and professional action designed to change societal values, structures, policies, and practices, such that disadvantaged or marginalized groups gain increased access to these tools of self-determination" (p. 795).

Stigma and "Othering"

One of the key problems addicted persons encounter is the problem of stigma, which is one of the areas advocacy programs normally seek to address (WHO, 2003). Sociologists have long been concerned about the potential consequences of stigma. In the 1960s, sociologist Erving Goffman (1963) described how stigma creates a "spoiled identity" in the minds of others, which can result in their mistreatment by ostracism, marginalization, and other negative responses. When people are stigmatized, they are labeled in a negative way and othered, which makes a clear distinction between them and other people or groups. The process of othering involves two steps, beginning with the creation of a clear distinction ("us and not them") followed by identification of the "othering" group ("us") as normal and the "othered group ("them") as abnormal (Singer & Page, 2014).

Challenges for Advocacy

Some challenges for the advocacy for addicted populations involve the wide-spread belief that this group brought the problem on themselves and are undeserving of treatment considerations and advocacy. The stigma that exists with the population is worsened when the government continues to frame it in terms of morality by suggesting a "war" or "crusade" is needed to eradicate it (Taleff, 1999). The long-running war on drugs continues.

The recent opioid crisis provides an example of recent events that involve "othering" as it relates to substances of abuse. Opioids were prescribed by physicians producing alarming levels of addiction and record numbers of overdose. Buchman, Leece, and Orkin (2017) describe two classifications in the minds of the public that was produced during this current situation—the "deserving patients" and "undeserving patients," with the second category being the most stigmatized.

A Short History and Review of Advocates

This section provides a short review of the history of advocacy approaches in the field of addiction. Some aspects have been discussed previously but will be abbreviated while some new ones will be provided. This review will proceed chronologically in order to show an evolution of advocacy efforts.

Benjamin Rush

Benjamin Rush, mentioned several times already, was an early advocate for those addicted to alcohol and those with other mental health conditions in the American colonies. Rush advocated abstinence from alcohol and promoted prevention services. He sought to understand addiction when scientific information was severely lacking, and his early treatment methods, which are antiquated today, were based on knowledge of the period and did help addicted patients (Whitaker, 2002). He believed that a more moral and functional condition for addicted persons would occur if their condition was viewed as a disease capable of being cured (Lender & Martin, 1987).

After observing high levels of alcohol use by soldiers in George Washington's army, Rush wrote a widely distributed essay warning of the consequences of excessive drinking. He continued to write against alcohol use, and in 1784, he published *An Inquiry into the Effects of Spirituous Liquor upon the Happiness of Society*. Although *Inquiry* was a small 36-page pamphlet, it remained the country's most influential work on addiction for generations. His insistence that alcohol was a disease led to the unusual recommendation that special places, called sober houses, be created for addicted persons instead of placing them in jails. This was at a time when even regular hospitals were rare. In an era when America was excited about freedom, he cautioned that people could not be free if they were under the control of spirits (Lender & Martin, 1987; White, 2014).

The Washingtonians

The group known as the Washingtonians, whose name was an homage to George Washington, was a major voice for abstinence in the years after the greater temperance movement was losing its prominence. This occurred when temperance groups shifted their focus from condoning moderate use of alcohol ("tempered" drinking) to focus on total abstinence. The new group based in Maryland took the name Washington Total Abstinence Society and consisted of working-class citizens (as opposed to earlier temperance groups that were of higher social status). The organization, whose name was unofficially shortened to the Washingtonians, was the first mutual aid group to focus on alcoholism and used the strategy of entering bars and taverns to enlist patrons to join the group and pledge abstinence. Some of the new recruits were famous and wealthy, changing the constitution of the organization over time. Private meetings became public, and the number of participants grew (Lender & Martin, 1987; White, 2014).

A spin-off from the group, the Martha Washington Societies, focused on the needs of the wives of alcoholic husbands and of addicted women (anticipating Al-Anon); they provided many goods and services to those seeking to abstain from alcohol. The general Washingtonian movement grew rapidly but ended after only a few years when strategic mistakes led to its demise. However, after the Washingtonians ended, they were quickly followed by other groups such as secret temperance societies, reform clubs, and early moderation societies. And, nearly a hundred years later, the ideas of this group reemerged in the most famous advocacy organization in the country, Alcoholics Anonymous (Lender & Martin, 1987, White, 2014).

Frederick Douglass

Frederick Douglass is primarily remembered as a great orator, author, news editor, and reformer in the movement to emancipate slaves. He is less known as an advocate for many slaves and freed slaves that experienced alcohol addiction. Douglass had been a heavy alcohol user before signing a temperance pledge in 1845 and remained alcohol-free afterward (White, 2014). He realized the role alcohol played in maintaining slavery as slave masters used it for that purpose (Lender & Martin, 1987; White, 2014). Douglass advocated temperance for persons of African descent in order to stop their additional oppression from alcohol use. He promoted the temperance movement in the United States generally but was critical of those groups that failed to recognize the plight of slaves and freed slaves (Douglass, Taylor, & Foner, 1999). Due to his influence, several temperance and mutual aid societies for freed slaves sprang up in the nineteenth century (White, 2014).

The Salvation Army

The Salvation Army is another major group in the advocacy of those addicted to alcohol. Founded in 1885 in England by Methodist minister William Booth, the organization is a mixture of Christianity and quasi-military force. In 1880, the group came to the U.S., where it set up street outreach programs focusing mainly on homeless male alcoholics. It began to professionalize in the mid-twentieth century, integrating medicine, counseling, twelve-step programming, and religious services to a growing number of men addicted to alcohol, eventually opening inpatient treatment programs. In the 1970s, the organization expanded its outreach to women and set up "drunk tanks" to divert people from jail (White, 2014). The program continues today, serving communities across the country in many areas other than addiction services, such as disaster assistance, employee services, interpersonal violence intervention, hunger relief, and many others (Salvation Army USA, n.d.).

Alcoholics Anonymous

Throughout this book, the role of Alcoholics Anonymous and the related twelve-step self-help movements has been presented as a treatment modality. Through the collaboration between founders Bill W and Dr. Bob format, the AA philosophy began in the twentieth century and is still a primary treatment modality, but it is also an advocacy group for the many people affected by addiction. In 1939, this new movement acquired its name, and with financial support from John D. Rockefeller, Jr. was able to achieve publicity on a national scale. With this publicity came the establishment of numerous AA groups which were formed all over the country and abroad. The principles of anonymity, surrender, amends, a spiritual rebirth, and an accepting, supportive community appealed to many people addicted to alcohol (White, 2014).

Related but independent groups Al-Anon (for families of alcoholics) and Ala-Teen (for teens of alcoholic parents) were formed for a variety of addictions that will be explored in the following chapter. Other substance addiction programs that have followed the lead of AA are Narcotics Anonymous (NA), Cocaine Anonymous (CA), and some that deal with behavioral conditions such as Gamblers Anonymous (GA), Overeaters Anonymous, and Sexaholics Anonymous (SA), among many others.

Narcotics Anonymous

Many other groups use the AA twelve-step philosophy, but one was especially influential, not with a focus on alcohol but on narcotics. After the successes of AA, another group based on a similar format was formed in 1949 in New York City, originally named Addicts Anonymous. It changed its name to Narcotics Anonymous (NA), the original incarnation of the organization that went by that name existed until the 1970s. Another organization with the same name on the West coast began to grow into the organization now known as NA, also modeled on the AA philosophy. This program was formed due to the growing use of opiates, cocaine, and marijuana. There were administrative discussions between AA and NA over whether another organization based on the twelve steps was needed. Since there was a strong distinction made between alcoholics and "dope addicts" (even by AA founder Bill W), a separate organization was created (White, 2014).

Gamblers Anonymous

Gamblers Anonymous, sometimes referred to as Gam-Anon, began in 1957 when a couple of men who were concerned with their compulsive gambling held regular meetings in order to help them abstain from their pastime. Adopting the philosophy of substance addictions, a twelve-step program was created for people whose gambling was deemed to be uncontrollable. The program included a strict series of guidelines regarding abstinence from the activity. Promoting the idea that behavior could produce similar conditions as substance use and, therefore, should be treated similarly, the idea of behavioral addiction became more crystallized. It should probably be noted, however, that on their website, the organization refers to problem gambling as a compulsion rather than an addiction but does consider it an illness (Gambler's Anonymous, n.d.).

The Haight Ashbury Free Clinic

The Haight Ashbury Free Clinic began in 1967 in San Francisco over concerns that the hippie counterculture movement would bring chaotic drug use and drug abusers to the area (White, 2014). The Haight Ashbury district was the epicenter of the new counterculture movement, and the clinic was the result of medical volunteers coming together to provide services to people, often young, who were suffering from overdose and other harmful consequences of hallucinogens, amphetamines, barbiturates, opiates, and many other drugs. The philosophy of the program was to be free of judgment of the people who used the clinic; this philosophy evidences a true spirit of advocacy. Other clinics of this type began after the Haight Ashbury program, which is still in existence today.

Late Twentieth-Century Figures

First Lady and wife of Gerald Ford, the 38th President of the United States, Betty Ford, became an unexpected advocate for substance abuse treatment and well as other causes, such as women's equality, reproductive rights, and other issues. Dealing with her own addiction involving alcohol and prescription medications, she entered treatment and, in 1982, founded the Betty Ford Clinic (now Center). The clinic became a nationally acclaimed addiction program, and the name Betty Ford became associated with addiction treatment and advocacy. Because she was so transparent with this personal information, many celebrities faced their own addictions and entered treatment programs.

New Recovery Movement

White (2007) describes a "new recovery movement" beginning in the late 1990s resulting from a backlash of the growing professionalization and commercialization of addiction treatment that had taken place in the 1970s and 1980s, and in response to the rejection of the grassroots activities that sustained them prior to this time. The new movement promotes a shift of focus from the problem to a solution, and advocates for political involvement stressing personal recovery strategies, grassroots activism, the formation of leadership structures at local and national levels, and more diversity in understandings of different addiction styles and pathways to recovery (religious, spiritual, and secular). Recovery is viewed as a voluntary process that flourishes in communities that support recovery measures and as a reciprocal process in which addicted persons give back to supportive communities at the micro- and meso-levels and that link resources into a national model.

Advocacy for Special Groups

Social and Identity Categories

Social and identity categories reflect those characteristics such as race, ethnicity, sex, gender, age, sexual identity, and social class, among others. While most characteristics are socially constructed and have little meaning outside what society places on them, it is important to note these differences in order to better advocate for them. This idea builds upon another the concept of social justice, mentioned earlier, which seeks to promote equality in laws and in social institutions, including the institutions and systems that advocate for addicted persons. Social justice "is guided by the moral principles of truth, reason, justice and fairness" (Badley, 1996, p. 73) through activities that promote a reduction of stigma, an increase in access to accommodations and treatment services, and provision of treatment services in a manner equivalent to medical services. Reviewed next will be how these identity characteristics are related to addiction.

Women

Women were very involved in early movements to stop addiction to alcohol and other drugs. One of those reasons was that the second-rate status of women meant they often suffered the consequences of addiction, such as husbands getting criminal charges, losing their jobs, ending up in jail or prison, or otherwise neglecting their families. In the mid- and late-1800s, women were often in leadership roles in the anti-saloon protests and were prominent in the fights favoring prohibition. At home, women were often dependent on their husbands and their incomes at this time; having seriously addicted husbands often created a lifestyle-threatening situation. Many psychiatrists during the mid-twentieth century, especially those with a psychoanalytic bent, faulted the mothers of male alcoholics, due to inappropriate attachments during parenting (McClellan, 2004).

The lesser power of wives of addicted persons was evident in the mid-twentieth century when groups such as Al-Anon were created and when the codependency movement began. Women after World War II were expected to be supportive of their husbands as they suffered through the "disease of alcoholism." As noted earlier in this book, the codependency movement emphasized the role of women in addicted spouses as "enabling" their husbands' addiction—many today feel this was simply a situation of blaming the victim.

Then there is the issue of female addiction, which has traditionally been perceived as a sign of social breakdown. Since women have historically been considered the gatekeepers of morality (Doyal, 1995), their use of addictive sources was perceived as an extreme form of deviance in early periods of American history. During the Victorian era, women who consumed alcohol did so secretly due to the extreme stigma involved. Doctors determined (mistakenly, of course) that female addiction was much more difficult to treat than male addiction and that women were less likely to be rehabilitated (Lender & Martin, 1987). After prohibition was repealed, many thought (despite the absence of evidence) that women were drinking more and, as a result, were becoming more masculine, hardly a desirable trait for women at that time. Men have historically had more access to power and economic resources than women, therefore greater access to addiction sources resulted in a double standard. However, some of the constraints were removed after World War II, and more women were able to enjoy the pleasures of drinking.

Female use of other drugs became a national issue and related directly to the problems of female health (or ill health). Physicians were often guilty of overprescribing for females, whereby they had a "pill for every ill" (Doyal, 1995, p. 182). Decisions about prescribing medication were based on several factors, including:

- gender stereotypes

- the orientation of the biomedical model

- lobbying efforts by drug companies

- the higher number of consultations by women

These factors led to female use of various "drugs of solace" (Doyal, 1995, p. 195). From dependence on laudanum in the Victorian era to the tranquilizing effects of "mother's little helpers" in the mid-twentieth century, drugs have often been used to "correct" the unique problems of womanhood, problems that promoted and maintained the notion of the general lower status of women.

Women have greater economic power and access to drugs than when they were sedated into conformity in America's past. Doyal (1995) argues the entrance into the high-stress occupational landscape has created greater opportunities for pharmaceutical companies to target women once more. For this reason, she advocates a comprehensive program for gender-based educational and support programs, treatment strategies, and greater restrictions on advertising and promotion by drug companies.

Racial and ethnic minorities

Race refers to biological characteristics, including physical features, that have been combined and given special significance, while ethnicity refers to the cultural aspects that have been passed down by custom through generations, including a common language, religion, and traditions. Modern sociological understandings of race see the concept as being socially constructed. People of racial and ethnic groups have been subjected to both individual and institutional prejudice and discrimination, as well as stereotyping. The maltreatment of people in these categories has produced some very disturbing chapters in the nation's history and still exists today. Recent events involving minorities affirms that race and ethnicity still guide how many people are viewed. Drugs have often figured into racial and ethnic stereotypes, further complicating the national dialogue on race.

Arrest for substances of abuse such as marijuana is higher for blacks than whites, which is primarily the result of racial profiling and enhanced supervision of minority communities. Intoxicated driving has resulted in what has been called "DWB" Driving While Black (or Brown). While the use and arrest of other drugs are about the same for whites and blacks, incarceration rates are much higher for the latter group. Alexander (2012) states that to simply ascertain there is discrimination in our society against racial minorities overlooks the obvious and calculated activity that has, in effect, removed them, especially black men, from our society through a system of mass incarceration. The targeted policing of people in communities of color, using tactics that would be inexcusable in white communities, is due in large part to the national war on drugs. Minorities are incarcerated in large numbers and, upon their release, find it increasingly difficult to find adequate housing, employment, educational opportunities, and other things necessary to remain drug-free. When an entire group of people are labeled criminals, the outside world sees them as such (reflecting the Thomas theorem mentioned in the previous chapter).

Children and Adolescents

Children and adolescents have long been a major concern for people advocating for addiction issues. In fact, the juvenile justice system, as asserted in chapter seven, was created by a group of advocates known as the "child savers" to address the idea that young people can be diverted from the misery of punishment that has been reserved for those who have lived a "hardened criminal's life." While the juvenile programs that were connected to the rehabilitation ideal were progressive and created positive changes, more retributive models have come about in recent decades that punish children like adults. Slobogin & Fondacaro (2011) advocate a preventative justice approach that resembles the older "child saving movement" of the early twentieth century but rejects some of the more paternalistic aspects of the movement. Developmental aspects regarding drug use and other criminal acts should be considered in all criminal legislation that affects young people.

So-called "scared straight" programs, in which adolescents with delinquency problems are subjected to the harsh reality faced by adult inmates in prisons, became popular in the late 1970s and 1980s due to movies and TV shows. Despite the programs' ineffectiveness and the efforts by many criminologists to redirect attention to programs that work, TV viewers seemed to enjoy watching juveniles, including those with drug possession and use charges, endure the frightening effects of exposure to incarcerated adult populations. Maahs and Travis (2017) advocate for better communication for TV viewers and lawmakers, purporting that actual research findings do not support the value of these programs.

People in the LGBTQ community

The LGBTQ community consists of people who are lesbian, gay, bisexual, transgender, or questioning (the q can also stand for queer). LGBTQ individuals, while not a monolithic group, face stigma at very high levels and suffer negative self-image due to this. With a long history of prejudice, discrimination, and stereotyping, it is not surprising many people who are LGBTQ suffer from alienation and seek to alleviate this condition using addictive substances that only worsen their feelings of alienation (Schulte, 2015).

Castro and Fritchle (2013) note these special problem areas:

- discrimination and stigma

- internalized stigma and homophobia

- family issues that include safety at home

- employment-related problems

- health-related concerns, including HIV/AIDS

- problems within correctional institutions

- bullying and harassment issues in educational settings

Referring to general mental health advocacy, but including addictions as well, Castro and Fritchle (2013) offer the strategy of mobilizing diverse individuals and groups in the community to include LGBTQ people to help regain acceptance and security. The goals of these groups can include:

- provision of community-based projects

- adoption of safe-space areas

- support groups

- referral networks

- a rejection of pathologizing conversion and reparation type therapies (Castro & Fritchle, 2013).

Homeless Populations

As with other groups dealing with poverty situations, the homeless often experience problems with substance addictions. Since before the days of skid row, the homeless and drugs have been intertwined in the addiction landscape. Homelessness is the result of many external factors, such as:

- housing inflation

- insufficient welfare and support systems

- racial and gender discrimination

- substandard assistance for the addicted and mentally dis-tressed (Baumohl, 1992).

Certainly, the deinstitutionalization efforts beginning in the 1960s that emp-tied many people from institutions to communities also created a situation where they were rejected by families (if they were even around) and ended up homeless. Since the homeless often live on city streets, they experience physi-cal and emotional pain that is often medicated by drugs they encounter on the street. Boredom also causes the homeless to seek out drug experiences. These drug experiences are both a cause and symptom of homelessness and create many barriers that deter any efforts to seek out treatment for addiction (Flanagan & Briggs 2016).

Advocacy for addicted persons who are homeless can include:

- encouraging business owners to become involved with social entrepreneurship programs that can assist the homeless with employment

- increasing access to medical services to mitigate the desire to self-medicate on the street

- increasing access to psychological services for the distress that contributed to and resulted in homelessness

- assisting them with acquiring financial skills and knowledge of insurance programs (Flanagan & Briggs, 2016).

Incarcerated Populations

There are many reasons for the dramatic increase in incarceration that has been occurring over the past few decades, including the deinstitutionalization of mental health facilities, changes in insurance coverage, and the war on drugs in the 1980s that resulted in an increase in harsh punishments, and mandatory and determinant sentencing.

People with substance addictions are highly represented in jails and prisons, and African Americans comprise a disproportionate number of incarcerated people, primarily resulting from the policies related to the war on drugs (Brin-kley-Rubenstein, 2014). There have been some positive changes recently for minority offenders such as the shortening of some sentences, an increase in prison diversions to treatment programs, the decriminalizing of some drug offenses, and an increase in the use of drug courts. Brinkley-Rubenstein (2014) advocates:

- a health-centered approach in which there is a micro-level drug addiction/overdose emphasis and meso-level risk mitigation initiatives in communities

- decriminalization of drug use to address the AIDS crisis (due to intravenous drug use) in minority communities

- community organizing that is centered around programs to deter racial profiling

Sentences for drug crimes and other non-violent offenses by Latinx citizens, like those for African Americans, are more severe than those for whites. Added problems include possible communication problems and immigration status issues, which can result in deportation for some members of this population. The undermining of Latinx families, communities, physical and mental health problems, and the lure of gang activity are all problems experienced by this group (Velasquez & Funes, 2014).

Native Americans are another racial group that is also overrepresented in the prison system and which has a long history with addiction and imprisonment. Many cultural ways were obliterated in attempts to force assimilation, and those refusing to conform often endured severe punishments. Many of the sacred traditions (such as the use of sweat lodge and the sacred pipe, and participation in the sun dance) and grooming customs (such as traditional hair length) have been prohibited for Native American inmates due to stated security concerns (Root & Lynch, 2014).

As noted earlier, young people have long been a concern for addiction, and an entirely new criminal justice detention system was created for this purpose. For minority youth who are detained in the juvenile justice system, the following recommendations have been made as advocacy for this group:

- increased recruitment of racial and ethnic minority personnel employed in juvenile justice agencies

- institution of cultural sensitivity training for personnel in the juvenile system.

- the establishment of drug and gang prevention programs

- the articulation of specific guidelines for policymakers with oversight of juvenile programs

- supervision of policy and decision-makers to hold them accountable for inappropriate behavior when it occurs (Barringer & Bruster, 2014).

Incarcerated addicted women have special problems and barriers. Many are single parents, lack supportive extended family, are already in involved in welfare programs, and must deal with the feelings of powerlessness and boundary violations resulting from past experiences of violence and incest; these experiences have often led to psychological disturbances other than the use of addictive sources (Kelly & Empson, 1999). Those problems are not necessarily unique to women but are certainly experienced by female addicted populations to a large degree.

Kelly and Empson (1999) recommend administratively based strategies on key critical issues for incarcerated addicted women:

- family reunification programs

- greater access to health care

- preventative counseling for HIV/AIDS

- counseling for coexisting mental distress

- pregnancy-related programs

- educational and vocational skills training

- recruitment, training, and hiring of skilled treatment providers

Also recommended for female inmates are more localized strategies such as letter-writing campaigns to judges, prison administration, or family members who could assist with reentry efforts upon release. Empowerment schemes, including providing inmates with guidance through the changes and transitions of incarceration, are also advocated (Kelly & Empson, 1999).

The current opioid crisis has prompted much discussion and action directed at advocacy for drug addiction. For example, recently, Csete (2019) proposed the following for incarcerated people who are addicted to opioids:

- adequate training, information, and support for treatment providers in the prison system, at least at a level commensurate to those outside prisons

- increased use of drug courts

- promotion of and use of medication-assisted treatment (MAT)

- reduction in sentencing for lesser, non-violent offenses

- advocacy for innovative programs such as the Law Enforcement Assisted Diversion (LEAD) program that diverts offenders directly into treatment programs instead of proceeding first through the criminal justice system

Conclusion

Advocacy refers to work by people or organizations in which pleas or arguments are made in favor of those who lack the social and political power and influence to be heard on their own. There are many barriers to creating a strong system of advocacy for persons with addiction, but there are also many positive benefits. Stigma is a continuing problem for addicted persons, and speaking on behalf of those who are seen by many to be at fault for their own miseries can be difficult. Advocacy is a worthwhile endeavor for all those who hope for the betterment of not only individuals but for society.

The United States has a long history of people and organizations advocating for people with addiction. From Benjamin Rush to the various twelve-step programs, to innovative programs such as the free clinic program, to the new recovery movement, there has been a continuation of programs and strategies. All seek to assist those with addiction and to gather new knowledge about this still enigmatic (and stigmatic) condition.

Groups that deserve some special consideration for addiction advocacy include women, racial and ethnic minorities, children and adolescents, people in the LGBTQ community, the homeless, and incarcerated populations. All of these have a unique relationship with addiction. Advocacy, as well as counseling strategies, require an understanding and subjective appraisal of these groups in a social justice framework in order to assure they receive treatment on par with other groups and individuals. The stigma and othering that often already exists with addicted populations is amplified with people with these additional discriminant characteristics, creating even more prejudice, discrimination, and stereotyping.

Chapter 10

Concluding Thoughts

"Any deviation from the pattern (of excessive conformity resulting from alienation) …arouses fear and insecurity; one is always dependent on the approval of others, just as a drug addict is dependent on his drug."

(Erich Fromm, 1955/1990 p. 197)

How Should Addiction be Defined?

Addiction is an enduring social problem, and as with all social problems, it must be defined prior to determining a way to alleviate it. Like the concept of deviance (a way addiction is often classified, by the way), the concept of addiction is difficult to define. Walters (1999) suggests addiction is the "Frankenstein monster of modern American life" (p. 1) in that it has taken on more and more components in the way it is defined. Beginning with problems resulting from various forms of alcohol to including loosely defined drugs known as narcotics, to more and more substances, natural and synthetic. Recently, additional considerations have been given to a host of what are known as behavior addictions—gambling, unofficially (for now) Internet gaming, and potentially excessive eating, problematic sexuality, and other behaviors previously designated as compulsions rather than addictions.

In this book, some explanations of addiction were provided through observations of common analogies:

- addiction as disease
- addiction as habit
- addiction as excessive appetite
- addiction as lifestyle
- addiction as deviance
- addiction as symptom
- addiction as ritual
- addiction as construction
- addiction as culture

- addiction as risk

- addiction as virtue

Analogies are beneficial in that they provide information regarding meaning that is often hidden beneath our common-sense understandings of social phenomena—in this case, addiction. However, analogies do not provide concrete explanations, just ideas.

Addiction is what society says it is. The introductory chapter of this book began with a decades-old quote by E.M. Jellinek, one of the early addiction researchers, explaining that addiction is officially defined by the medical establishment; he went on say that the medical definition stands regardless of what the non-medical laypersons or even dissenters in the medical field say it is. Written decades ago, the term addiction was defined by the medical field and had been so defined since medical doctor Benjamin Rush made the declaration. It is, therefore, a disease, or perhaps an illness. Either way, it is a medical problem because it has been officially designated as such.

It was another powerful player that augmented the powerful force of the medical establishment. This was a group of people who decided they had to take control of their own lives with a distinct philosophy (though not new at the time) and a treatment protocol (which was new) and who adopted the idea of addiction as disease to be dealt with through a series of steps with strong moral underpinnings. Addicted persons were viewed by the AA as powerless to disease and, therefore, not deviant; thus, the medical model created a positive mood and safe place for addiction to reside.

Psychoanalysis, another a major force in the twentieth century, developed during the repressive Victorian era in Europe, and spread rapidly to America and beyond. Sigmund Freud, a medical doctor and the founder of psychoanalysis, adopted the medical model as well in his new therapy, though he ventured out in unchartered territory to do so. In this conception, addiction is better defined as a symptom of problems, blocked from a person's consciousness. But symptoms still fall under the medical model.

So, addiction became placed under the authority of the medical field. However, medicine must have concrete definitions from which to make choices for diagnosis and treatment. It should be obvious that addiction does not have concrete definitions, at least based on our current knowledge of it. It can be a disease, or deviance, or lifestyle choice, or social construction, or any of the other analogies mentioned.

Addiction is better viewed as a social construction, constructed by whoever has the authority to construct it. Authority, as Max Weber (1947/1964) taught us, is power that has been legitimized, or determined to be deserved. In an ever troubling and risky world, society places faith in the medical field—which is understandable, since lives are saved in that arena—therefore it is that field that is the definer.

Expanding the Concept of Addiction

Peele (1995) provides this description of addiction: "an experience that people can get caught up in, but that still expresses their values, skills of living, and personal resolve—or lack of it" (p. 3). Addiction, then, is like other experiences one can get "caught up in." What then makes these experiences addiction? Can any human activity be a potential addiction source? Before a condition can be successfully examined—especially a condition that can lead to loss of a normal healthy lifestyle and for which many people have indeed lost their lives because of—it must be accurately defined. If addiction cannot be definitively quantified or differentiated from other conditions, any efforts to treat it or to control its deleterious effects on society will be fruitless. Peele and Brodsky (2015) provide some interesting insights into the world of behavioral addictions; while they believe all "consuming experiences" can be addictions, it could also be that these experiences are normal human responses to their environment and that when performed to access, create problematic consequences. But are the non-drug involvements the same in terms of their effects on the body, the effects on the families of other primary groups, their communities, or on society generally? This direction is the way psychiatry is obviously going.

Not everyone agrees that behaviors can be addictive in the same way substance addictions that have a chemical source. Many, in fact, believe that common behaviors are being medicalized. The term medicalization refers to "defining a problem in medical terms, using medical language to describe a problem, adopting a medical framework to understand a problem, or using a medical intervention to 'treat it'" (Conrad, 2000, p. 105). Therefore, the concept refers to framing a problem previously not considered a medical problem as an issue to be turned over to the medical profession, or at least be placed in the context of such a medical problem. Rantala and Sulkunen (2012) ask if these behavioral conditions should be classified with substance addictions because the properties are essentially the same, or if they are simply social constructions that were classified in this way with the purpose of medicalizing these problems. That's a good question.

Adler and Adler (2011) are quite blunt in their assessment of the issue of medicalization. They believe the field of psychiatry has claimed ownership over an increasing number of behaviors (as represented in the growth of the DSM series) in order to conduct therapy and bill insurance companies. As more and more behaviors are medicalized, more specialists are needed, entire treatment industries, including pharmaceuticals, of course, are developed to accommodate the new disorder categories. And while the medicalization movement removed some of the stigma attached to behaviors previously perceived as deviant, it also took away individual agency in response to these behaviors.

Gambling, for example, has now been officially placed under the control of the medical establishment with its inclusion in the DSM-5. As noted, earlier, gambling has historically been considered a form of recreation, or when taken to the extreme, a personal problem. Now it has officially determined a psychiatric issue. Related in some ways to gambling, Internet gaming, is now in the hopper to become the next behavioral addiction; this "disorder," of course, has a much more recent origin and it appears it is felt that this activity poses enough of a threat to be considered a medical disorder. It has even been accused by some politicians of leading to the mass shootings in America. That is quite a disease.

Although sexual addiction has not been given official addiction status, yet, it can certainly claim unofficial status and could well be made official in the future. Though not yet included in the DSM, the issue of potential sex addiction (or hypersexuality) has long been eyed by the medical profession (or those who operate within this mindset) as a medical issue. Sexuality, however, presents a unique case for medicalization. Conrad makes an important claim on this point; "medicalization occurs when a medical frame or definition has been applied to understand or manage a problem; this is as true for epilepsy as for 'gender dysphoria'" (2000, p. 105). Few would doubt that epilepsy is appropriate within the medical frame, but what about gender dysphoria?

Described in the DSM-5 as "the distress that may accompany the incongruence between one's experienced or expressed gender and one's assigned gender" (APA, 2013, p. 451) the issue of gender dysphoria reflects the larger issue of transgenderism—does the distress that comes with this condition differ to a large enough degree that it should be a separate form of "illness" than other types of distress, such as social anxiety? Does this type of distress require a separate treatment regime or a specialized group of professionals to "treat" it? Or does this simply refer to medicalization? Another example is the DSM-5 designation of a transvestic disorder as a psychiatric disorder. Included with the other DSM designated sexual problems of voyeurism, exhibitionism, sadism, masochism, and pedophilia is transvestic disorder, described as dressing as the "opposite sex" in which sexual excitement is obtained. The other behaviors in this group constitute deviance, and even criminality, so would this disorder belong there? Equally questionable, is it a disorder at all, or the result of a social proscription? While neither of these "ailments"—gender dysphoria or transvestic disorder—are currently considered addictions, they represent how conditions of a sexual nature (deemed as negative by society) can be

framed as medical conditions to be treated in the medical field by professionals, often with specializations.

Eating is another category that would appear problematic as an addiction. As
with the ingestion of alcohol and other drugs, food is taken directly into the
body. And eating disorders also have serious physiological consequences that fit
within the medical model. But should it be regarded as an addiction? There is
not a traditional type of intoxication involved. The feelings from bingeing can
invoke feelings of pleasure (as can gambling, Internet use, and sex but so can
watching a play, fishing, and teaching a college course); do these supply the
same "intoxication" received from heroin or cocaine? Overeating, binge eating,
and purging can certainly be problematic; eating disorders are real and psychologically distressing. And they can be medical problems. But should they be
classified as addictions? Are the factors similar enough to lump these together?

There are many consuming hobbies that bring pleasure to people such as
antique collecting, record collecting, metal detecting, the refurbishing of old
cars: are these diseases that need medical attention? Music is very fulfilling,
and many people get much pleasure from listening to or playing it. If music is
played "excessively," do listeners/players need treatment by a specialist, a
musicologist perhaps? This is, of course, meant to be sarcastic, but when
many types of behaviors have been given serious consideration as addictive:
exercise addiction, workaholism, entrepreneurship addiction, cell phone
addiction, tanning addiction, even "street addiction," it must be considered
that this idea has been expanded a bit too far. And if so, why. As Forbes (1994,
p. 3) notes, "to declare everyone an addict can be even more psychobabble
about people's compulsive, self-indulgent habits in need of the one true cure
from the latest self-help regimen." Addiction can be trendy.

The Medicalization of Anxiety in a Risk Society

The common thread that ties together all the various understandings and types
of addiction that have been discussed in this book is the element of anxiety,
which is experienced at micro-, meso-, and macro-levels. It was mentioned
earlier that the medicalization of addiction became a major factor in the early
and mid-twentieth centuries. As discussed throughout the book, this idea did
not start then, but much earlier. However, the flowering of the addiction as
disease concept appeared when psychiatry, in its attempts to legitimize itself in
the medical community (see Steverson, 2018), began a strict professionalization
scheme in which a new manual, the DSM, was published in 1952. Though addiction was inadequately addressed, it did set in motion a classification process
(which was needed, no doubt) that would expand its tentacles into more and
more behaviors and processes over the years. AA was formed in the 1930s when
two people met to take alcoholism treatment into their own hands (one, inci-

dentally was a medical doctor). By mid-century, the movement had grown incredibly, gaining a national and later international following.

Around the same time, Freudian psychoanalysis gained notice not only in clinical circles but also in popular culture and was presented in books, movies, television shows, and many other media. However, was there a reason the convergence of these factors happened during this time? The early part of the American twentieth century was marked by two major wars and by mid-century a military conflict in North Korea. There was also a huge economic depression in the 1930s, following the carefree 1920s. Anxiety was high because the idea of living in an unpredictable world became very real. The economy got much better after the second World War and heralded the beginnings of an age of consumerism, consumerism that was available to a larger number of people than in the past. And new inventions were making life easier as well on the domestic front. Faith in science was revived. Medicine represented science, psychoanalysis represented curing our individual problems, and AA proved that solidarity could produce results that people on their own cannot.

However, the century did not live up to its curative promise. Psychoanalysis fell from grace as other treatment modalities seemed to render it archaic. The twelve-step philosophy of AA grew and expanded to new areas but was met with alternatives that appealed to many because they did not have the strict demands of AA. Yet medicine, emblematic as science, remained. Even in the face of newer, non-Western approaches to health, these have not offered a challenge to its authority. The anxieties of the age were addressed by medicine in areas involving mental health, and particularly addiction.

As discussed in chapter eight, anomie theory and other theories of social disorganization infer that society has done an ineffective job of making sure the workings of that society are functional and contributing to the welfare of its citizens. The breakdown of norms can result on a psychological level, to an extreme degree, in the form of suicide. On a larger scale, social institutions are "sometimes disturbed by some painful crisis or by beneficent but abrupt transitions" (Durkheim 1897/1951, p. 252). The concern over societal breakdown creates social anxiety—not anxiety from a clinical perspective where an individual has a so-named diagnosis from the DSM—but a deep-seated fear of a state of anomie, where the norms are confused, or not clearly articulated, resulting in a state of chaos.

However, our responses to these conditions are not based merely on nature but on culture. Shorter (1992) describes "symptom pools" that provide the cultural understandings from which are drawn understandings of the experience of anxiety along with ways to mitigate it. Addiction is an ambiguous concept and seems to shapeshift as culture changes, which can possibly be most easily observed in the incidence of moral panics. Culture also shapes our understandings of various types of illness—the "shaping of symptoms" occurs when various aspects of culture create our "knowledge" (Shorter, 1992).

This clinical type of anxiety has been described in our current society by the DSM-5 as an anticipation of a future threat, as compared to fear, which is described as a response to a current one (APA, 2013). Horwitz describes the groups that benefit from this designation of anxiety as a medical problem:

- mental health practitioners who are paid for their services treating it
- drug companies who profit from medications
- social science researchers who receive funding and possibly academic advancement
- politicians who are safe in making policy on this perspective
- advocates who have a well-defined cause to promote
- patients able to receive treatment and less stigma (Horwitz, 2013).

These groups benefit from the way the therapeutic substructure is arranged. But it is not a natural process—it is based on factors that could be very different had different historical events and encounters occurred. This is also true with addiction. If Bill W and Dr. Bob had never met, or if Benjamin Rush didn't have negative family experiences with alcohol as a child, things could have been very different in the addictions field.

Pitirim Sorokin (1941), in *The Crisis of our Age*, notes the role of social cohesion with a concern that when moral and religious values and contractual obligations break down, "if his hunger for pleasures and sensory values is paramount, what can guide and control his conduct toward other men. Nothing but his desires and lusts." (p. 205). Could these sensory pleasures include addictive behavior? Or is that a stretch?

Mills (1959) states when people feel threats in society and lack cherished values, they experience a "deadly unspecified malaise" (p. 11). Wilkerson explains that "we are kept in a state of anxiety so long as we are left struggling to define the threatening situation in which we find ourselves" (2001, p. 19). Anxiety produces malaise, and malaise produces confusion. And many people in society turn to addiction sources to deal with this condition.

Forbes (1994) places the compulsive desire for drugs in a larger consumerist society, which also creates a cycle of craving, tolerance, withdrawal, and demand for more of the addiction source. Drugs become a cure for living in a world full of uncertainty, boredom, and potential pain. It is society, then, that is sick and in need of a cure (to further extend the medical analogy).

Anxieties of This Age

For the purpose of this examination of addiction, a list of current anxieties at the macro-level that might have some effects on addiction problems at the micro- and meso-levels will be described. A nation's zeitgeist refers to that region's "spirit of the times" that represent the salient cultural aspects of the period. Our current zeitgeist is represented by many factors that add to our national anxiety, anxiety that could be reflected in problems with addiction.

Health Care

Health care is a major issue in American society currently and hotly debated in American politics. Health care is expensive, and our society expects the medical field to take care of a growing number of ailments. The health care system has implications for mental health and addiction, and the fact that even prescribed medications have the potential for serious consequences to individuals, communities, and society generally, certainly has the potential to increase anxiety at all levels.

Immigration

The current national discussion around immigration represents a long history of the fear of "the other." The discussions of moral panics reveal that this is not a new phenomenon, but it is certainly experiencing a revival. The issue of immigration is also at the forefront in American politics, symbolized in debates over a physical wall at the country's southern border. Demographic shifts have created anxiety in some majority groups as well as minority groups, further creating a split between people regarding racial and ethnic categories.

Economic concerns

The Great Recession of 2007-2008 made it clear that economic stability is not a given in the United States, even as the economy has made an increasingly positive trajectory. Economic inequality exists, and the gap between the very wealthy and the working classes continues to grow. Students often graduate from college with large amounts of educational debt, creating anxiety and thwarting their ability to find their place in society; they often take jobs that will allow them to repay their loan debt, in the process redirecting them from jobs for which they can self-actualize and find meaning and purpose. People in debt are also forced to worry about micro-level anxieties and unable to critically evaluate macro-level ones, meaning that decisions are made at the top with little input from below.

Military Activity and Terrorism

Wars in the Middle East have gone on for decades, creating generations of people who have grown up with the real fear of war, which is always an anxiety provoker. The terrorist attacks on September 11, 2001, set into place an additional level of anxiety through the potential for subsequent attacks on American soil. Fears of terrorism, foreign and domestic, continue to create anxiety. And the global wars continue.

Political Division

Although there has traditionally been a political division in the country—that is a mark of democracies—the current political discord between parties is extremely high. Partisan 24/7 news media networks and different types of media have increased knowledge of political issues and increased incivility. The past few years have seen increased anxiety over a very uncertain and unpredictable political landscape. Interference by hostile foreign agents in the American democratic system is a recent concern. Additionally, concerns that news stories are fake has also led to citizens not being sure of the veracity of the material conveyed to them, further creating anxiety and political distance between people.

Mass Shootings

The continued occurrence of mass shootings in schools and other public areas has created deeply felt anxiety mixed with the added emotions of anger, sadness, frustration, and even despair. As with other major issues, people are taking sides on how to address the problem adequately. As the problem is political, the solution must be political.

A World at Risk

The idea of risk is closely related to the issue of anxiety. It can be found at both the clinical and cultural levels. And using the sociological imagination, the concepts of anxiety and risk can be examined to acquire a more comprehensive understanding of addiction. Risk has become a major area of focus for many social scientists in the last few years. It has been developed and elaborated upon by many social science scholars, notably Ulrich Beck (1992). Mythen (2004) describes certain elements that represent the concept of risk:

- danger

- uncertainty

- futurity

- probability

- opportunity

The last factor, opportunity, implies there is a potential for positive outcomes, a potential that can be missed is appropriate social policy interventions are not applied.

The issue of risk is ubiquitous and embedded in all social institutions: government, economy, family, education, and religion, and made more threatening when media depictions create a sense of danger. Political risk is consistent as parties are constantly jockeying for power in a challenging time. The risks to the economy were evident during the Great Depression and, more recently, with the Great Recession. Risks in the educational institution are demonstrated by declining student performance in many educational institutions and lower levels of research funding in graduate research institutions, in addition to piling student loan debt. Threats to the religious institution can be seen in the growing intolerance and xenophobia that exists nationally and abroad, evidenced by the targeting of people and places of worship for harm. The family has long been viewed from the prism of risk as traditional forms of marriage and sexuality are being challenged (which could be a positive outcome but still presents anxiety for many). When the functions of social institutions become less defined and less "solid," people are living in what Bauman (2007) calls "liquid society," when the institutions are not firm enough to manage the various risks that are encountered.

Addiction is a social phenomenon that results from various institutional risks, such as poverty, lack of adequate housing, moral decline, family dysfunction—basically forms of social disorganization or anomie—and perceived as a risk to society. The current situation in the U.S. involving opioids is a case in point in that addiction to opioids for medical reasons represents a failure to deal with the problem of pain management.

The world is becoming more rationalized and is producing more risks in this evolution. Risks must be managed, and addiction, either to substances or behaviors, creates a series of challenges. A side effect of great medical advancements is greater susceptibility to addiction. New technology creates the possibility of compulsive behavior related to this technology (such as with Internet addiction). The effects of social disorganization and structural problems contribute to escapist behavior such as eating problems, sexual compulsions, gaming, and the ingestion of addictive substances. Everyone is "at-risk" in that the possibility of addiction is open to all people who choose to use addictive substances, even prescribed ones, or become involved in addictive behaviors.

Final Thoughts: Addiction Reimagined

Society will continue to grapple with the types of behaviors it considers addiction. While on the one hand, classifying behaviors or processes in a similar fashion as substance addiction might provide more research data, treatment options, preventative measures, and a lessening of stigma. On the other, classifying more and more behaviors as addictions detracts from the more serious conditions society has already defined as addictions. There is a risk in over-medicalizing behaviors that, while problematic, have little in common with addiction. For example, it has been proposed that gang activity is a "street addiction" (Bergen-Cico et al., 2014). One must wonder what psychotherapeutic modalities and possible psychopharmacological treatments that might be utilized to deal with street addiction. Or tanning addiction. Or entrepreneurship addiction. Defining non-clinical human behaviors as medical problems just adds more behaviors to an already crowded field. Throughout this work, the term behavioral addiction was used—this was done for consistency and to avoid confusion. At this point, it is appropriate to note the author's opinion that behavioral addictions have little in common with substance addictions and would do well to remain under the category of compulsions.

Despite the ambiguity of the addiction concept and its questionable status as a disease, substance addictions have a place in the medical model due to the various physiological consequences that result from it. Therefore, substance addiction's continued placement under the medical model is probably the best society has to offer currently. However, since there are cultural aspects that are often neglected or ignored outright in clinical explanations, it is recommended that culture play a larger role in the addictions field. Sociologists, social psychologists, cultural anthropologists, criminologists, and others should be involved in the diagnosis, treatment, and prevention efforts of persons addicted to substances. Social workers have filled this void in the past and still need to be involved, augmented by these other groups. These "sociotherapists" should be licensed to perform addictions treatment and included in clinical decision-making, prevention measures, on treatment teams, and on panels such as those that create the DSM. Graduate school curricula should include diagnosis, treatment, and prevention, and advocacy. It should also include coursework that includes understandings of addiction at the macro-level to encompass issues such as culture, risk, globalization, the drug trade, poverty, crime and criminal justice, racism, sexism, classism, ageism, sexual identity, and family systems analysis. It should include addiction coursework at the micro-level, which provides information on communities, community health, social service provision, local adult and juvenile justice systems, and volunteerism. It should also include coursework at the micro-level, including the effects of drugs on the body, the psychological effects of drug use and abuse, and information on labeling, stigma, addiction and families, and self-image. As noted earlier, it should be multidisciplinary. Licensure should follow along these lines rather than simply focusing on the clinical aspects of addiction. Too many clinicians are not taught to see the bigger picture, and that's not helpful to clients, communities, or society.

Living in a risk society, or a liquid modern society, people must deal with the many potential problems that occur as society evolves and changes. Cultural lag occurs when values and beliefs are delayed in the creation of new technology (which creates new risks). Imagining a world without risk, however, is futile. But what about alleviating some degree of risk? What about removing some of the risks that come with psychopharmacology companies unleashing a host of dangerous opioids into a public seeking relief from pain? Society has a role in the well-being of its citizens beyond leaving all matters of addiction to the field of psychiatry. As Alexander (1963) stated, "psychotherapy can only do so much. Its work must be complemented by society in that society must provide opportunities for an individual to fulfill essential needs" (p. 8).

Reimagining a society in which risk is addressed rather than provided with a band-aid intervention should be sought. In fact, reimagining a society that addresses poverty, homelessness, family problems, racism, sexism, classism, homophobia, the cost of education, climate change, and the various other social problems head-on can assist in preventing the conditions that affect, and are affected by, addiction. Concepts need to be better articulated. And the idea of making profits from addiction needs to be addressed; if you perform an Internet search of "addiction," your search will initially produce mounds of information about numerous private treatment programs—many of them very expensive. Access to addictions treatment should be made available to all as it is a cultural, as well as a personal issue. The societal approach to addiction must be reimagined. Zygmunt Bauman states, "*whatever* is made by humans can be remade by *humans* (2007, p. 56, italics in text). The addictions field should learn the lessons of history, be reflective, take a larger cultural view, be reimagined, and then be remade.

References

Adler, P. A., & Adler, P. (2011). *The tender cut: Inside the hidden world of self-injury.* New York and London: New York University Press.

Alexander, B. K. (2000). The globalization of addiction. *Addiction Research, 8*(6), 501-526.

Alexander, B. K. (2008). *The globalization of addiction: A study in poverty of the spirit.* Oxford, UK: Oxford University Press.

Alexander, B. K. (2012). Addiction: The urgent need for a paradigm shift. *Substance Use and Misuse, 47.* 1475-1482. DOI: 10.3109/10826084.2012.705681

Alexander, T. (1963). *Psychotherapy in our society.* New York: Prentice-Hall.

Alexander, M. (2012). *The new Jim Crow: Mass incarceration in the age of colorblindness* (Rev. ed.). New York: New Press.

American Psychiatric Association. (2013). *Diagnostic and statistical manual of mental disorders* (5th ed.). Arlington, VA: American Psychiatric Publishing.

American Psychiatric Association. (2013). Diagnostic and Statistical Manual of Mental Disorders (5th ed.). Arlington, VA: American Psychiatric Association.

American Society of Addiction Medicine. (n.d.) *Definition of addiction.* Retrieved from https://www.asam.org/quality-practice/definition-of-addiction.

Ames, G. M. (1985). American beliefs about alcoholism: Historical perspectives on the medical moral controversy. In L.A. Bennett, & G.M. Ames (Eds.), *The American experience with alcohol: Contrasting cultural perspectives.* (pp. 23-29). New York and London: Plenum Press.

Ancrum, C. (2014). Drug Dealing. In R. Atkinson (Ed.), *Shades of deviance: A primer on crime deviance, and social harm* (pp. 70-73). London & New York: Routledge.

Anderson, D. (1996). Hurrah for habits. *Human Psychopharmacology. 1*(11), S6-S8. DOI: 10.1002/(SICI)1099-1077(199602)11:1+<S3:AID-HUP746>3.0.CO;2-R

Anderson, R. E., & Carter, I. (1990). *Human behavior in the social environment: A social systems approach* (4th ed.). New York: Aldine de Gruyter.

Antze, P. (1987). Symbolic action in alcoholics anonymous. In M. Douglas (Ed.), *Constructive drinking: Perspectives on drink from anthropology.* (pp. 149-181). University of Cambridge Press.

Armstrong, E. G. (2007) Moral panic over meth. *Contemporary Justice Review, 10*(4), 427-442. DOI: 10.1080/10282580701677519

Arnold, E. P., Valentine, M., McInnis, M., & McNeese, A. (2000). Evaluating drug courts: An alternative to incarceration. In G.L. Mays, & P.R. Gregware (Eds.), *Courts and justice: A reader* (pp. 419-431). Prospect Heights, IL: Waveland Press.

Badley, K. (1996). *Worldviews: The challenge of choice.* Toronto: Irwin.

Bahr, H. M. (1973). *Skid row: An introduction to disaffiliation.* New York and Toronto: Oxford University Press.

Baldwin, J. M., Miller, B. L., Stogner, J., & Hach, S. (2012). The night the raving died: The social construction of a moral panic. *Deviant Behavior. 33*(9), 675-698. DOI: 10.1080/01639625.2011.636723

Barr, A. (1999). *Drink: A social history of America.* New York. Carrol & Graf.

Barringer, T. A., & Bruster, B. E. (2014). The juvenile justice system: An analysis of discretion and minority overrepresentation. In S.W. Bowman (Ed.), *Color Behind Bars: Racism in the U.S. Prison System.* (pp. 191-205). Santa Barbara, CA: Praeger.

Bauman, Z. (2007). *Liquid times: Living in an age of uncertainty.* Cambridge, UK: Polity Press.

Baumohl, J. (1992). Addiction and the American debate about homelessness. *British Journal of Addiction, 87*(1), 7-10. Retrieved from http://dx.doi.org.research.flagler.edu/10.1111/j.1360-0443.1992.tb01889.x

Beck, U. (1992). *Risk society: Towards a new modernity.* London, Thousand Oaks, New Delhi: Sage.

Becker, G. S., & Murphey, K. M. (1988). A theory of rational addiction. *Journal of Political Economy, 96*(4), 675-700. Retrieved from https://www-jstor-org.research.flagler.edu/stable/1830469

Becker, H. S. (1973). *Outsiders: Studies in the sociology of deviance* (New ed.). New York: Free Press.

Beecher, L. (2002). Six sermons on the nature, occasions, signs, evils and remedy of intemperance. (Original work published 1826). In D.F. Musto (Ed.), *Drugs in America: A Documentary History.* (pp. 44 86). New York and London: New York University Press.

Benfield, J. (2018). Sex addiction: The search for a secure base. *Healthcare Counseling & Psychotherapy, 18*(4). 14-17. Retrieved from http://content.eb scohost.com/ContentServer.asp?EbscoContent=dGJyMNXb4kSeprU4v%2 BvlOLCmr1Gep7NSsKu4SrOWxWXS&ContentCustomer=dGJyMPGusUuxp7 NNuePfgeyx43zx1%2B6B&T=P&P=AN&S=R&D=asn&K=1325 12778

Ben-Yehuda, N. (1990). *The politics and morality of deviance: Moral panics drug abuse, deviance science, and reversed stigmatization.* State University of New York Press.

Berczik, K., Szabo, A., Griffiths, M. D., Kurimay, T., Kun, B., Urban, R., & Demetrovics, Z. (2012). Exercise addiction: Symptoms, diagnosis, epidemiology, and etiology. *Substance Use and Misuse, 47*, 403-417. Received from http://eds.a.ebscohost.com.research.flagler.edu/eds/pdfviewer/pdfviewer? vid=1&sid=e4b95433-7c76-4ac9-b990-7f71386df196%40sessionmgr4006

Bergen-Cico, D. K., Haygood-El, A., Jennings-Bey, T. N., & Lane, S. D. (2014). Street addiction: proposed theoretical model for understanding the draw of street life and gang activity. *Addiction research and theory, 22*(1), 15-26. DOI: 10.3109/16066359.2012.759942

Berger, L. S. (1991). *Substance abuse as symptom: A psychoanalytic critique of treatment approaches and the cultural beliefs that sustain them.* Hillsdale, NJ: The Analytic Press.

Berger, P. L., & Luckmann, T. (1966). *The social construction of reality: A treatise in the sociology of knowledge.* New York: Anchor Books.

Bernhard, B. J., & Preston, F. W. (2007). Introduction: Sociologies of Problem Gambling. *American Behavioral Scientist, 51*(1), 3-7. DOI: 10.1177/0002764207305502

Bertalanffy, L. (1968) *General system theory: Foundations, developments, applications.* New York: George Braziller.

Best, J. (2004). *Deviance: Career of a concept.* Belmont, CA: Thomson Wadsworth.

Birchard, T. (2011). Sexual addiction and the paraphilias. *Sexual addiction and compulsivity, 18,* 157-187. DOI: 10.1080/10720162.2011.606674

Black, C. (1984). *Process of recovery: Al-anon and the adult child.* In Al-Alon Faces Alcoholism (2nd ed). New York: Al-Anon Family Group Headquarters.

Bloch, H. A. (1951). The Sociology of Gambling. *American Journal of Sociology, 57*(3), 215- 221. Retrieved from https://www-jstor.org.research.flagler.edu /stable/pdf/2771641.pdf?refreqid=excelsior%3A33ac69c3dc7a929a90ed8120 f364a5bc

Booth, M. (1996). *Opium: A history.* New York: St. Martin's Press.

Boskind-White, M., & White, W. C. (2000). *Bulimia/anorexia: The binge/purge cycle and self-starvation* (3rd ed). New York and London: W.W. Norton and Co.

Bourdieu, P., & Wacquant, L. J. D. (1992). *An invitation to reflexive sociology.* University of Chicago Press.

Brinkley-Rubenstein, L. (2014). Historical perspectives on race and the war on drugs and the prolonged effects of racially based laws and policies. In S.W. Bowman (Ed.), *Color Behind Bars: Racism in the U.S. Prison System.* (pp. 171-190). Santa Barbara, CA: Praeger.

Brown, N. W. (2013). *Creative activities for group therapy.* New York and London: Routledge.

Brown, S. L. (2017). *Families in America.* Oakland: University of California Press.

Brumberg, J. J. (1984). Is running an analogue of anorexia nervosa? An empirical study of obligatory running and anorexia nervosa. *Journal of the American Medical Association, 252*(4), 520-523. DOI: 10.1002/1098-108X(198711)6:6<771::AID-EAT2260060612>3.0.CO;2-V

Brumberg, J. J. (2000). *Fasting girls: The history of anorexia nervosa.* New York: Vintage Books.

Buchman, D. Z., Leech, P., & Orkin, A. (2017). The epidemic as stigma: The bioethics of opioids. *Journal of Law, Medicine, and Ethics, 45*(4), 607-620. DOI: 10.1177/1073110517750600

Bureau of Justice Statistics. (n.d.a). *Drugs and Crime.* Retrieved from https://www.bjs.gov/index.cfm?ty=tp&tid=35

Bureau of Justice Statistics. (n.d.b). *Law Enforcement.* Retrieved from https://www.bjs.gov/index.cfm?ty=tp&tid=7#summary

Burroughs, W. S. (2003). *Junky: The definitive text of 'junk'.* O. Harris (Ed.). New York: Grove Press. (original work published 1953).

Burroughs, W. S. (2001). *Naked Lunch.* New York: Grove Press.

Buser, T. J., & Buser, J. (2013). Conceptualizing nonsuicidal self-injury as a process addiction: Review of research and implications for counselor training and practice. *Journal of Addictions and Offender Counseling, 34*, 16-29. DOI: 10.1002/j.2161-1874.2013.00011.x

Carnes, P. (2001). *Out of the shadows.* Center City, MI: Hazelden.

Castellani, B. (2000). *Pathological gambling: The making of a medical problem.* Albany: State University of New York Press.

Castro, D., & Fritchle, M. (2013). Working with the queer community: Advocacy as a therapeutic intervention. In D. Maller, K. Langsam, & M. L. Fritchle (Eds.), *The Praeger Handbook of Community Mental Health Practice* (pp. 67-83). Santa Barbara, CA: Praeger.

Cavanaugh, C. (1998). *AA to z: Addictionary of the 12-step culture.* New York: Main Street.

Center on Addiction. (2017). *Definition of addiction.* Retrieved from https://www.centeronaddiction.org/what-addiction/addiction-disease

Center on Addiction. (2018). *Addiction as a disease.* Retrieved from https://www.centeronaddiction.org/addiction

Centers for Disease Control and Prevention. (2019). *CDC'S response to the opioid epidemic: A public health crisis.* Retrieved from https://www.cdc.gov/opioids/strategy.html.

Chapman, A. L. (2006). Dialectic Behavior Therapy. *Psychiatry, 3*(9), 62-68. Retrieved from https://www.ncbi.nlm.nih.gov/pmc/articles/PMC2963469/

Cherlin, K. (1985). *The hungry self: Women, eating, and identity.* New York: Times Books.

Clegg, J. W. (2012). Teaching about mental health and illness through the history of the DSM. *History of Psychology, 15*(4), 364-370. DOI: 10.1037/a0027249

Clinard, M. (1957). *The sociology of deviance.* New York: Rinehart.

Cohen, S. (2002). *Folk devils and moral panic.* (3rd ed). London and New York: Routledge.

Collins, R. (2014). *Interaction ritual chains.* Princeton, NJ: Princeton University Press.

Conrad, R. (2000). Medicalization and social control. In P. Brown (Ed.), *Perspectives in Medical Sociology* (3rd ed). (pp. 114-129). Prospect Heights, IL: Waveland Press.

Cornwell, B., & Linders, A. (2002). The myth of "moral panic": an alternative account of LSD prohibition. *Deviant Behavior: An Interdisciplinary Journal, 23*. 307-330. DOI: 10.1080/01639620290086404

Coser, R. L. (1964). Introduction. In R. L. Coser (Ed.), *The family: Its structure and functions.* (pp. xiii-xxviii). New York: St. Martin's Press.

Coser, L. (1981). "The Uses of Classical Sociological Theory" In B. Rhea (Ed.), *The Future of the Sociological Classics.* London: George Allen and Unwin.

Cosgrave, J. F. (2006). Editor's introduction: Gambling, risk, and late capitalism. In J. F. Cosgrave (Ed.), *The Sociology of Risk and Gambling Reader.* (pp. 1-24). New York & London: Routledge.

Costandi, M. (2014). A brief history of psychedelic psychiatry. *Psychologist, 29*(9), 714-715. Retrieved from http://content.ebscohost.com/ContentServ er.asp?EbscoContent=dGJyMNXb4kSeqa84yOvqOLCmr1GeprVSsK64SrOWx

WXS&ContentCustomer=dGJyMPGusUuxp7NNuePfgeyx43zx1%2B6B&T=P
&P=AN&S=L&D=asn&K=97722222

Courtwright, D. T. (2001). *Forces of habit: Drugs and the making of the modern world.* Cambridge, MA, and London: Harvard University Press.

Cramblett, H. G. (1953). The uses of and poisoning by the barbiturates. *Journal of Law, Criminology and Police Science, 43*(3), 390-395. DOI: 10.2307/1139181

Csete, J. (2019). Criminal justice barriers to treatment of opioid use disorders in the United States: The need for public health advocacy. *Public Health Law, 109*(3), 419-422.

Csikszentmihalyi, M. (1975). Play and Intrinsic Rewards. *Journal of Humanistic Psychology, 15,* 41-63.

Csikszentmihalyi, M. (2000). *Beyond Boredom and Anxiety: Experiencing Flow in Work and Play.* San Francisco: Jossey-Bass. (Original work published 1975).

Curra, J. (2014). *The relativity of deviance* (3ʳᵈ ed). Los Angeles: Sage.

Davis, D. M., & Hayes, J. A. (2011). What are the benefits of mindfulness? A practice review of psychotherapy-related research. *Psychotherapy, 48*(2), 198-208. DOI: 10.1037/a0022062

De Quincey, T. (2009). *Confessions of an opium-eater Being an extract from the life of a scholar.* The Floating Press. Original work published 1822. Retrieved from http://eds.a.ebscohost.com.research.flagler.edu/eds/ebookviewer/ebook/bmxlYmtfXzM Mzg0M19fQU41?sid=278cc62f-3fa3-4c2a-a194 936e832f58d5@sessionmgr4008&vid=0&format=EB&rid=1

Denham, B. E. (2008). Folk devils, news icons, and the construction of moral panics. *Journalism Studies, 9*(6), 945-961. DOI: 10.1080/14616700802227811

Dies, R. R. (2003). Group psychotherapies. In A. Carr, & M. McNulty (Eds.), *The handbook of adult clinical psychology: An evidence-based practice approach.* London and New York: Routledge.

Dobkin de Rios, M (1984). *Hallucinogens: Cross-cultural perspectives.* University of New Mexico Press.

Dombrink, J. (1996). Gambling and the legalization of vice. In J. McMillan (Ed.), *Gambling cultures: Studies in history and interpretation.* (pp. 43-64). Routledge: London and New York.

Douglass, F. T., Taylor, Y., & Foner, P. S. (1999). *Frederick Douglass: Selected Speeches and Writings.* Chicago: Lawrence Hill Books.

Doyal, L. (1995). *What makes women sick: Gender and the political economy of health.* New Brunswick, NJ: Rutgers University Press.

Dualdiagnosis.com. (2018). *Acceptance and Commitment Therapy.* Retrieved from https://www.dualdiagnosis.org/treatment-therapies-for-dual-diagnosis-patients/acceptance-commitment-therapy/

Durkheim, E. (1951). *Suicide: A study in sociology.* (Trans. and Ed. by J. A. Spaulding and G. Simpson). New York: Free Press. (Original work published 1897).

Durkheim, E. (1965). *The elementary forms of religious life.* New York: Free Press. (Original work published 1912).

Dyer, N. O. (2003/2004). Durkheim, Mead and heroin addiction. *Human Ar-chitecture: Journal of the Sociology of Self-Knowledge, 2*(2), 99-104. Retrieved from http://eds.b.ebscohost.com.research.flagler.edu/eds/pdfviewer/pdfviewer?vid=1&sid=0837da20-5e55-4b79-8ad6-366adc0bcb80%40pdc-v-sessmgr02

Ehmer, K., & Hindermann, B. (2015). *The school of sophisticated drinking: An intoxicating history of the seven spirits.* Vancouver and Berkeley, CA: Grey-stone Books.

Elkin, M. (1984). *Families under the influence: Changing alcoholic* patterns. New York & London: W.W. Norton & Co.

Elster, J. (2003). Gambling and addiction. In A. Alexander, & M.S. Roberts (Eds.), *High culture: Reflections on addiction and modernity.* (pp. 309-337) New York: SUNY Press.

Erickson, K. (1966). *Wayward puritans: A study in the sociology of deviance.* New York: Wiley.

Esteicher, S. K. (2006). *Wine: From Neolithic times to the 21st century.* New York: Algora Publishing.

Eversman, M. H. (2016). Feeding of fear: Edible marijuana and disproportion-ality in U.S. media. *Drugs: Education, Prevention and Policy, 23*(6). 462-470. DOI: 10.1080/14616700802227811

Fatayer, J. (2008). Addiction types: A clinical sociology perspective. *Journal of Applied Social Sciences, 2*(1), 88-93. Retrieved January 21, 2018 http://research.flagler.edu:9101/openurlsid=EBSCO%3asih&genre=article&issn=19367244&ISBN=&volume=2&issue=&date=20080401&spage=88&pages=883&title=Journal+of+Applied+Social+Sciences+(19367244)&atitle=Addiction+Types%3a+A+Clinical+Sociology+Perspective.&aulast=Fatayer%2c+Jawad&id=doi%3a&site=ftf-live

Federal Drug Administration. (2019). *2018 NYTS Data: A startling rise in Youth E-Cigarette Use.* Retrieved from https://www.fda.gov/tobacco-products/youth-and-tobacco/2018-nyts-data-startling-rise-youth-e-cigarette-use

Finestone, H. (1964). Cats, kicks, and color. In H.S. Becker (Ed.), *The other side: Perspectives on deviance.* (pp. 281-297). New York: Free Press.

Finlay, S. W. (2000). Influence of Carl Jung and William James on the origin of Alcoholics Anonymous. *Review of General Psychology, 4*(1), 3-12. DOI: 10.1037//1089-2680.4.1.3

Flanagan, M. W., & Briggs, H. E. (2016). Substance abuse recovery among homeless adults in Atlanta, Georgia, and a multi-level drug abuse resiliency tool. *Best Practices in Mental Health, 12*(1). 89-109. Retrieved from http://eds.a.ebscohost.com.research.flagler.edu/eds/pdfviewer/pdfviewer?vid=1&sid=c79e30f6-151a-41f6-9961-dae5efa7e647%40sdc-v-sessmgr03

Flinders, M., & Wood, M. (2015). From folk devils to folk heroes: Rethinking the theory of moral panics. *Deviant Behavior, 23*, 307-330. DOI: 10.1080/01639625.2014.951579

Forbes, D. (1994). *False fixes: The cultural politics of drugs, alcohol, and addic-tive relations.* New York: State University of New York Press.

Foucault, M. (1960). *Madness and civilization: A history of insanity in the age of reason.* New York: Vintage.

Foucault, M. (1963). *Birth of the clinic: An archaeology of medical perception.* New York: Vintage.

Fraser, S., Moore, D., & Keane, H. (2014). *Habits: Remaking Addiction.* Basingstoke, UK: Palgrave Macmillan.

Freimuth, M. (2008). *Addicted? Recognizing destructive behavior before it's too late.* Lanham, MA: Rowman and Littlefield.

Freud, S. (1914). *Remembering, Repeating, and Working Through.* Retrieved from http://marcuse.faculty.history.ucsb.edu/classes/201/articles/1914FreudRemembering.pdf

Fromm, E. (1990). *The Sane Society.* New York: Henry Holt and Co. (Original work published 1955).

Gambler's Anonymous. (n.d.) *About us.* Retrieved from http://www.gamblersanonymous.org/ga/content/history

Germer, C. K. (2013). Mindfulness: What is it? What does it matter? In C. Germer, R. D. Siegel, & P. R. Fulton, (Eds.), *Mindfulness and psychotherapy* (2nd ed.) (pp. 3-29). New York & London: The Guilford Press.

Giffin, P. J. (1966). The revolving door: A functional interpretation. *Canadian Review of Sociology and Anthropology, 3*(3), 154-167. Retrieved from http://eds.a.ebscohost.com.research.flagler.edu/eds/pdfviewer/pdfviewer?vid=1&sid=b3430e10-97bd-47c1-ac01-8bf679b6ff17%40sdc-v-sessmgr03

Giorgi, L. (2012). Lifestyle risk: The challenging marriage of two thorny subjects. *European Journal of Risk Regulation, 3*(1), 97-103. DOI: 10.1017/S1867299X00001872

Glasser, W. (1976). *Positive Addiction.* New York, Evanston, IN, San Francisco, & London: Harper & Row.

Goffman, E. (1961). *Asylums: Essays on the social situation of mental patients and other inmates.* New York: Anchor Books.

Goffman, E. (1963). *Stigma: Notes on the management of a spoiled identity.* Englewood Cliffs, NJ: Prentice-Hall.

Goffman, E. (1967). *Interaction ritual: Essays on face-to-face behavior.* New York: Pantheon Books.

Goode, E. (2008). Moral panics and disproportionality: The case of LSD use in the sixties. *Deviant Behavior, 29*, 533-543. DOI: 10.1080/01639620701839377

Goode, E., & Ben-Yehuda, N. (1994). Moral panics: Culture, politics, and social construction. *Annual Review of Sociology, 20*, 149-171. DOI: 10.1146/annurev.so.20.080194.001053

Goodman, L. A., Liang, B., Helms, J. E., Latta, R. E., Sparks, E., & Weintraub, S. R. (2004). Training Counseling Psychologists as Social Justice Agents: Feminist and Multicultural Principles in Action. *The Counseling Psychologist, 32*(6), 793-837. DOI: 10.1177/0011000004268802

Gottfredson, M., & Hirschi, T. (1990). *A general theory of crime.* Stanford University Press.

Griffiths, M. (2011). Workaholism—a 21st century addiction. *Psychologist, 24*(10), 740-744. Retrieved from http://content.ebscohost.com/ContentServer.asp?EbscoContent=dGJyMNHX8kSep7Y4yNfsOLCmsEieprZSrqy4TLKWxWXS&ContentCustomer=dGJyMPGusUuxp7NNuePfgeyx43zx1%2B6B&T=P&P=AN&S=L&D=asn&K=66609111

Grob, G. N. (1991). Origins of DSM-1: A study in appearance and reality. *American Journal of Psychiatry. 148*(4). 421-431.

Grove, V. E. (1979). Painless self-injury after ingestion of 'angel dust'. *Journal of the American Medical Association, 242*(7), 655. DOI: 10.1001/jama.1979.03300070051023

Gusfield, J. R. (1986). *Symbolic crusade: Status politics and the American temperance movement.* Urbana: University of Illinois Press.

Haaken, J. (1993). From Al-anon to ACOA: Codependence and the reconstruction of caregiving. *Signs, 18*(2), 321-345. Retrieved from https://www-jstor-org.research.flagler.edu/stable/3174978

Hamachek, D. E. (1978). *Encounters with the self* (2nd ed.). New York: Holt, Rinehart, and Winston.

Harris, O. (2003). Introduction. *Junky: The definitive text of junk.* New York: Grove Press.

Hartogsohn, I. (2017). Constructing drug effects: A history of set and setting. *Drug Science, Policy, and Law.* Retrieved from https://journals.sagepub.com/doi/full/10.1177/2050324516683325#articleCitationDownloadContainer.

Henderson, E. C. (2000). *Understanding addiction.* Jackson: University of Mississippi Press.

Henderson, R., & Pochin, M. (2001). *A right result? Advocacy, justice, and empowerment.* Bristol: Policy Press.

Herman, J. (2015). *Trauma and recovery: The violence of violence—from domestic abuse to political terror.* New York: Basic Books.

Herring, S. (2014). *The hoarders: Material deviance in modern American culture.* Chicago & London: University of Chicago Press.

Hickman, T. A. (2007). *The secret leprosy of modern days: Narcotic addiction and cultural crisis in the United States, 1870-1920.* Amherst: University of Massachusetts Press.

Hier, S. P. (2002). Raves, risks, and the ecstasy panic: A case study in the subversive nature of moral regulation. *The Canadian Journal of Sociology, 27*(1), 33-57. DOI: 10.2307/3341411

Higgins, S. T., & Petry, N. M. (1999). Contingency management: Incentives for sobriety. *Alcohol Research and Health. 23*(2). Retrieved from https://pubs.niaaa.nih.gov/publications/arh23-2/122-127.pdf

Hillman, D. C. A. (2008). *The Chemical Muse: Drug Use and Roots of Western Civilization.* New York: Thomas Dunne Books.

Himmelstein, J. L. (1983). *The Strange career of marihuana: Politics and ideology of drug control in America.* Westport, CN, and London: Greenwood Press.

Hirschi, T. (1969). *Causes of delinquency.* Berkeley: University of California Press.

Hirschi, T., & Gottfredson, M. (2001). Self-control theory. In R. Paternoster, & R. Bachman (Eds.), *Explaining criminals and crime.* (pp. 81-96). Los Angeles: Roxbury.

Holstein, J. A. (2009). Defining deviance: John Kituse's modest agenda. *American Sociologist, 40,* 51-60. DOI: https://doi.org/10.1007/s12108-008-9058-6

Horwitz, A.V. (2013). *Anxiety: A short history.* Baltimore: Johns Hopkins University Press.

Irvine, J. (1995). Reinventing perversion: Sex addiction and cultural anxieties. *Journal of the History of Sexuality, 5*(3), 429-450. Retrieved from http://www.jstor.org/stable/4617181

James, W. (1985). *The varieties of religious experience: A study in human nature.* Garden City, NY: Masterworks Program. (Original work published 1902).

Janet, P. (1925). *Psychological healing: A historical and clinical study.* (Trans. by E. Paul & C. Paul) (pp. 661-663). New York: MacMillan.

Jellinek, E. M. (2010). *The disease concept of alcoholism.* Mansfield, CN: Martino Publishing. (Original work published 1960).

Jenkins, P. (1994). The ice age: The social construction of a drug panic. *Justice Quarterly, 11*(1), 7-31. Retrieved from https://doi.org/10.1080/07418829400092111

Jenkins. P. (1998). *Moral panic: Changing concepts of the child molester in modern America.* New Haven & London: Yale University Press.

Johns Hopkins University Bloomberg School of Public Health. (2018). *Policing and the opioid crisis: Standards of care.* Retrieved from https://americanhealth.jhu.edu/article/policing-and-opioid-crisis-standards-care

Jones, M. B., Viswanath, O., Peck, J., Kaye, A. D., Gill, J. S., & Simopoulos, T. T. (2018). A brief history of the opioid epidemic and strategies for pain medicine. *Pain & Therapy, 7,* 13-21. DOI: 10.1007/s40122-018-0097-6

Jourard, S. M. (1971). *The transparent self* (Rev. ed). New York: D. Van Nostrand Co.

Kaminer, W. (1993). *I'm dysfunctional, you're dysfunctional: The recovery movement and other self-help fashions.* New York: Vintage Books.

Kantor, D., & Lehr, W. (1975) *Inside the family: Toward a theory of family process.* San Francisco: Jossey-Bass.

Karim, R., & Chaudhri, P. (2012). Behavioral addictions: An overview. *Journal of Psychoactive Drugs, 44*(1), 5-17. DOI: 10.1080/02791072.2012.662859

Katherine, A. (1996). *Anatomy of a food addiction: The brain chemistry of overeating* (3rd ed.). Carlsbad, CA: Gurve Books.

Kelly, B. (2007). Club drug use and risk management among 'bridge and tunnel' youth. *Journal of Drug Issues, 37*(2), 425-444. Retrieved from http://dx.doi.org.research.flagler.edu/10.1177/002204260703700210

Kelly, K., & Empson, G. (1999). Advocating for women in the criminal justice and addiction treatment systems. In J. Lewis, & L. Bradley (Eds.), *Advocacy in Counseling, Counselors, Clients, and Community.* Retrieved from https://eric-ed-gov.research.flagler.edu/?id=ED435916

Keys, D. P., & Galliher, J. F. (2000). *Confronting the drug control establishment: Alfred Lindesmith as a public intellectual.* State University of New York.

Kline, P. (1984). *Psychology and Freudian theory: An introduction.* London and New York: Methuen.

Koop, P. (2008). The symbolic power of "healthy lifestyles". *Health Sociology Review, 17,* 18-26. DOI: 10.5172/hesr.451.17.1.18

Kourosh, A. S., Harrington, C. R., & Adinoff, B. A. (2012). Tanning as a behavioral addiction. *The American Journal of Drug and Alcohol Abuse. 36.* 284-290. DOI: 10.3109/00952990.2010.491883

Krafft-Ebing, R. V. (1997) *Psychopathia Sexualis.* London: Velvet Publications. (Original work published 1886).

Kubey, R., & Csikszentmihalyi, M. (2004). Television addiction. *Scientific American Mind, 14*(1), 48-55. Retrieved from https://www.jstor.org/stable/10.2307/24939365?seq=1&cid=pdfreference#references_tab_contents

Kuhn, C., Swartzenwelder, S., & Wilson, W. (2008). *Buzzed: The straight facts about the most used and abused drugs from alcohol to ecstasy* (3rd ed.). New York & London: W.W. Norton and Company.

Lab, S. P., Williams, M. R., Holcolm, J. E., Burek, M. W., King, W. R., & Buerger, M. E. (2016), *Criminal justice: The essentials* (4th ed.). New York & Oxford: Oxford University Press.

LaBruzza, A. L. (1997). *Using DSM-IV: A Clinician's Guide to Psychiatric Diagnosis.* Northvale, NJ and London: Jason Aronson Inc.

Laing, R. D. (1971). *The politics of the family and other essays.* New York: Pantheon Books.

Lembke, A. (2018). Why addiction should be considered a disease. *Judge's Journal, 57*(1), 4-8. Retrieved from http://research.flagler.edu:9839/eds/detail/detail?vid=0&sid=a7ff6d92- 127e-4658-98c93eb9723249a%40sessionmgr4006&bdata=JnNpdGU9ZWRzLWxpdmUmc2NvcGU9c2l0ZQ%3d%3d#AN=127674546&db=lgs.

Lender, M. E., & Martin, J. K. (1987). *Drinking in America: A History,* (Rev. and expanded ed). New York: The Free Press.

Lesch, O. M., Kefer, J., Lenter, S., Mader, R., Marx, B., Musalek, M., … Zach, E. (1990). Diagnosis of Chronic Alcoholism - Classificatory Problems. *Psychopathology, 23*(2), 88-96. DOI: 10.1159/000284644

Levine, H. G. (1978). The discovery of addiction: Changing conceptions of habitual drunkenness in America. *Journal of Studies on Alcohol. 15.* 493-506. Retrieved from https://qcpages.qc.cuny.edu/~hlevine/The-Discovery-of-Addiction.pdf

Levine, J. (1995). Reinventing perversion: Sex addiction and cultural anxieties. *Journal of the History of Sexuality, 5*(3), 429-450. Retrieved from https://www.jstor.org/stable/4617181

Lindesmith, A. (1938). A sociological theory of drug addiction. *American Journal of Sociology, 43*(4), 593-613. Retrieved from http://www.jstor.org/stable/2768486.

Lindesmith, A. (1963). Torture by Law. In Dan Wakefield (Ed.), *The addict and us.* (pp. 33-40). New York: Fawcett World Library.

Little, J., Franskoviak, P., Plummer, J., Lavender, J., & Berg, A. (2013). Come as you are: Harm reduction therapy in community drop-in centers In D. Maller, K. Langsam, & M. J. Fritchle (Eds.), *The Praeger Handbook of Community Mental Health Practice.* (pp. 45-61). Santa Barbara: Praeger.

Lo, H., & Harvey, N. (2014). Compulsive buying: Obsessive acquisition, collecting, or hoarding? *International Journal of Mental Health & Addiction, 12*, 453-469. DOI: 10.1007/s11469-014-9477-2

Loscalzo, Y., & Giannini, M. (2018). Problematic overstudying: Studyholism or study addiction? *Journal of Behavioral Addiction, 7*(4), 867-870. DOI: 10.1556/2006.7.2018.124

Lovald, K., & Stubb, H. R. (1968). The revolving door: Reactions of chronic drunkenness offenders to court sanctions. *The Journal of Criminal Law, Criminology and Police Science. 59*(4), 525-530. DOI: 10.2307/1141833

Maahs, J., & Travis, T. C. (2017). "I hate these little turds": Science, entertainment, and the enduring popularity of scared straight programs". *Deviant Behavior, 38*(1), 47-60. DOI: 10.1080/01639625.2016.1190619

MacMaster, S. A. (2004). Harm reduction: A new perspective on substance abuse services. *Social Work, 49*(3), 356-363. Retrieved from http://doctor deluca.com/Library/AbstinenceHR/HarmReductionNewPerspective04.pdf

Malik, M. L., & Beutler, L. E. (2002). The emergence of dissatisfaction with the DSM. In M.L. Malik, & L.E. Beutler, (Eds.), *Rethinking the DSM: A Psychological Perspective* (pp. 3-15). Washington, DC: American Psychiatric Association.

Marlatt, G. A., & Witkiewitz., K. (2009). *Addictive behaviors: New readings on etiology, prevention, and treatment.* Washington, DC: American Psychological Association.

Maroukis, C. (2013). The peyote controversy and the demise of the Society of American Indians. *American Indian Quarterly, 37*(3), 158-180. Retrieved from https://www.jstor.org/stable/10.5250/studamerindilite.25.2.0161

Marshall-Lee, E. D., Hinger, C., Popovic, R., Miller Roberts, T. C., & Prempeh, L. (2019). Social Justice Advocacy in Mental Health Services: Consumer, Community, Training, and Policy Perspectives. *Psychological Services.* Advance online publication. http://dx.doi.org/10.1037/ser0000349

Martinson, R. (1974). What works? Questions and answers about prison reform. *The Public Interest, 3*, 22-54.

Matusow, H., & Rosenblum, A. (2013). Psychoanalytic theories of addiction: Can the talking cure tell us anything about substance use and misuse? *Substance Use and Misuse, 48*, 239-247. DOI: 10.3109/10826084.2012.753548

McClellan, M. (2004). "Lady Tipplers": Gendering the modern alcoholism paradigm, 1933-1960. In S.W. Tracy, & C.J. Aker, (Eds.), *Altering American consciousness: The history of drug use in the United States, 1800-2000.* (pp. 267-297). Amherst and Boston: University of Massachusetts Press.

McGovern, P. E. (2009*). Uncorking the past: The quest for wine, beer, and other alcoholic beverages.* Berkeley: University of California Press.

McMillen, J. (1996). Understanding gambling. In J. McMillen (Ed.), *Gambling cultures: Studies in history and interpretation.* Routledge: London and New York.

Merriam-Webster Online. (2018). *Habit.* https://www.merriam-webster.com/dictionary/habit.

Merton, R. K. (1938). Social structure and anomie. *American Sociological Review, 3*(5), 672-682. Retrieved from http://links.jstor.org/sici?sici=0003-1224%28193810%293%3A5%3C672%3ASSAA%3E2.0.CO%3B2-8

Miller, D. (2014). A downside to the entrepreneurial personality? *Entrepreneur-ship: Theory and Practice, 39*(1), 1-8. DOI: 10.1111/etap.12130

Miller, T., & Leger, M. C. (2003). A very childish moral panic: Ritalin. *Journal of Medical Humanities, 24*(1/2), 9-33. DOI: 10.1023/A:1021301614509

Miller, T. (2006). A risk society of moral panic. *Cultural Politics, 2*(3), 299-318. DOI: 10.2752/174321906778531682.

Miller, W. R., & Rollnick, S. (1991) *Motivational interviewing: Preparing people to change addictive behavior.* New York: Gilford Press.

Mills, C. W. (1959). *The sociological imagination.* New York: Oxford University Press.

Mitenbuler, R. (2015). *Bourbon empire: The past and present future of America's whiskey.* New York: Penguin.

Muller, T. (2014). Chicago, jazz, and marijuana: Howard Becker on Outsiders. *Symbolic Interaction, 37*(4), 576-594. Retrieved from https://www-jstor-org.research.flagler.edu/stable/symbinte.37.4.576

Musto, D. F. (1973). *The American disease: Origins of narcotic control.* New Haven, CT & London: Yale University Press.

Musto, D. F. (2002). Introduction. In D.F. Musto (Ed.), *Drugs in America: A Documentary History.* (pp. 3-13). New York and London: New York University Press.

Myers, P.L., & Salt, N.R. (2007). *Becoming an addictions counselor: A compre-hensive text* (2nd ed.). Sudbury, MA: Jones & Bartlett Publishers.

Mythen, G. (2004). *Understanding the risk society: Crime, security, and justice.* UK: Palgrave McMillan.

Napier, A. Y., & Whitaker, C. (1978). *The family crucible: The intense experience of family therapy.* New York: Harper & Row.

National Center for Biotechnical Information. (2005). *Substance abuse treat-ment for persons with co-occurring disorders.* Appendix C. Glossary of terms: Substance abuse. Retrieved from https://www.ncbi.nlm.nih.gov/books/NBK64200/

National Institute on Drug Abuse. (2014). *Principles of drug abuse treatment for criminal justice populations-A research-based guide. Is legally mandated treatment effective?* Retrieved from https://www.drugabuse.gov/publica tions/principles-drug-abuse-treatment-criminal-justice-populations/legal ly-mandated-treatment-effective

National Institute on Drug Abuse. (2018a). *Opioid Overdose Crisis.* Retrieved from https://www.drugabuse.gov/drugs-abuse/opioids/opioid-overdose-crisis

National Institute on Drug Abuse. (2018b). The Science of Drug Abuse and Addiction: The Basics. Retrieved from https://www.drugabuse.gov/publica tions/media-guide/science-drug-use-addiction-basics

National Institute on Drug Abuse. (2019). *Prescription Opioids.* Retrieved from https://www.drugabuse.gov/publications/drugfacts/prescription-opioids

National Institute of Justice. (2018). *Drug Courts.* Retrieved from https://www.nij.gov/topics/courts/drug-courts/Pages/welcome.aspx

National Institute of Mental Health (n.d.) *The science of drug abuse actions and addiction: The basics.* Retrieved from https://www.drugabuse.gov/publications/media-guide/science_drug-abuse-addiction-basics.

Newbigging, K., Ridley, J., McKeown, M., Sadd, J., Machin, K., Cruse, K., ... Poursanidou, K. (2015). *Independent mental health advocacy: The right to be heard.* London and Philadelphia: Jessica Kingsley Publishers.

Nichols, M. P., & Swartz, R. C. (2016). *Family therapy: Concepts and methods* (5th ed.). Boston: Allyn & Bacon.

Oates, W. (1971). *Confessions of a workaholic: The facts about work addiction.* New York: World Publishing Co.

Ogburn, W. F. (1966). *Social change: With respect to cultural and original nature.* New York: Dell Publishing.

Olson, P. (1970). *The study of modern society: Perspectives from classic sociology.* New York: Random House.

Orford, J. (1985). *Excessive appetites: A psychological review of addiction.* UK and New York: John Wiley & Sons.

Osco, B. (2003/2004). Anomie or alienation?: A self-exploration of the roots of substance ab/use. *Human Architecture: Journal of the Sociology of Self-Knowledge, 2*(2), 105-108. Retrieved from http://eds.a.ebscohost.com.research.flagler.edu/eds/pdfviewer/pdfviewer?vid=1&sid=83c5b945-1a37-468f-8764-fe2984c888be%40sessionmgr4007

Peele, S. (1985). *The meaning of addiction: Compulsive experience and its interpretation.* Lexington, MA: Lexington Books.

Peele, S. (1995). *Diseasing of America: How we allowed recovery zealots and the treatment industry to convince we are out of control.* San Francisco, CA: Jossey-Bass Publishers.

Peele, S., and Brodsky, A. (2015). *Love and addiction.* Watertown, MA: Broadrow.

Phillips, D. C. (1970). Organicism in the late nineteenth and early twentieth centuries. *Journal of the History of Ideas, 31*(3), 413-432.

Pratt, A. M. (1969). *The child savers: The invention of delinquency.* Chicago & London: University of Chicago Press.

Price, C. (2018). *How to break up with your phone.* CA & NY: Ten Speed Press.

Prochaska, J. O., & DiClemente, C. C. (1982). Transtheoretical therapy: Towards a more integrative model of change. *Psychotherapy, theory, research, and practice 19,* 276-288. *Psychiatry, 148*(4), 421-431. Received from https://pdfs.semanticscholar.org/cffa/a1c2198954646deeca25646720b24a435cd6.pdf Publishing.

Quinney, R. (1974). *Critique of legal order: Crime control in capitalist society.* Boston: Little, Brown & Co.

Rantala, V., & Sulkunen, P. (2012). Is pathological gambling just a big problem or also an addiction? *Addiction Research and Theory, 20*(1), 1-10. DOI: 10.3109/16066359.2011.552819

Rapaport, A. (1968). Systems analysis: General systems theory, In *International Encyclopedia of the Social Sciences.* (p. 454). New York: Macmillan and Free Press.

Rasmussen, N. (2017). Controlling 'America's opium': Barbiturate abuse, pharmaceutical regulation, and the politics of public health in the early postwar United States. *The Journal of Policy History, 29.* 543-568. DOI:10.1017/S0898030617000264

Redfield, M., & Brodie, J. F. (2002). "Introduction". In J. F. Brodie, & M. Redfield, (Eds.), *High anxieties: Cultural studies in addiction.* Berkeley, Los Angeles, and London: University of California Press.

Reiss, S., Leviton, G. W., & Szyskzo, J. (1982). Emotional disturbance and mental retardation: Diagnostic overshadowing. *American Journal of Mental Deficiency, 86*(6), 567-574.

Reith, G. (1999). *The age of chance: Gambling in Western cultures.* London: Routledge.

Riemersma, J., & Sytsma, M. (2013). A new generation of sexual addiction. *Sexual Addiction & Compulsivity, 20,* 306-322. DOI: 10.1080/10720162.2013.843067

Rodgers, T. (2014), Video-gaming. In R. Atkinson (Ed.), *Shades of deviance: A primer of crime, deviance, and social harm.* (pp. 87-90). London & New York: Routledge.

Roizen, R. (2012). Ron Roizen on Bruce Alexander's "Addiction: The urgent needs for a paradigm shift": A measurement nightmare. *Substance Use and Misuse 47,* 1485-1489. DOI: 10.3109/10826084.2012.724614

Rooij, A. J. et al. (2018). A weak scientific basis for gaming disorder: Let us err on the side of caution. *Journal of Behavioral Addictions, 7*(1), 1-9. DOI: 10.1556/2006.7.2018.19

Root, C., & Lynch, M. J. (2014). We shall not forget this: Native Americans and colonial racism in America's prisons. In S. W. Bowman (Ed.), *Color Behind Bars: Racism in the U.S. Prison System.* (pp. 171-190). Santa Barbara, CA: Praeger.

Rorabaugh, W. J. (1979). *The alcoholic republic: An American tradition.* New York: Oxford University Press.

Rosecrance, J. (1985). Compulsive gambling and the medicalization of deviance. *Social Problems 32*(3). 275-284.

Ruben, D. H. (2001). *Treating adult children of alcoholics.* San Diego: Academic Press.

Rush, B. (2002). An inquiry into the effects of ardent spirits upon the human body and mind In D. F. Musto (Ed.), *Drugs in America: A Documentary History.* (pp. 27-43). New York & London: New York University Press. (Original work published 1784).

Salerno, R. A. (2004). *Beyond the enlightenment: Lives and thoughts of social theorists.* Westport, CN: Praeger.

Salvation Army USA. n.d. What we do. Retrieved from https://www.salvation armyusa.org/usn/home/#whatwedo

Sanders, M. W. (1998). The empirical status of psychological interventions with families of children and adolescents. In L. L'Abate (Ed.), *Family psychopathology: The relational roots of dysfunctional behavior.* (pp. 427-465) New York and London: Guildford Press.

Sayegh, C. S., Huey, S. J. Jr., Zara, E. J., & Jhaveri, K. (2017). Follow-up treatment effects of contingency management on substance abuse: A meta-analysis. *Psychology of addictive behaviors, 31*(1), 403-414.

Schaef, A.W. (1987). *When society becomes an addict.* New York: Harper and Row.

Scholtz, H. (2015). Rational choice theory in comparative sociology. *Comparative Sociology,* 14, 587-608. DOI: 10.1163/15691330-12341359

Schreiber, K., & Hausenblas, H. A. (2015). *The truth about exercise addiction: Understanding the dark side of thinspiration.* Lanham, Boulder, New York, and London: Rowman and Littlefield.

Schulte, P. (2015). *Paths to recovery for gay and bisexual drug addicts: Healing weary hearts.* Lanham, MD: Rowman & Littlefield.

Schwitzer, A. M. (2012). Diagnosing, conceptualizing, and treating eating disorders not otherwise specified: A comprehensive practice model. *Journal of Counseling and Development, 90*(3), 281-289. DOI: 10.1002/j.1556-6676.2012.00036.x

Siegelman, E. Y. (1990). *Metaphor and meaning in psychotherapy.* New York and London: Guilford Press.

Shapiro, S. L., & Carlson, L. E. (2017). *The art and science of mindfulness: Integrating mindfulness into psychology and the helping professions* (2nd ed). Washington: APA.

Shaw, V. N. (2002). *Substance use and abuse: Sociological perspectives.* Westport, CN: Praeger.

Shorter, E. (1992). *From paralysis to fatigue: A history of psychosomatic illness in the modern era.* New York: Free Press.

Sinclair, T. R., & Sinclair, C. J. (2010). *Bread, beer, and the seeds of change: Agriculture's imprint on world history.* Oxfordshire, UK & Cambridge, MA: CABI.

Singer, M., & Page, J. B. (2014). *The social values of drug addicts: The uses of the useless.* Walnut Creek, CA: Left Coast Press.

Slobogin, C., & Fondacaro, M. R. (2011). *Juveniles at risk: A plea for preventative justice.* Oxford & New York: Oxford University Press.

Smelser, N. (1962). *Theory of collective behavior.* New York: Free Press of Glencoe.

Smith, S. R., & Hamon, R. R. (2012). *Exploring family theories* (3rd ed.). New York and Oxford: Oxford University Press.

Sorokin, P. (1941). *The crisis of our age: The social and cultural outlook.* New York: E. F. Dutton & Company.

Spivack, A., & McKelvie, A. (2018). Entrepreneurship addictions: Shedding light on the manifestation of the "dark side" in work-behavior patterns. *Academy of Management Perspectives, 32* (3), 358-378. DOI: 10.5465/amp.2016.0185

Steverson, L. (2018). *Madness reimagined: Envisioning a better system of mental health in America.* Wilmington, DE: Vernon Press.

Steverson, L. A., & Melvin, J. E. (2019). *Debating social problems.* New York & London: Routledge.

Stewart, N. R., Winborn, B. B., Burks, H. M. Jr., Johnson, R. C., & Engelkes, J. E. (1978). *Systematic counseling.* Englewood Cliffs, NJ: Prentice-Hall, Inc.

Substance Abuse and Mental Health Services Administration. (2015). *Detoxification and substance abuse treatment. A Treatment Improvement Protocol.* Retrieved from https://store.samhsa.gov/shin/content//SMA15-4131/SMA15-4131.pdf

Substance Abuse and Mental Health Services Administration. (2019). *Medication-assisted treatment.* Retrieved from https://www.samhsa.gov/medication-assisted-treatment

Sutherland, E. H. (1924). *Criminology.* Philadelphia: J.J. Lippincott Co.

Sutherland, E. H. (1950). The diffusion of sexual psychopath laws. *American Journal of Sociology, 56*(2), 142-148. Retrieved from http://www.jstor.org/stable/2772162

Szablewics, M. (2010). The ill effects of "opium for the spirit": A critical cultural analysis of China's internet addiction moral panic. *Chinese Journal of Communications, 3*(4), 453-470. DOI: 10.1080/17544750.2010.516579

Szasz, T. (2010). *The myth of mental illness: Foundations of a theory of personal conduct.* New York: Harper Perennial.

Szasz, T. (2007). *The medicalization of everyday life: Selected essays.* New York: Syracuse University Press.

Taleff, M. J. (1999). Advocacy on issues related to addictions. In J. Lewis, & L. Bradley (Eds.), *Advocacy in Counseling, Counselors, Clients, and Community.* Retrieved from https://eric-ed-gov.research.flagler.edu/?id=ED435916

Thornton, M. (1991). *The economics of prohibition.* Salt Lake City: University of Utah Press.

Tiger, R. (2011). Drug courts and logic of coerced treatment. *Sociological Forum. 26*(1). 169-182. DOI: 10.1111/j.1573-7861.2010. 01229.x

Timascheff, N. S. (1967). *Sociological theory: Its nature and growth* (4th ed.). New York: Random House.

Tracy, S., & Acker, C, J. (2004). Introduction. In S.W. Tracy, & C. J. Acker (Eds.), *Altering American consciousness: The history of alcohol and drug use in the United States, 1800 2000.* (pp. 1-30). Amherst & Boston: University of Massachusetts Press.

Trimpey, J. (1996). *Rational recovery: The new cure for substance addiction.* New York: Pocket Books.

Trivedi, R. H., & Teichert, T. (2017). The Janus-faced role of gambling flow in addiction issues. *CyberPsychology, Behavior, & Social Networking, 20*(3), 180-187. DOI: 10.1089/cyber.2016.0453

Tunney, R. J., & James, R. E. J. (2017). Criteria for conceptualizing behavioral addiction should be informed by the underlying behavioral addiction. *Addiction, 112,* 1716-1724. Retrieved from http://eds.a.ebscohost.com.research.flagler.edu/eds/pdfviewer/pdfviewer?vid=2&sid=a858e6bb-ea62-40ba-8cb6-eddf0d0eff56%40sessionmgr4008.

Twelve Steps and Twelve Traditions. (1989). New York: Alcoholic Anonymous World Services, Inc. (Original work published 1952).

Velasquez, R. J., & Funes, S. M. (2014). The mass incarceration of Latinos in the United States: Looking ahead to the year 2050. In S.W. Bowman (Ed.), *Color Behind Bars: Racism in the U.S. Prison System.* (pp. 273-289). Santa Barbara, CA: Praeger.

Vold, G. B., Bernard, T. J., & Snipes, J. B. (2002). *Theoretical Criminology* (5th ed). New York & Oxford: Oxford University Press.

Walker, J. (2014). A short history of game panics. *Reason. 46*(2). 30-36. Retrieved from http://eds.b.ebscohost.com.research.flagler.edu/eds/detail/detail?vid=0&sid=53855889-445e-4a1a-a880-fcd9fd19695f%40pdc-v-sessmgr04&bdata=JnNpdGU9ZWRzLWxpdmUmc2NvcGU9c2l0ZQ%3d%3d#AN=edsgcl.367198236&db=edsgbc

Walker, M. (1996). The medicalization of gambling as an 'addiction'. In J. McMillen (Ed.), *Gambling cultures: Studies in history and interpretation.* (pp. 223-242). London and New York: Routledge.

Walters, G. D. (1999). *Addiction concept, the working hypothesis or self-fulfilling prophecy?* Boston: Allyn & Bacon.

Warner, J., Her, M., Gmel, G., & Rehm, J. (2001). Can legislation prevent debauchery? Mother gin and public health in 18-century England. *American Journal of Public Health, 91*(3), 375 384. DOI: 10.2105/AJPH.91.3.375

Warner, T. D., & Kramer, J. H. (2009). Closing the revolving door? Substance abuse treatment as an alternative to traditional sentencing for drug-dependent offenders. *Criminal Justice and Behavior, 36*(1), 89-109. DOI: 10.1177/0093854808326743

Weber, M. (2003). *The Protestant ethic and the spirit of capitalism.* (Trans.by T. Parsons). New York: Dover Publications. (Original work published 1930).

Weber, M. (1964). *The theory of social and economic organization.* (Ed. & Trans.by T. Parsons). New York: Free Press. (Original work published 1947).

Wegscheider-Cruse, S. (1989). *Another chance: Hope and healing for the alcoholic family.* (2nd ed.). Palo Alto, CA: Science and Behavior Books.

Weidner, R. R. (2009). Methamphetamine in three small midwestern cities: Evidence of a moral panic. *Journal of Psychoactive Drugs, 41*(3), 227-239. DOI: 10.1080/02791072.2009.10400533

Weil, A. (1972). *The natural mind: A new way of looking at drugs and the higher consciousness.* Boston: Houghton Mifflin.

Weil, A. (1980). *The meaning of the sun and moon: A quest for unity in consciousness.* Boston: Houghton Mifflin.

Weil, A. (2004). *The natural mind: A revolutionary approach to the drug problem.* Boston & New York: Houghton Mifflin.

Weinberg, D. (2011). Sociological perspectives on addiction. *Sociology Compass, 5/4*, 298-310. DOI: 10.1111/j.1751-9020.2011.00363.x

Whitaker, R. (2002). *Mad in America: Bad science, bad medicine, and the enduring mistreatment of the mentally ill.* New York: Basic Books.

White, M., & Epston, D. (1990). *Narrative means to a therapeutic ends.* New York: W.W. Norton and Co.

White, W. L. (2007). The new recovery advocacy movement in America. *Addiction, 102*, 696-703. DOI: 10.1111/j.1360-0443.2007.01808.x

White, W. L. (2014). *Slaying the dragon: The history of addiction treatment and recovery in America* (2nd ed). Bloomington, IL: Chestnut Health Systems/Lighthouse Institute.

Whitfield, C. L. (1987). *Healing the child within: Discovery and recovery for adult children of dysfunctional families.* Deerfield Beach, FL: Health Communications.

Whitfield, C. L. (1991). *Co-dependence: Healing the human condition.* Deerfield Beach, FL: Health Communications.

Wilkinson, I. (2001). *Anxiety in a risk society.* London & New York: Routledge.

Wilson, D. B., Mitchell, O., & MacKenzie, D. L. (2006). A systematic review of drug court effects on recidivism. *Journal of Experimental Criminology, 2,* 459-487. DOI: 10.1007/s11292-006-9019-4

Wincup, E. (2014). Drugs. In R. Atkinson (Ed.), *Shades of deviance: A primer of crime, deviance, and social harm.* (pp. 105-107). London & New York: Routledge.

Woititz, J. G. (1983). *Adult children of alcoholics.* Pompano Beach, FL: Health Communications.

Woo, C. (1997). *The principles of desirable society.* New York: Vantage.

Woolfolk, R. L. (1998). *The care of souls: Science, values, and psychotherapy.* San Francisco: Jossey-Bass.

World Health Organization. (n.d.). *Dependence syndrome.* Retrieved from http://www.who.int/substance_abuse/terminology/definition1/en.

World Health Organization. (2003). *Advocacy for mental health: Mental health policy and service guidance package.* Retrieved from https://www.who.int/mental_health/policy/services/1_advocacy_WEB_07.pdf

World Health Organization. (2018). *International statistical classification of diseases and related health problems* (11th Rev). mental_healthresources/en/Advocacy.pdf. Retrieved from https://icd.who.int/browse11/l-m/en.

Zajac, K., Ginley, M. K., Chang, R., & Petry, N. M. (2017). Treatments for internet gaming disorder and internet addiction: A systematic review. *Psychology of Addiction, 31*(8), 979-994. Retrieved from http://dx.doi.org.research.flagler.edu/10.1037/adb0000315

Zajdow, G. (2008). Moral panics: The old and the new. *Deviant Behavior.* 29. 640-664. DOI: 10.1080/01639620701839476

Zellner, M. R. (2014). Preliminary steps toward a neurobiology of the repetition compulsion. *Modern Psychoanalysis, 39*(1), 1-25. Retrieved from http://eds.a.ebscohost.com.research.flagler.edu/eds/pdfviewer/pdfviewer?vid=1&sid=c8281746-3755-47c4-8174-31267979d622%40sessionmgr4008

Zinberg, N. E. (1984). *Drug, Set, and Setting: The Basis for Controlled Intoxicant Use.* New Haven, CT: Yale University Press.

Index

Lightning Source UK Ltd.
Milton Keynes UK
UKHW021631020720
365920UK00003B/251

9 781648 890352